Alec Nove on Communist and Postcommunist Countries

Alec Nove on Communist and Postcommunist Countries

Previously Unpublished Writings, 2

Alec Nove

Edited by

Ian D. Thatcher

Lecturer, Institute of Russian and East European Studies, University of Glasgow, UK

Edward Elgar

Cheltenham, UK · Northampton, MA, USA

Published by
Edward Elgar Publishing Limited
Glensanda House
Montpellier Parade
Cheltenham
Glos GL50 1UA
UK

Edward Elgar Publishing, Inc.
6 Market Street
Northampton
Massachusetts 01060
USA

A catalogue record for this book
is available from the British Library

Library of Congress Cataloging in Publication Data
Nove, Alec.
    Alec Nove on economic theory : previously unpublished writings /
Alec Nove ; edited by Ian D. Thatcher.
    Includes indexes.
    1. Nove. Alec. 2. Economic theory. 3. Marxian economics.
4. Socialism. 5. Soviet Union—Economic conditions. 6. Soviet
Union—Economic policy. 7. Soviet Union—Politics and government.
I. Thatcher, Ian D. II. Title. III. Title: Alec Nove on communist
and postcommunist countries
HB171.N72 1998
330'.01—dc21   98–17086
                                                          CIP

ISBN 1 85898 862 4

Printed and bound in Great Britain by Bookcraft (Bath) Ltd.

Contents

Preface

Alec Nove's knowledge of communist systems and their economies was not drawn purely from statistical reports, archives, and contemporary news media. He loved above all to travel to the countries themselves, inspecting factories, meeting reformers and their advisers, attending conferences, delivering papers and discussing matters with colleagues from around the world, noting prices in the local markets, using the local transport networks, and visiting the restaurants and theatres. It is our good fortune that he kept accounts of these visits, for there was no better qualified observer of life in the communist and postcommunist world. Read overall, the diary accounts of visits to Eastern Europe and beyond, from the late 1960s to the early 1990s, not only reveal the extent of change, taken individually they are a crucial source for an account of a particular point in a country's history. Alec was willing to travel to countries beyond his immediate specialism, and he was open minded enough to travel to and learn from China. His evaluation of China as an emerging great power seems obvious enough now, but if only more had heeded his urgings to become interested in China, Britain itself might have profited more from its rise.

It is clear from his papers on the USSR and its successor states that well before 1983 Alec expected a reform of the post-Brezhnev economy (although he was uncertain about how radical an attempt it would be), that he supported Gorbachev's introduction of market mechanisms into the Soviet centrally planned economy (while noting both the difficulties of this and the failings of Gorbachev's economics), and that he rejected the application of laissez-faire ideology to the postcommunist economies. It is difficult to find fault with most of Alec's prognoses, although fortunately we have witnessed less violence in postcommunist Russia than Alec sometimes feared. His analyses of the confusion and corruption of its government, political in-fighting, and lack of a clear and well-based economic policy, though, remain as topical as ever. Anyone seeking to understand the difficulties of the postcommunist transition will find Alec's post-1991 writings indispensable. His letters to Morgan Stanley – not all of which could be included – are a masterpiece of day-to-day reporting on what were the latest developments in Russia and Ukraine.

The final, short piece in this volume reveals some of Alec's humour, and of his humorous approach to life. This sense of fun, his clarity of analysis of the most complex issues and his good sense in suggesting the way ahead, are sorely missed.

Ian D. Thatcher

PART I

Travels to Communist and Postcommunist Countries

Russian report: March–April 1969

I spent the period 24 March to 30 April 1969 in Moscow. The following are some very mixed impressions, which could be of interest. While there is nothing secret about it, it is plainly undesirable that copies should be circulating in Moscow, and I should be grateful if the recipients would treat it as confidential.

OBJECT AND FACILITIES

I was there under academic exchange arrangements, to study Russian and Soviet economic thought. For this purpose I was attached to Moscow University (though I had originally asked for *Leningrad*), and placed in the care of Professor Tsagolov, head of the *Kafedra* (department) of Political Economy. While he was not personally particularly informative, he did help me make contacts with other institutions (telephoning Gatovsky and Pashkov, and also Gorfan at TsEMI) and ensuring that I had all the necessary library facilities. He was friendly and helpful, and his staff also. The atmosphere at the Kafedra was conducive to good human relations and to informal discussions. Far from having to ask to attend Kafedra discussions, I was always informed of them and invited to come along. There can be no possible complaint, therefore, about the way the university looked after me.

I used the 'professorial reading room' at the Gorki Library, which is in the precincts of the old university. It was so rich in the sort of materials I needed that in fact I never went to the Lenin Library. The Gorki library holdings would have kept me busy for many more months. The library staff could not have been more helpful.

Tiresomely, I was put in the Ostankino hotel. The hotel itself is quite adequate. The trouble is its remoteness. One has compulsory lessons in the working of the public transport system. An Intourist bus nominally leaves the hotel at 8 and 8.30 a.m., but it frequently failed to run. Coming back in the evening was tiring and tiresome. Demianova, the University administrator who deals with foreigners, apologised and blamed the Ministry for not pressing for more suitable accommodation. She would welcome protests, to strengthen her hand.

Unlike some visiting scholars, I had no requests to make either to visit a university or to travel. Therefore I was not refused anything.

THE UNIVERSITY

Until next year, the Economics faculty is in the old university complex opposite the Kremlin; a great convenience.

I gave four lectures or seminars during my stay. One, on 'devaluation', was in English, for the Kafedra of English language in the Faculty. One was on British economists, another was on the British economy, and the last one concerned 'Efficiency criteria in nationalised industries and private corporations'. There were questions and much discussion, especially in corridors afterwards. Audiences included some undergraduates and some research students. One of the talks was in the Kafedra dealing with western economies, whose head is Professor Dragilev.

Several discussions which I attended were of interest. One such was based on a paper by *docent* (senior lecturer) M. Malyshev, on the teaching of Political Economy. There were familiar complaints: some lectures are dull, students saw little point in them. 'We now have greater freedom to start new courses; we do not need the consent of the ministry. We should use this right to devise optional specialised courses which would interest the students.' He also said that 'let us be frank', not only do we have too many *troiki* (that is, 'threes', a Russian equivalent of a bare pass), but many of our troiki are really *dvoiki*, that is, 'failures'. 'Our students know that we have a plan to fulfil, and that therefore we will not dare fail them. When they come to the university, they work hard and worry about passing. But by their third and fourth years they realise that, if they are not totally ignorant, we will pass them anyway.'

A student notice board had pinned on it a typed article criticising dull lectures, asking for more discussion seminars, and also challenging the system of discipline. Non-attendance is occasionally punished, but attendance is none the less irregular. Punishment creates friction, students should have greater voice in what goes on. What is needed is a *studencheski dekanat*, that is, a kind of student representative council or students' union. The Komsomol (communist youth organisation) is evidently thought to be unable (or unwilling) to act in this capacity.

But student grievances at no time emerged as a threat to order. The atmosphere was peaceful, though evidence will be cited of strong feelings on various matters.

One participant in another Kafedra discussion spoke of the desirability of 'cleansing' (*ochistka*) of the concept 'profit' from extraneous elements, and another faculty member interjected: 'cleansing profits from Ota Šik'.

In still another the lecturer (Prof. Osadko) sought to define 'legitimate' profits in such a way as to *exclude* profits arising from a change in the product mix. He insisted that bonuses based on profitability should be payable only if the *assortiment* plan is fulfilled. This casts some light as to his picture of what the economic reform is about.

A long and fascinating debate raged around the draft thesis on *Technical Progress and Employment in Agriculture* defended by Bulochkina, Lidia Andreevna. Her conclusions were, among others, that agriculture has no reserves of labour suitable for non-agricultural work. A high proportion of the labour force consists of unskilled older women, while farms are short of skilled and young labour.

The official *opponent* was the rather dull Osadko, who ended a soporific contribution by saying: 'of course American agriculture is far more productive than Soviet agriculture', but this is explicable by the fact that 'socialism was achieved in a country of semi-developed capitalism'. He also asserted that collective farms (*kolkhozy*), given equal conditions, tended to be more efficient than state farms (*sovkhozy*).

The second discussant, Shkredov, was eloquent and woke up the audience. He criticised Bulochkina for some of her thesis statements. While expressing approval of her demographic, employment and mobility studies, he took her to task for using vague phrases like 'work suited to ability' and 'rational employment'. Might there not be some over-education of the rural population in relation to the totally unskilled work required of it? This is a cause of migration from village to town; an educated villager may find no suitable work. Maybe in Soviet society as a whole there is 'over-education and over-qualification'. Is the annual migration of townsmen (paid by their urban employers) to help with the harvest 'rational'? Shkredov also complained that there is a tendency to ignore similarities between 'production relations' in east and west, such as those arising from the introduction of automation. It is also nonsense to assert that there was 'stagnation' (*zastoi*) in capitalist agriculture. He considered that socialist 'regularities' (*zakonomernosti*) should *not* be based on Soviet agricultural experience, which was affected by historical peculiarities, such as the very hard burdens Soviet farms had to carry.

At this point there was a light-hearted exchange of views. Shkredov said: 'And anyway, which one of us knows villages at all?' A voice: 'Khessin visits a village sometimes' (laughter and cheers). Another voice: 'But without education surely a tractor can easily be broken. We need *more* education.' Shkredov: 'I have actually driven a tractor (cheers). Of course you need a mechanics' course, but that is a few weeks' training' (Some shouts of 'no').

Another discussant joined in, Gerkovets. The USA had 4.6 per cent of the population employed in agriculture, the USSR still had 30 per cent (he later agreed that the 30 per cent does not include the 'millions' of townsmen who help bring in the harvest). Furthermore the Soviet percentage is falling *more slowly* than in many western countries. Why so? Insufficient investment? Wrong investment? Admittedly, drastic economy of labour would cause intolerable unemployment.

Another discussant spoke of history and its influence on the village and on rural productivity. The author of the thesis was accused of obtaining her US statistics from Soviet sources.

Bulochkina replied with vigour, after politely thanking her critics. Her American figures were from *American* sources. US figures are fuller and more accessible than Russian ones. She used America as her comparison, because this showed the greatest technical advance. 'We certainly have some concealed unemployment, though there are big variations by region and by seasons.' She studied labour utilisation on private plots too. The *average age* of agricultural labourers is *50*. Men should do more work. 'It is a disgrace that the heaviest unskilled work is done by women.' Central Asia has labour surplus, but how can it be redistributed to other areas? 'Only the law of value will do it, nothing else can or will.' (Interrupter: 'There too the city does the harvesting. A law of socialist agriculture: "they sow, they watch the rain, and then townsmen will come and reap"'). We should not blame history for our difficulties. Contradictions (she concluded) are mainly the creation of socialism.

I have reported this session at some length to indicate the sort of discussion which seems quite acceptable – and presumably not abnormal – at the Faculty of Economics. The atmosphere was relaxed and, although people did put much feeling into their arguments, basically good-humoured.

On another occasion Osadko spoke at length and said nothing worthwhile. He developed a (much-criticised) idea that under socialism the workers produce the 'necessary product', while under capitalism the object of production is 'surplus value'. These and other kinds of scholasticisms produced murmurs of dissent from graduate students: *'nelepo'* ('nonsense'). On another occasion there was a dissertation defence by one Dzavrasov, Sultan Skvarbeevich, who spoke of autonomy, centralisation and economic effectiveness. He introduced his 800-page thesis in ten good-humoured minutes. Discussants argued about prices and value theory, the contradiction between sectional and social interest, whether the size and growth of the consumption fund (net of administrative costs) should be *the* criterion of effectiveness, whether services should not be included as a separate item. An able and eloquent lecturer, Khessin, supported the industrial association (*obyedineniye*) as the basis of industrial management. He warned against adopting unrealistic pseudo-*khozraschyot* (cost accounting), 'like under the *sovnarkhozy*'. He also criticised 'marketeers' (*rynochniki*), and considered that the 1920s were logically followed by the 1930s. Other discussants referred to the need for use-value to be reflected in prices, so that higher costs should not necessarily imply higher prices.

Also at the University: a wall-newspaper with a big headline: OSIP MANDELSHTAM. Beneath, typed, and signed by the 'responsible editor', a series of articles on his poetry, his life, an extract from Ehrenburg's view of him, and six poems, including one of his Voronezh poems of 1937 'Kuda mne detsa v etom yanvarye' ('What shall I do with myself, now it is January?') and the excellent one about Leningrad 'Ya ver-nulsya v moi gorod, znakomyi do slyoz' ('I've come back to my city. These are my own old tears'). A poem – by Brodksy – was thrown in for good measure. The biography concludes with the statement that he was arrested in 1938. This because he had previously been arrested ('kak ranneye repressivovan') and sentenced to five years. He died near Vladivostok in a transit camp, 'shivering by the camp-fire, yearning for just a piece of sugar and declaiming his poems'. The biography ends with a few lines from another poem:

'Poprobuite menya ot veka otorvat'
Ruchayus' vam, sebye svernyote sheyu' ('Try, if you can to tear me from my time/I promise you that you will twist your neck'). Students were reading silently. One or two took out notebooks and copied the poems.

THE LIBRARY

The catalogue had no entries for such as Bukharin and Zinoviev. It did, however, include virtually all *academic* heretics of the 1920s, such as Kondratiev, Groman, Bazarov, and so on. All the journals of the 1920s were there, complete, so that even Bukharin and some other heretics could be read. The Gorki library had just this one catalogue. One or two of the books were labelled 'checked (*proverno*) 1936'. One – by Kondratiev and Oganovsky – was marked 'withdrawn by order of Glavlit order 68a/5, 11 Dec. 1938'; this was crossed out in rather inferior ink when the book was restored to the shelves on *8 March 1954* (but could still be deciphered).

My own works were represented in the catalogue by two entries, one of them *Was Stalin Really Necessary?*

The reading room contained, on open shelves, a wide range of Western periodicals, including the *Economic Journal*, the *English Historical Review*, *Mind*, almost every American law review I have ever heard of, the principal American economic quarterlies, *Welwirtschaftliches Archiv*, and so on. Among recent acquisitions exhibited was Archibald and Lipsey's

Mathematical Economics and two volumes of the Cambridge economic history. Also there were two separate sets of the pre-revolutionary encyclopaedia, Brokgaus and Efron.

My various economic 'discoveries' in this library will be the subject of a later note, time permitting.

THE DISCUSSION OF THE STATISTICAL HANDBOOK

This took place at the 'House of Statistics' (*Dom Uchyonykh*) and is an annual event. I was brought along by a member. The official side was represented by Starovsky (head of the TsSU), Genin (editor of the handbook) and Li (a Korean, editor of the RSFSR handbook).

Criticisms included the following: The irregularity of the issue of local and sectoral statistical handbooks. Poor paper, printing, arrangement. Delays in publication. Needless repetition. It could be much shorter. Why no 'industrial groupings' (*gruppirovki*)? Why so many comparisons with 1913, when in fact the 1913 statistics are so incomplete and inaccurate? Why meaningless notes such as 'data modified', or 'according to the methodology of the respective years', when no explanations are given? 'Why does the TsSU treat us as hostile?' Why so little about reform? Thus why not give figures to show who actually gets various bonuses, how 'funds' are used? Some indices are not comparable. Why so little on income differentiation? Why is the price of the statistical handbook 2.5 times the 1960 price, though the length has gone up only 50 per cent? Why no 'statistics of crime and morals?'

Starovsky replied very briefly and answered hardly any questions. He agreed that printing is not good, (and Li also spoke of the great difficulty in getting adequate printing done). He denied that he regards his audience as hostile. He himself worries about gaps in figures in respect of technical progress, effectiveness of capital investments and effectiveness of science.

A friend said that they never take any notice of criticism, and it was hardly worth complaining.

WAGES AND PRICES IN MOSCOW

By comparison with past visits, wage information was exceedingly plentiful. Many advertisements, printed and written, cite quite high rates, for a city in which an obvious labour shortage is partly due to the extreme difficulty for any outsider to get a residence permit (*propiska*). Cleaners (*uborshchitsy*) are offered 90 roubles a month, bus drivers 'a minimum of 240', trolleybus drivers a good deal less (140 and up). Typists are offered upwards of 80. Workers on semi-skilled jobs in repair shops get 110, skilled men a great deal more. All these rates seem to be well up on what I remember in the past. The first academic appointment (*Assistent*) is worth 105 roubles.

No doubt the substantial rise in money incomes contributes to the general tendency to queues, and to large increases in prices for jewellery, furs and perhaps other luxuries, while prices of basic foodstuffs are held steady and some textiles are sold a little cheaper. Imported Spanish nylon shirts were going for 20 roubles in GUM, with no queue.

Long queues for oranges (1.50 per kilo), eggs, sometimes meat. Huge numbers of shoppers come into Moscow daily from near and far. Supplies elsewhere said to be very much less varied, hence journeys to Moscow. A woman near a station complained bitterly to me that in her town (Alexandrov) there were no canned goods, no fruit, nothing. She had to go to Moscow to shop during holidays (*na prazdniki*) (this was just before 1st May).

I have the impression that popular restaurant prices are higher. In cafeterias I frequently paid well over a rouble for indifferent food, whereas I could get better quality sitting down in second-class restaurants for much less than this ten years ago. But luxury restaurants are still *relatively* inexpensive. Thus a good meal in the Natsional or the Ararat (without drinks) can be had for 2 or 2.5 roubles. No wonder there are queues at the good restaurants!

Since there was not really enough time to do even a major part of the necessary reading, I did not make any systematic notes on wages or prices, but there are certainly ample data for those who are interested in walking around the city with a notebook.

UNIVERSITY AGAIN: REJECTED DISSERTATIONS

Shkredov, who happens to be the party secretary of the Faculty of Economics, read a paper on 'Property Relations and Socialism', which unfortunately clashed with another date and which I missed. Several graduate students said that it was very good, also that Shkredov had a dissertation on the subject of 'law, economics and ownership' rejected by the VAK (All-Union Attestation Commission), after it had been approved by the Academic Board of the Faculty at Moscow University. Inquiry produced the information that *every* dissertation for a higher

degree from every university in all the USSR needs to be approved by
VAK, whose economics committee has 15 members.

A discussion with Shkredov quickly showed where the problem lay. He
wrote of Western corporations, with their vastly spread shareholdings.
Legally the firm belongs to the shareholders. They really do own their
shares. But in what economic–social sense is the corporation theirs? This
line of thought was regarded as revisionist, although even Marx (as
Shkredov duly pointed out) had noted over 100 years ago the special and
growing role of salaried managers in large firms.

Another dissertation was approved by the Academic Board by 15 votes
to 9, which meant rejection, as this was less than a two thirds majority.
This thesis concerned the pricing system required for a mathematical pro-
gramme-plan. The thesis had had strong support from the external
examiner, Novozhilov. This in itself, said Pashkov, ensured opposition,
though he (Pashkov) had voted 'for', or so he said.

It is interesting to note that *all* university teaching appointments are
[now] for five years only. There is then a renewal-of-appointment procedure, which is not automatic and calls for a positive vote by the Faculty.

REFORM

Discussed this with TsEMI (Petrakov, Gorfan, Perlamutrov) and also
with both Gatovsky and Khachaturov, though with the last two I discussed mainly the economic thought of the 1920s.

The TsEMI meeting was in some respects disappointing. It may have
been my own fault, in beginning the proceedings by citing the view – heard
often enough in Prague and Budapest – that the Soviet reform has
changed things very little. This put them uneasily on the defensive.
Petrakov, with whom I had a very frank discussion two years earlier,
seemed cautiously apologetic. Gorfan – described by one person in a
chance encounter as 'that KGB man' – said little. Petrakov asserted that
the present is only one stage of reform, that it would be wrong to hurry,
that greater autonomy of sub-units requires 'psychological reconstruction'
of all concerned. Planning is becoming more flexible. They are feeling
their way (*nashchupyvayut*) to the proper degree of decentralisation.

His colleagues concurred. Three years is not a long time. The restored
ministries had to be established on a firm footing first, which added to
delays. Important gains have been made. *Glavki* (chief departments) will
increasingly be put on *khozraschyot*, then ministries; pricing is now better,
more attention is paid to supply and demand, and in prices of new equipment they now try to measure value-in-use (*potrebitelski effekt*). Marginal

use, that is, the least effective use for which there is sufficient supply, would determine price of a new machine. Then, as supply increases, prices will be cut to make some less effective uses profitable.

They would advocate a wider range of wholesale prices being subject to variation by agreement. One idea likely to be adopted is not to fix wholesale prices for intra-ministry purchases and sales. There should be more right to negotiate discounts and surcharges for quality, especially for machinery and equipment. Perhaps there should be more *inter*-ministerial direct contracts, with details left to be negotiated between enterprises. They all agreed that *too many* prices are now centrally fixed, which causes delays and inflexibilities. One further idea is to control the prices of the finished products only, letting prices of inputs be settled by lower-level negotiation within the limits so set.

Retail prices are another problem. There is a drive for price stability, which does run counter to the aim of flexibility. This is particularly so where, as in the case of meat and many other products, there is no 'cushion' of turnover tax which facilitates variations in the wholesale price without any necessary alteration in retail price.

They agreed that prices ought to be more rational, but even with wrong prices one could have *glavk* and ministerial *khozraschyot*, provided the built-in constraints included '*plan po nomenklatura*' (product mix plan). I naturally objected that the product mix is in practice a variable which depends, indeed must depend, on initiatives taken at ministerial, *glavk* and enterprise levels. They agreed. They cited the experiment now being undertaken by the Ministry of Equipment-Building (*priborost-royeniya*), within which wide powers exist to decide the product mix and also to fix temporary prices for the many new products of this ministry.

I asked about the powers of Gossnab (state supply commission), and the survival of administrative allocation of materials. Petrakov laughed when I expressed the view that this must be the subject of argument. 'Yes, and Gossnab likes the present situation very much.' No, there is not yet any significant growth of wholesale trade in producers' goods, and some move in this direction is indeed (in his view) desirable. But 'Gossnab will be with us for many years yet.' Even big construction sites sometimes cannot get materials and implements, and *their* supplies do not and should not depend on prices. It is, however, deplorable that under the present system the user is often indifferent as to the price of inputs, and might even prefer high prices, provided they are incorporated in his plan.

Excess demand, they pointed out, still requires allocation on a priority basis, but it is certainly an intolerable situation that building materials and implements are often unavailable for decentralised or unplanned investments. So Petrakov has advocated a sort of interim solution: let the priority, planned investments take their share of inputs at the fixed official prices – at which supply and demand does not balance – and let the enterprises buy freely for extra-plan investments at higher prices at which non-priority supply and unplanned demand *will* balance. He did not defend this dual-price idea as economically very sound, but saw its advantages over the present situation. This is *in principle* the same as charging a smaller rate of interest on credits to finance centrally planned investments (0.5 per cent against the 'unplanned' 2 per cent) which is already operating (except that, of course, neither of the interest rates is high enough to affect the volume of demand for credits).

I asked, was not the incentive fund system clumsy and complex? They agreed that it should be altered and simplified. Perhaps *rentabel'nost'* (profitability rate) will be abandoned as an indicator, leaving only net profit (that is, net of capital charges and rent) and sales (*realizatsiya*). It is appreciated that the latter indicator may reward unnecessary inputs, insofar as it shares the deficiencies of gross output, and so TsEMI has been arguing for net profit as the sole indicator on condition of fulfilling the product mix plan (*nomenklatura*). It would be better, they think, if the payment into the incentive funds would just be a percentage of profits.

We discussed prices. The lists now cover 5 million prices. No more *general* price-changes will occur. Gradual revisions are essential. TsEMI favours, for some goods such as machinery, price changes by stages fixed in advance (*stupenchatye tseny*), so that potential buyers will know that new machines would cost less, and how much less, in two years' time. Existing prices are still in the main those of July 1967. Some are known to be 'wrong': thus the Moscow coal basin prices make use of Moscow coal unprofitable, yet the coalfield cannot be abandoned because of the need to provide work for miners.

Petrakov agreed that unfinished capital projects remain a source of waste. One trouble is that it pays the building enterprises to start and not to finish.

He confirmed that the wages fund plan remains linked with the gross output indicator, though this will be changed in his view. One of *the* problems of reform was the issue of *responsibility*. How can management be made to feel responsible and be *held* responsible?

I formed the impression in the end that TsEMI economists are more than a little embarrassed by the slowness of the process of change. The traditionalists are strongly entrenched. They know very well that something very different is going on in Hungary.

Gatovsky was relatively uncommunicative about reform – though very helpful in giving advice and opinions about economists of the early Soviet period. Khachaturov readily admitted that the essentials of the old system have been retained, and argued that the far-reaching Hungarian-style reforms are not suitable for the USSR at present: bigger country, less reliance on foreign trade, bigger priority projects.

OTHER ECONOMIC NOTES

The difference between produced and utilised national income: it was explained that much of it consists of the results of the revaluation of imports and exports into domestic rouble prices. In view of the wide and variable gap between foreign-trade ('world') prices and domestic prices, it follows that a net balance of zero in terms of the former could be a substantial plus or minus in terms of the latter.

The three-queue system in retail food stores has been replaced, to the benefit of all concerned, by a two-queue system: one looks at price-tags, goes at once to the cashier, asks for a bill for the requisite amount (say '35 kopecks, second counter'), presents this bill to the assistant at the counter (saying '100 grams of Cracow sausage', or whatever) and takes the purchase away. Clearly an improvement, if long overdue. Snag: it is not always possible to see what one is buying before paying for it.

Cafeteria food is dominated by the rissole. This comes in many verbal disguises: *bitochki, tefteli, rublennye kotley, bifshteks, lyulya-kebab*. All rissoles. The last of them is flavoured with herbs and guaranteed to give you heartburn. The others are all harmless, if not exactly grande cuisine. For some reason, there was plenty of duck on all menus, but the problem was very small and bony. Vegetables consisted of *Kvashennaya Kapusta* (hot sauerkraut), very occasionally carrots, far too often tasteless mashed potatoes. Cucumber and sour cream made a pleasant change. There were ample supplies in the cafeterias of tinned calamares, shproty, herring. Shops were amply supplied with tinned goods, especially fish. Some Far-Eastern fish called salaka was well worth eating.

Shortage of vegetables reduced the range of soups. Borshch was occasionally available, there was never any *zelyonye shchi* or *rassolnik*, though *solyanka* was often 'on' (at the National it was extremely tasty). A peppery concoction with rice and mutton-bones misnamed Kharcho turned up in cafeterias. The Ararat restaurant served a good *shashlyk*.

The book trade is as bad as ever. Popular or interesting works vanish speedily. A well-laid-out bookshop in Prospekt Kalinina is a great step forward, but in the end it is hard to find what one wants. Enterprising young men sell books in the pedestrian subways, shouting out their wares in a manner suggesting that they have a substantial material interest in the proceedings. Are they unofficially trading, doubtless with the connivance of the shops? (All good for turnover statistics.) One young man was selling a detective story by two authors, titled *Ubiistvo v biblioteke* (Murder in the Library). Later I was told that it was excellent, and tried to find it, but alas, it was totally sold out and no bookshop had it. They do, however, have plenty of dull books. The children's books sections are well stocked, though.

Several new specialised shops have appeared for men's and women's clothing, also footwear. Many shops exist in outlying areas, which is very necessary owing to Moscow's rapid growth. Thus I accompanied a resident into a food shop in a new housing estate a couple of miles north of the Economic Achievements Exhibition, and it had adequate stocks and no unusual queues.

The great housing drive has produced results, and indeed created problems, for example, transport to and from work. I visited several of the new apartments in different parts of the new outer Moscow, some municipal and others cooperative. They are quickly erected by assembly of prefabricated parts. They are usually now about 9 or 10-storey, with a lift that works. The external finish is poor; visually the effect is not as ugly as a Glasgow corporation estate. Inside the actual flats the finish is quite adequate, the parquet floors much better than previously seen in new flats in Russia. The rooms are small, usually two of them. The kitchen is minuscule, the entrance hall in one flat was so small that the host has to get into a room to allow the guest to take his coat off! But the happiness due to privacy ('our own front door, our own kitchen and bathroom!'), after years of communal apartments, represents a big gain in human welfare.

The improvement in Moscow has been contributed to by the very severe restrictions on movement of people into the city. Never has a *propiska* been more difficult to obtain.

INTERNATIONAL POLITICS: COMMENTS AND ATTITUDES

I arrived just after the Damansky island incidents. The newspapers were playing up the 'hero frontier guards' who had defended 'the sacred soil of our *rodina*', and so on. All persons to whom I talked were unanimously distrustful, fearful, hostile – and puzzled. 'What on earth is going on in China? We cannot understand it.' But *of course* they thought that the China problem would exercise a big influence in Soviet foreign-policy attitudes. Several people, including a Soviet journalist encountered at a party, said that China was *the* menace. America one could, at a pinch, live with. I was confirmed in my opinion that all this *must* affect Soviet attitudes to European and other problems. (At the Königswinter conference, which I attended just before going to Moscow, I expressed this view, but found myself in a minority in my group.)

Attitudes to Germany, however, remain hard, suspicious, hostile. Official propaganda here finds a fertile soil. Wildly exaggerated screeds about revanchism, neo-Nazism, plots, and so on, appear in the press. Some of it is believed.

This has a big effect on public attitudes to Czechoslovakia. Needless to say, opinions differ. One man said, cynically: 'of course we had to go in, to save democracy, don't you know'. People knew that the Soviet troops had a hostile reception; many could quote friends or relatives who had experienced it. It was widely believed that Soviet soldiers had been killed by snipers; one person referred to bodies in coffins arriving from Czechoslovakia. Yet these same persons sometimes linked the 'unpleasant necessity' of troop movements with some ill-defined menace from West Germany. What other reason could there be? They could not imagine any other rational answer to the question 'why'.

I was shaken to find that one Soviet friend was quite unaware that Dubček, Černik and co. had been arrested in August. In fact to this day the Soviet press had not reported it.

I gave a couple of lectures on the British economy at the university (also one on British economists and one on 'operational criteria for nationalised industries'). There was interest in Britain, but also a kind of pitying sympathy with our difficulties. Some of the students specialising on Britain (in Professor Dragilev's Kafedra) were very well-informed. I got a question about the import deposit scheme, and a whole series of arguments about American investments in this country.

I met, among many others, two hard-line ideologists, both middle-aged, both of them quite good-humoured about it. One – Akhmanova, the linguist – roundly asserted that literature should be 'life-asserting and optimistic'. Both took the line that the USSR is in a worldwide conflict, that there are therefore 'fronts' and 'barricades', and all things should be seen in the context of the great struggle. To such persons references to China are embarrassing, for in a two-sided, one-barricade world where is China?

The Middle East crisis is reported from a 100 per cent Arab point of view. Israeli villainy is played up daily in the press. Some Jewish acquaintances are alarmed, partly because they cannot understand what the Israeli government is up to, partly because they fear that all this will react unfavourably upon the situation of Jews in Russia. But I felt no sense of people being acutely worried about *Soviet* intervention.

One 'odd' individual did say: 'if we kick up such a fuss about remote Damansky island, how can we expect the Israelis to give up Jerusalem?'

JEWS

Widespread feeling that Jewish nationality makes things difficult, some things more difficult than others, but little to suggest anything more definite.

Large numbers of Jewish economists, in many age-groups, encountered in person and on paper.

Someone told story of a Jewish student giving his result as 'two fives', a five mark in the examination modified by the consequences of the fifth paragraph (that is, the 'nationality' entry on his passport).

Some stories heard of the anti-semitic policies of the 1948–53 period. Some evidently feel that what had happened once would happen again, but hope that it will not.

Conversation piece: 'And I told him that with his nose he would never be admitted into the Faculty of Philosophy. Chances are better in Psychology.'

'Temptation always exists to blame any troubles on Jews, and it is all too easy to play on old prejudices.'

However, the most general complaints among the public about black-marketeers relate, in that order, to Georgians and Armenians. Georgian dealers hang around the car and car-spares shops near the Baumansky metro station.

Not a single Jewish concert or poetry evening was advertised when I was in Moscow.

Two recent issues of *Sovietisch Heimland* were on sale at kiosks near Red Square.

Some foreigners, remarking on *Pravda*'s journalists Zhukov and Mayevsky, said that while Zhukov could relax and make disrespectful off-the-record remarks, Mayevsky, 'as a Jew', always felt he had to stick to every word of the official line.

Total silence in the press or in theatre on anything Jewish, except perhaps that, in *Bolsheviki* (see later) the Jewish features of Sverdlov, and Uritsky's very Jewish name (Moisei Solomonovich) were given unmistakable emphasis, as also were the names of the two doctors, Mints and Veissbrod, who attended Lenin.

General impression: unhappy situation, people worried, but nothing seen or heard that could be described as outrageous. I speak only of my direct experience. For some reasons, Russians tend to take me for an Armenian, and I was once criticised by a drunken passenger for being one.

MISCELLANEOUS

Pashkov complained that not only did the Americans publish a translation of volume 1 of the *History of Russian Economic Thought*, which he edited, without even informing him, and not only did they put someone else's name on the cover, but when he asked them for a copy they sent him the book *and* a bill for $12, and two reminders thereafter. He was happy to hear that the translation had been attacked by Gerschenkron.

Pashkov shocked me when, in conversation, he asserted that Rubin, a theoretician of the 1920s denounced in 1930, was 'a menshevik who had plotted with mensheviks abroad to organise armed intervention against the USSR'. Cor! He even claimed that Kondratiev was still alive, but later found occasion to withdraw this statement.

Most people, including even Pashkov, spoke with great respect about the economists of the 1920s, and urged the study of their works. One man – I think it was F. Polyansky, said: 'we cannot at present take our history of thought beyond 1917, so it is good that someone [abroad] should write it'. Several spoke of the need to analyse the ideas of Bukharin and Preobrazhensky, among others. So it was odd to read an article in *Ogonyok* (No. 15, April, 1969) by a Professor Razumny, denouncing Trotskyism as 'the enemy of Leninism' in the harshest terms, including the phrases 'pryamoe predatel'stvo' ('direct betrayal').

One author told me that he was able to refer to Bergson's computations in a published work only if the word 'computations' were put in inverted commas.

Radio announcements and also small-ads of all kinds refer job-seekers to the '*upolnomochennyi po trudodovym resursam*', that is, to labour exchanges run by the city Soviet, which are clearly playing an important role in job placement.

Many stories of unusual storms in the Ukraine and the South generally which blew off snow cover and led to severe crop damage. '80% winter kill', said one person. South-east winds so strong that soot from Donetz basin blew all over the Dnieper.

A US writer reportedly asked to speak to Liberman. Intourist offered him an hour for $100! Bargaining reduced the price (evidently this was *not* Liberman's doing).

A Soviet citizen said: 'Among Uzbeks the Russians are respected, there is real affection for them, people are friendly to visitors.' Me: 'Is it different in the Baltic states?' Soviet citizen: 'Of course, yes. *They* think they would have done better if we had not pulled them down to our level.'

Unconscious humour department! In one article in *Novaya i noveishaya istoriya* (No. 1, 1969, p. 118), there is a reference, in English, to 'Rostow's fake-off'.

In my hotel there were some Iraqis, pilots in training, apparently from Tashkent on holiday.

One person said: 'Beria's hold over Stalin was connected with the fact that he supplied him with his needs. He had odd tastes.'

A small but tiresome point. It seems that many areas quite near Moscow are out of bounds to foreigners, but nothing whatever is done to inform the 'academic' visitors of this. Thus I visited a professor in his dacha, and unwittingly (as I discovered from an embassy map) almost trespassed on a 'black' area. One day an incident can be made out of unintentional transgression.

All papers, radio, television, speeches, dwell endlessly on the coming '100th anniversary of the birth of Vladimir Ilych Lenin' (spoken with just the right tone of affectionate awe). Since his 99th birthday was celebrated in April, it follows that the campaign will get more and more effusive with time. Surely people will get heartily fed up, even given the high respect in which the name of Lenin is held?

Can any press be duller than the Soviet daily press? Or so uninformative? At the university, the *Morning Star* is under the counter because of heavy demand. Students often read English. Compared with *Pravda* it is a real newspaper! A Soviet journalist (works for *Novoe Vremya*) readily agreed, regretted as a *journalist* the departure of Abzhubei from *Izvestiya*, and also the fact that *Pravda*'s present editor is not a journalist.

CONCLUSIONS

1. Academically the trip was emphatically worthwhile, with both courtesy and cooperation from Soviet colleagues. The British Embassy too was very helpful. So were journalists, British and American. Opportunities to see life in Moscow in general, in the university in particular, were ample. People did not seem nervous about talking to suspicious foreigners.
2. There is continuing progress with living standards, but shortages are created by an imbalance between money incomes and the volume of goods and (especially) services available at established prices. This conceals and distorts the improvements. (But it may be dangerous to generalise from Moscow.)
3. The cultural–political scene is bleak. Intellectuals must be in a state of great irritation. Censorship is tough. Economic reform is stalled. Nationalist conservatism does, however, evoke some responding chords among many people.

I would like to go again soon.

CULTURAL APPENDIX

'Moscow theatre is in a bad way just now', said some Russian friends. A look at the month's programmes suggested that my friends had perhaps excessively high standards. Four plays by Bulgakov, the usual selection of Russian classics (*The Seagull, The Three Sisters, A Month in the Country*, two different productions of *The Inspector General* and also adaptations of *Dead Souls, The Brothers Karamazov*), but also some promising-sounding modern pieces, not to speak of the Bolshoi and the concert hall, would surely occupy all my free evenings? 'The censorship is so tight just now that no contemporary plays can say anything that needs saying', my friends told me.

There seems no doubt that censorship is tight indeed, and not only in the theatre, as social scientists, historians and novelists are well aware. None the less the *Sovremennik* ('Contemporary') theatre was still there, and it was playing a modern and highly controversial trilogy, by three different playwrights: *The Decembrists, The Narodnovoltsy (People's Will)*, and *The Bolsheviks*, which, so a critic had told us, had much to say about revolutionary morality. So obviously they had to be seen, particularly *The Bolsheviks*: this was set in the day in 1918 when Lenin was shot and dangerously wounded, and the rights and wrongs of Red Terror were debated on the stage.

Theatre tickets are sold all over Moscow in kiosks, but the more popular shows are always sold out. The foreign visitor can usually rely on a good seat via the Intourist hotel office, but this time I drew a blank. 'The whole theatre is booked, it is a closed performance', they said. Since all Moscow theatres show plays in repertory, it was necessary to wait for the next time; a western journalist promised to get tickets, by direct approach to the management. Result: nil. 'Closed performance'. It looked as if foreigners were not meant to see *The Bolsheviks*. I read the play and saw why they might take such a view. But then a stroke of luck: a Russian friend had a spare ticket.

The play opens in the meeting-place of the Council of People's Commissars. Historical characters argue, joke, quarrel, among them Sverdlov, Lunacharsky, Pokrovsky, Kollantai, Krestinsky, Enukidze. The missing men were specifically accounted for in the script: 'Stalin is in Tsaritsyn, Trotsky is at the front.' Zinoviev was referred to several times as an addressee of telegrams to Petrograd. Bukharin, in the printed text, is addressing a meeting but in the play he was mentioned by Krupskaya as having dined with Lenin.

It is 30 August 1918. Lenin is shot. Some demand Red Terror. But the Jacobins destroyed themselves by terror – 'They perished at the hands of

those with whom they travelled the long and hard road of revolution! The
terror snowballed.' The historian Pokrovsky is shown trying to sidetrack
the argument. To discuss the excesses of the Jacobins would weaken their
determination to act, he asserted. Sverdlov retorted: 'We cannot say that
we may discuss some things and not others! By this route we might even-
tually come to remember only what is convenient at the given moment!'
And Chicherin added: 'By selective silence we will turn history into a
prostitute, who will sell herself to the highest bidder. This is a slippery
slope, and we will fall!' Lunacharsky, brilliantly played by the actor
Evstigneyev, spoke of the Jacobins' political degeneration: 'If the organs
of terror were at one time elected and responsible to the revolutionary
masses, by the end of Jacobinism all this changed . . . The Committee of
Public Safety carried out a thorough centralisation of the coercive apparatus . . . The organs of terror merged with those of the state. This new
terroristic bureaucracy seizes control of everything. The abuses of power
are immense, but no one, not Robespierre or St. Just, can do anything
about it. They cannot challenge bureaucratic officialdom because this has
become their only support. In such circumstances, even personal dislike
can cause disastrous conflicts.' Chicherin is made to add a quotation from
St. Just: 'The revolution congealed, its ideology grew weak, there
remained only intrigue covered by red caps.' Two future victims of the
Stalin terror speak. Krestinsky says the cause was not just ambition, but
the logic of struggle, which 'seems to lead us to results which no one ever
dreamt of. This is the key to the tragedy.' While Enukidze is made to
explain: 'Enough talk of Jacobins! We face no such danger! Whom am I
to suspect? You? You? Myself?' To this Allexandra Kollantai replies: 'But
don't we hear people advocate making terror into the weapon of our
social policy, that is to use terror as the method of administration, just as
the Jacobins did?' Lunacharsky joins in: 'I fear that our local Robespierres
and Dantons will make the bullet the cure for all conflicts', and Sverdlov
comments: 'They will, of course, unless we stop them.'

These and other passages came over powerfully, and the audience lis-
tened raptly. This was a discussion of Russian revolutionary history,
hardly disguised at all by being about the Jacobins, since the argument
precisely concerned the applicability *to Russia* and to Bolsheviks of the
lessons of French revolutionary terror. At the end, the cast were given an
ovation. Their final bow they took without makeup, unsmiling, serious,
as if they had had a heart-to-heart talk with their audience.

An odd detail: throughout the performance two armed soldiers stood
rigidly on guard at each side of the stage. At regular intervals throughout
the play they were relieved, with smart, goose-stepping guard-changing.
The soldiers wore the full dress uniform of 1969. What was this meant to

convey? The present paying respect to the past? Or was it meant to point to the contrast between the informal, argumentative and unkept revolutionaries of 1918 and the stiff, hierarchical formality of today? Or . . .

This play – by Shatrov – made an exciting evening.

I saw three of the four Bulgakov plays (missing, alas, the farce *Ivan Vasilievich*). The first and most famous *Dni Turbinykh* (*The White Guard*), was poorly presented and indifferently performed by the Moscow Arts Theatre. I met no less than three separate Russians who told me that they had walked out after the first act. I could see why. The charm was missing, the actors (perhaps with two exceptions) below par, the production dull, the scenery and settings ugly. There were indefensible changes in the text. Thus a sarcastic reference by one character to Tolstoy was changed to Dostoevsky, for instance. Yet the prewar production of this play by this theatre is legendary, and Stalin was supposed to have seen it fourteen times. A Russian thought that the graceless ugliness was deliberate, because the present management of the theatre is too timid to present a White-guard family in a favourable light, and this, of course, would wreak havoc with Bulgakov's picture of warm and civilised domesticity. This seemed to me hardly a credible explanation. More probably it just is an unimaginative, mediocre production.

Very much better, indeed excellent, was the production of *Beg* (*Flight*) at the Yermolova theatre. This play 'in eight dreams' by Bulgakov is a beauty, and it was staged with skill and originality and acted with imagination. The principal character, the White general Khludov, the cruel hangman who returns to Russia from Constantinople after the flight of the White armies, is admirably played by Solovyov. No liberties were taken with the text or with Bulgakov's very detailed stage directions.

'Molière', by Bulgakov, with the Armenian actor Dzhigarkhanyan in the name part, went well at the Komsomol theatre. The production, by Efros (since sacked, or rather transferred), included some highly unusual music by Andrei Volkonsky – a mixture of modern quasi-electronic and the seventeenth-century idiom.

Volkonsky, a member of the aristocratic family, was educated in Switzerland. His great service to music in Russia has been to found, inspire and lead the 'Madrigal' ensemble. I had the good fortune to attend one of their concerts. Schütz, Orlando Gibbons, Campion, extracts from very early Italian opera, exquisitely sung and played. A Spanish Christmas carol, sung in procession with candles on the darkened stage, was the final encore. The ensemble includes three members of one family, the Lisitsyans, and their visit to this country ought not to be long delayed.

In the 'Soviet army' theatre Alexei Tolstoy the elder's *Death of Ivan the Terrible* was distinguished by an impressive Ivan by Alexei Popov, and by ultra-modern staging and music, but disfigured by the inability of the cast, except for Ivan and one old priest, to speak blank verse. The passages relating to Ivan's execution of all his best generals had a modern ring and received some emphasis.

At the Vakhtangov theatre a much more talented company was playing a dramatised version of Babel's *Red Cavalry* (*Konarmiya*). Production and acting were on a high level, but the play was a travesty of Babel. No Jews. The nasty bits smoothed out. Thus in the story 'Salt' the black-marketeering salt-smuggling woman is shot, by a soldier from a train. In this play the soldier puts his rifle down and says: 'I can't! She is a woman, after all.' Furthermore Babel's gentle and compassionate humour about the ignorant and illiterate cavalrymen is turned into a sort of upper-class giggle reminiscent of *Punch*'s attitude to Old Bill in World War I, and surely hardly proper in the circumstances.

How much better it was to hear that very same story recited, in full and as it was written, by a student at an evening of amateur theatricals put on by the Psychology faculty at the university. The acts were of very variable quality, but there was one excellent satirical playlet, including such harmless cracks as: 'The patient is suffering from solipsism, eclecticism and empirio-criticism.' Also what I assume to have been good imitations of certain lecturers, judging from audience reaction. I was later told the show was given low marks (it was entered for an inter-faculty competition) owing to 'ideological inadequacies' (*nevyderzhannost'*).

A professional variety show of quality was provided by the visiting 'Teatr miniatyur' of Leningrad, led by the great Raikin. One or two sketches had economic points. Here is one.

Director, to chief engineer: 'Telegram received, ordering us to make and deliver a hundred pumps. Can we do it?' Engineer: 'No. No materials. No machines. Shall we reply telling the ministry this?' Director: 'What, and be sacked at once? No.' Engineer: 'Shall we just not reply?' Director: 'Then we would be sacked tomorrow.' Engineer: 'Then what can we do?' Director: 'I know. Just watch me.' There follows an exchange of telegrams with the ministry. From Director: Consignment of wheels ready for despatch on Monday. Sidorov proposed for Order of Red Banner. From Ministry: Pumps, repeat pumps, not wheels. Who is Sidorov? From Director: Wheels sent by air, plane crashed in mountains of Azerbaijan. Goods stolen by hill tribes. Sidorov dismissed. And so on. Finally the director explains: 'If we go on long enough, then there are three possibilities. We will be transferred; they will change the plan; or they will abolish the ministry.'

At the Taganka theatre, reportedly modern and go-ahead, saw *Pugachev* by Yesenin. Yesenin was a fine lyric poet, but as a playwright, alas, he is quite second-rate. The production was imaginative and well acted, but there seemed little point in devoting ingenuity to such a play, full of loud declamation.

Other visits were to a very fine concert by Barshai and the chamber orchestra, and to the Bolshoi's magnificently staged *Khovanshchina* and *Boris Gudonov*. The experienced bass Ognivtsev made an impressive Dosifey in the former, and had short notice to sing Boris too, when Boris Christoff called off at the last moment. Reason: that Rozhdestvensky, the conductor who took the rehearsal, fell ill and would not conduct the performance, and, after some dithering, it was decided to go ahead under another conductor. Christoff was furious and returned to Italy, thereby cancelling two other appearances in the part the following week. With no rehearsal Ognivtsev sang well and acted superbly, especially in the last act, when he conveyed a haggard wreck of a man in the grand manner.

One very agreeable evening was spent in the Arts club (*Klub rabotnikov isskustv*), when various singers and instrumentalists performed works of an almost-forgotten nineteenth-century Russian composer, Verstovsky. A contemporary of Pushkin, and later the director of the Bolshoi theatre, he wrote an opera which is apparently due for a revival, 'Askoldova mogila'. The composer's great-grandson was present and was greatly moved.

Cultural life in Moscow is rich, and, one hears from all sides, hamstrung and frustrated by pettifogging censorship.

China: 1983

It was four years since I had visited China. What had changed? Superficial impressions first. Women more smartly dressed, often with elegant, colourful blouses and more complex hairdos. Fewer political slogans. Hardly any political portraits. I saw *one* of Mao Tse-Tung in sixteen days. Opposite the entrance to the Forbidden City there had been huge portraits of Marx, Engels, Lenin and Stalin – which provided me with a perennial discussion topic! I would point to Stalin's crimes and ask what he was doing there. Now, no Marx, or Engels, or Lenin or Stalin: all gone. Then – and this is perhaps no coincidence – what one did see were many more street traders, the first visible sign of economic reform, new ways of thinking, more flexible ideology. Small-scale private trade is now legal, and this in addition to the free peasant market. Peddlers can buy goods, anything from saucepans to sweets, and resell them for profit in town and village. In Russia, this would still be 'speculation', punishable by, say, four years imprisonment. It *was* illegal in China, but no more so. In a speech, prime minister Zhao envisaged leasing small state-owned stalls and workshops to private operators. There are already many thousands of small family workshops in existence, producing for the market. Could they employ labour, I asked? The answer came with a slight smile: open employment of labour by private enterprise might be characterised as exploitation, but a few apprentices or 'partners' would be acceptable. I must stress that these are very small workshops, maybe just in a back room, hardly capitalism raising its ugly head.

Two more positive developments must be mentioned: the appearance of a remarkably well-produced English language newspaper, *China Daily*, and the appearance, at long last, of a volume of official statistics. The visitor is thus much better informed. The *China Daily* not only prints a most useful survey of world news – from it I had learned not only the date of the general election, but also that Manchester United had won the Cup – but also a digest of the Chinese press, including some sharply critical or satirical material. Thus, one short piece related to the habit of weekly political study in factories and offices. These have long ago degenerated into tea-drinking, smoking and gossip. Why then continue this so-called study? Because, the author said, no orders have been received to stop it, and besides, the study takes place in work time! Also reported were more serious matters, such as the apparently widespread scepticism of the peasants about whether the latest agricultural reforms would last. But more about the peasants in a moment. The volume of official statistics makes fascinating reading. There are figures on the extent of overcrowding in urban housing, the size of the gold and currency reserves, the effects of the Cultural Revolution on education – higher education of all kinds virtually collapsed by 1970 – and also the catastrophic effects of the Great Leap Forward on agricultural and industrial production. That there was a famine in 1961–62 is now openly recognised. Though natural disasters also played their part, the main blame is now assigned to ultra-leftism, or what they choose to call 'the communist wind'. But to return to the statistics, there are striking data on population. Very high birth-rates were a feature of the 1950s and 1960s. The population of China increased by *420 million* in the last 30 years. The total sown area in these 30 years did not increase at all. Every inch of cultivable land is cultivated. The fertile province of Szechuan alone now contains 100 million people, or the population of Great Britain and France combined. In all China there are 800 million peasants. How to feed the people, and how to prevent the population from rising too fast, these are *the* most vital problems for China. The birth rate has dropped, from 36 per thousand in the 1960s to 18 in 1981, but stern measures are seen to be needed, as the many children born in the 1950s and 1960s have reached the age of reproduction. *One* child per family is the much-advertised norm, with two tolerated in the villages. A second child in a city means financial penalties and opprobrium. A third child? I was simply told: 'This is forbidden'. Compulsory abortion, presumably. Yet even if all these measures are effective they expect the population to reach 1200 million by the end of the century. In villages the drive to reduce the number of children, at a time when land is being assigned to peasant *families*, has led to a disturbing reappearance of the age-old practice of letting girl-babies die, since girls that marry become, by long tradition, members of their husband's family. English-language publications in Peking admit that the problem exists, connecting it with prejudices about the inferiority of women, but claim that it is not very widespread and that steps are being taken to stop it. There are proposals to alter the law to protect the interests of those whose only child is a daughter.

I must now briefly describe the radical changes which have occurred in Chinese villages. Since these account for 80 per cent of the population, the matter is of quite fundamental importance. The point is that the Chinese leaders have recognised, first, that collectivisation and communes had been *imposed* upon an unwilling peasantry, that this had been 'premature, excessive socialisation'. Second, they have realistically noted that agricultural techniques remain medieval: indeed, to my eyes the methods of cultivation could not have changed since the Ming dynasty! Consequently, there are no economies of scale, only *dis*economies of scale. Third, for evident reasons, more food production is a vital and top priority. So they took the decision to decollectivise. Or perhaps this is the wrong word. The land has not been transferred to peasant *ownership*, nor are they left free to decide what to grow on it. In most of China what we now have is called 'the household responsibility system'. A field, or fields, is assigned to a peasant family for their long-term use. The family have imposed upon them a quota of compulsory delivery; for example, they must sell to the state a specified quantity of rice, or vegetables. But, anything they produce over and above the delivery quota is theirs to dispose of, and, most important, they dispose of their own labour time, that is, instead of working under orders as members of a brigade or team, they are free to organise and arrange their work as a family. The idea is to provide much more direct incentives, and so to stimulate better and more productive work. The peasants, understandably, prefer such a system. As already mentioned, some wonder how long it will last. What has been given can be taken away. I put this to a member of the Agricultural Economics Institute in Peking. He replied: 'If the peasants prefer it so, it will last till the end of the world.' There are great inequalities between areas, and between peasants in the same area, depending partly on location and fertility, and partly on the prices paid by the state for the different products the peasants are ordered to deliver. When I broached the subject, to my surprise the answer I got was that the party's policy actually favours the emergence of a stratum of *rich* peasants, as this will dramatise in peasants' eyes the possibilities of enrichment under the new system. If riches were the result of superior effort and skill, one might accept this argument. But is this so? As another official frankly told me: 'No one could get rich by cultivating rice . . .' And millions, of course, grow rice to order. In one village I visited the rich family was allowed to raise ducks.

Industrial reform, decentralisation, the greater use of the market mechanism, were already being discussed widely when I was there four years ago. In this area, progress has been patchy. On the one hand, the many small urban industrial cooperatives are now much freer to produce for their customers, and retain nearly half of their profits. There is also much talk of allowing the larger state enterprises to dispose freely of that part of their output which the central planners have not allocated for their purposes. A new *profits tax* was being introduced, giving some greater financial autonomy to state enterprises, by providing them with resources to finance decentralised investments, housing, bonuses for workers. But, on the other hand, state-fixed prices are irrational, so that many enterprises make a loss, while high profits are often due to price anomalies rather than to efficient operation. The proper balance between plan and market is being sought, but has not yet been found. A Chinese leader is reported to have said: 'The relationship between the two is like a bird in a cage. The bird should be allowed to fly, but within the cage. Otherwise the bird will fly away.' So presumably they are building a bigger cage. But will this work in practice? Visiting factories in Chungking, Nanking and Shanghai, we learned of many local differences, experiments, pilot projects. In other words, reform is not yet in full flight, but I think it is on the way, if I may change the metaphor. There are parallels between China's reform measures, and their frustrations, and the sometimes similar reforms attempted in the Soviet Union, which have also been very largely frustrated, not only by resistance from bureaucrats but also through the reforms' internal contradictions. We will soon see if the Chinese will overcome the obstacles which still stand in the way of genuine decentralisation.

Mention of the Soviet Union leads me to another topic, that of China's attitude to Moscow. This *has* changed. In my capacity as a Sovietologist I gave a number of lectures and seminar talks, in Peking and elsewhere, both four years ago and on this occasion. In 1979, Chinese attitudes were more hostile: the USSR was enemy No. 1, threatening China militarily, any enemy of the USSR was *ipso facto* a friend of China, and that included NATO. This was accompanied by a considerable degree of ignorance about Soviet internal affairs, explicable by the disastrous impact on research institutes of the Cultural Revolution: staff had been sent to shovel manure in villages; library acquisitions ceased. It is quite different today. Chinese specialists on the USSR seemed not only much better informed, but far less extreme in their judgements. No one spoke to me of the Soviet military menace. My Chinese colleagues, in their comments on my own papers, tended sometimes to be a little more optimistic than I am about the possibilities of reforming the Soviet system. I do not want for a moment to suggest that anyone took a *pro*-Soviet position, or believed in any real reconciliation. There are still some conflicts, for instance over Vietnam and Kampuchea. Perhaps we are not seeing a thaw, but the ice is becoming less cold, so to speak. Trade will surely increase. It is indeed absurd that Chinese trade with the Soviet Union has been little higher than with Switzerland in recent years. Why this change? I suggest the following reasons. First, the Chinese perception of *Soviet* hostility had been exaggerated. Second, the Soviets are alarmed by Reagan's anti-communist crusade, and are genuinely anxious to avoid trouble on their Asian flank, fearing particularly a link-up between America and China. Third, Reagan's exaggerated anti-communist rhetoric, and American relations with Taiwan, have irritated Peking, which has now become even more even-handed in its criticisms of the two super-powers. We have no reason to expect any sort of Sino–Soviet alliance, but relations have improved. This has been symbolised by several sports events in which Soviet *and* Chinese athletes competed. This should remind us of ping-pong diplomacy and its role in re-establishing relations between China and the United States.

Not surprisingly, China's biggest trading partner is Japan. Japanese consumer durables are making their appearance, at high prices, in Chinese shops. The statistical annual informs us, for instance, that in 1981 China imported nearly four million TV sets, mainly from Japan. Imports from Britain are much below those from West Germany, but they have been growing. It was sad to note that the biggest city and commercial centre of China, Shanghai, has no British consulate, though the Americans, the French, the Germans, and of course the Japanese, have them. While it is true that the Chinese have postponed major industrial developments until they have got their economy into balance, it will be a very important market indeed, and I trust that the Foreign Office and the Department of Trade are not overlooking its potential. At the moment priority is given to consumers' goods industries and agriculture and to coping with bottlenecks in energy and transport. The 'period of readjustment' announced in 1979 was due to last for three years, but it has been extended. Even a modest increase in the incomes of the peasantry, poor though they are, represents a major strain on supplies of industrial goods; as one of their economists put it, 'unfortunately we have 800 million peasants'. To avoid shortages and inflation their needs have been put before the development of heavy industry.

China is, of course, a very poor country, and urban living standards, low as they are, are well above those of the peasantry. Average wages have now reached about 70 yuan a month. At the official exchange rate this is the absurd sum of £23, or £6 a week. The official exchange rate is misleading, in that basic foodstuffs such as rice and cooking oil (rationed), cotton cloth (also rationed) and housing are very cheap. But goods which are not basic necessities are dear, at these low wages. Thus a bicycle, very widely used, costs 160 yuan or more, well over two months' pay. A television set averages 500 yuan. A cheap suit costs one month's wages at least, which is why most men still wear blue cotton jackets. But China's clothing industry has been producing some brightly-coloured and cheap blouses, which has had the effect of making the women look far smarter than their menfolk. Wages have become a little more flexible, with bonuses payable for higher productivity and regular attendance. But one thing the workers cannot do is to change their job at their own volition. They are assigned to factories and offices by the labour bureau, and there they stay, unless they can successfully apply for a transfer. When they reach retirement age, their pension is paid by the enterprise or institution that had employed them. Some factory directors complained to us that they had no right to recruit the workers they wanted, or to get rid of those they did not want, and we heard of experiments: enterprises would be allowed to negotiate a contract with a time-limit, at the end of which they could offer to renew it or the worker could leave. But this is not the rule. The rule is that one is tied to one's job. In this respect the Chinese system is more authoritarian than the Soviet. I heard of cases where wife and husband are tied to jobs in different towns and see each other once a year, two weeks' holiday being the entitlement of those whose family live far away; others make do with Sundays and the Chinese equivalent of bank holidays. Women work alongside men even in steelworks; I saw them there in large numbers. Peasants cannot move to town without permission, which is seldom granted. Were it otherwise, no doubt towns in China, like many in the third world, would be overwhelmed. As it is, the housing problem is acute, the overcrowding very serious, especially in big cities like Shanghai.

The Cultural Revolution did some moderate damage to industry; it did not greatly affect agriculture. But it had a devastating effect on intellectuals, and much can be heard, and read, about arrests, deportations, humiliations, the smashing of monuments, the drive against so-called bourgeois culture. The damage done to education of all kinds will take long to repair. To the credit of Mao's successors, these bitter memories are openly discussed, and are the subject of many a short story and poem. I was impressed by some verses by an American, Paul Engle, who has a Chinese wife and spent many months with her in China. Here, for instance, is a part of a poem with the title: 'Dialogue with widow of a persecuted Chinese writer who committed suicide'. The widow speaks: 'But that man's dead because he asked from life/What the wind has – the simple right to breath./Without that he preferred his own self-death./For such an action I am still his wife,/Proud of his love for me, proud of his death/By which he praised the power of life, our life.' This, be it noted, was published in Peking. So was this: 'The bones ideas broke are mostly mended/Hands numbed by torture once again can feel,/The hate and horror of their lives have ended/But scars bleed in their eyes and will not heal.' The contrast is great, is it not, with the enforced shamefaced silence of official Russia on the Stalin terror. It gives grounds for hope that it cannot happen again in China.

Few visitors with any imagination and sensibility, in the course of a tour around China, will fail to develop a real affection for this ancient

people, who had and still have a hard and difficult life. You see them in
the fields, old and young, early and late, carrying two buckets on a yoke,
filled with human excrement for the paddies, or baskets laden with cab-
bages, or bricks, or coal; human beasts of burden, since in most of China
there is neither fodder nor pasture for pack-animals. Yet their faces can
and do light up with smiles. An attractive people, who would not wish
them well?

Yet I would like to end with two criticisms, one directed at the Chinese
authorities and one at us. They claim that they have a classless society,
but one is struck by the number of places which seem to be barred to any
but select officials and foreigners. Indeed in Shanghai of all places there is
a large building, a so-called club, with a park attached, and at the
entrance a notice in two languages forbids ordinary Chinese to enter:
only foreign visitors and overseas Chinese admitted. In the bad old days
of the foreign concessions, it is said there was a notice: 'Entrance forbidden to Chinese and dogs.' True, now there is no mention of dogs, but one
would wish such things would disappear and not be resurrected. In fair-
ness, I should perhaps mention that a magnificent temple complex, in the
mountains some 50 miles from Peking, was – we were told – reserved
until recently as a rest area for high officials, but is so no longer. On a
Sunday it was indeed full of Chinese excursionists. The second criticism is
of us. China is and has always been the most populous country in the
world, with the longest continuous history of statehood ever known. Yet
how many schools and universities teach how many students *anything*
about the history of China, or for that matter its politics, its economy, its
society or its language? This is a great power-to-be, and it is about time
we started learning about it.

Hungary: February 1985

Discussions with: Eva Ehrlich, Gabor Revesz, Bela Csiko-Nagy, Janos Kovacs, Maria Kovacs, Adras Köves, Tamas Nagy, Marton Tardos, Andras Brody, Maria Augustinovics, Rejszo Nyers, Tamas Bauer, Attila Soos, Ivan Major, Josef Bognar, Janos Kis, Laszlo Szamuely, Istvan Salgo, Ivan Berend, David Young, Miklos Pulaj.
Lectures given: Four. Two at the Karl Marx Economic University, one at the Institute of Economics, one at the Institute of World Economy.
Institutions visited: The above plus the Planning Office (saw deputy-chief-planner, Pulaj), and the British Embassy.

IMPRESSIONS

The Fate of the Reform

Much has changed since my last visit (in 1980). In principle the reform policies remain, and in a few respects have even been strengthened (for example, the extension of the second economy, the beginnings of a bond market, of which more later). The industrial ministries have been combined into one, with the avowed intention of reducing ministerial interference. However, the unanimous view of all I spoke to was that in practice the autonomy of enterprise management has been significantly reduced, and that the number and types of (often informal) interventions by various state and party authorities has become a source of even greater frustration and a source of inflexibility. A major cause was certainly the acute balance of payments crisis of 1982. Vigorous measures had to be taken to increase exports at almost any cost, to cut imports, to cut investment, to cut real wages. Avoidance of default or rescheduling of debt was given top priority, in the knowledge that the measures taken would contradict the logic of reform and would do other damage too. The policy could be described as a remarkable success in achieving its main objective: debts have been reduced, imports cut, exports raised, the trade balance has become positive, and all this within the space of a year or two. But this could not possibly happen as a result of laissez-faire or

31

purely 'economic' levers. And although the immediate crisis is past, there
is little room for manoeuvre, there is constant danger of a speed-up of
inflation, of disequilibrium, so many controls remain, much informal
intervention continues. A manager was quoted as saying wearily that
within the previous week he had visits from every official organisation in
Hungary except the Red Cross and the League of Women. Many
examples were quoted of how enterprise autonomy is restricted. For
example, rights to enter foreign-trade transactions remain. There are
about 200 enterprises who are authorised to enter into foreign-trade
deals, plus several competing foreign-trade corporations, which may be
used or not according to convenience. But any attempt to import more, or
something different, could encounter problems; there is a sort of informal
import licensing scheme, affecting particularly Western goods, though
some limited relaxation of restrictions is expected in 1985. There is also a
strong tendency for those prices which are nominally free to be subject to
limits. The 1980 attempt to link internal prices with prices obtained in
export markets has apparently been replaced by a better formula: that
prices charged in Hungary should not exceed the price of a similar
import plus import duty. This is seen as the price effect of import competition which ought to exist, but which, for reasons of shortage of hard
currency, cannot in fact exist. The view was expressed that there were few
consumers' goods available from Comecon members which would satisfy
Hungarian demand (cars are an obvious exception, more of which in a
moment; so is Czech beer). There is little competition between Hungarian
state firms, despite a desire to encourage it (one positive example is the
appearance of competing travel agencies), and so some sort of limit on
price rises is seen as essential, the more so as there are some shortages of
industrial producers' and consumers' goods. Yes, everyone agrees that the
price controls that exist are often illogical, but what alternative is there?
Which did not prevent one eminent economist from saying roundly that
all these informal price controls are a curse; that investments cannot be
profitably made when to the price squeeze is added a sharply increased
interest rate on credits. Modernisation of the productive structure
requires more investment, and this is frustrated.

It is clear – no one disagrees – that there have been seven lean years,
that living standards are below 1979 levels, that prices have had to be
increased again in January 1985 (Budapest public transport, admittedly
too cheap, has raised charges by 100 per cent, heating is up, so is milk,
and so on). Wages have been held down to below the rate of inflation by
reinforced controls (not prohibition, but penal taxes hit any enterprise
that exceeds norms). In *this* situation the second economy becomes
inevitably the target for criticism, some from genuinely outraged workers,

some used by political opponents of reform and liberalisation. Several colleagues spoke of the difficulties caused to state enterprises by the strictness of wage control. Thus a major metallurgical factory has lost some of its most skilled workers, because they felt they had to supplement their low official wages in some way, and could not do so in this enterprise. They had to move to the second economy, where their special skills were probably less useful to society.

The growth of various kinds of 'second economy' in urban areas has continued, with one institutional change of significance. This is the emergence of contract work-groups *within* state enterprises. Roughly 180 000 workers are so engaged, so this is not a trivial phenomenon. They serve the purpose essentially of evading wage control, 'to preserve the labour force in state enterprises', by providing a means of earning extra by 'internalising' the second economy within the enterprise. The state-enterprise workers form groups of varying size and sign a contract with the enterprise management; the workers produce in accordance with this contract using the enterprise's materials and equipment, and deliver to the enterprise on payment of an agreed sum. This bypasses wage control, as this is regarded not as a wage but as 'production expenses'. In one sense this is pay for overtime work. There are also contract groups who work independently outside of 'their' firm, also negotiating an agreement to produce and deliver to a state enterprise, this being yet another form of second job, urgently needed to top up inadequate family incomes. Some even do a third job. One shudders to think what the average total hours of work per week in fact are in Hungary. One ingenious colleague, in describing the accounting and control-evasion which led to the contract work group, spoke of the 'non-convertible forint': thus a forint intended to be paid out as wages cannot in practice be used for this purpose if to do so exceeds the limit set. Similarly, strict controls over investment can prevent the use of enterprise funds for investment purposes; so these are 'hard' forints, that is, hard to get authorisation to spend them. A 'soft' forint, however, is one which can be said to be usable to cover production expenses. The three kinds of forint are not (or almost not) mutually transferable under present practice. This is, of course, totally alien to the spirit and the letter of the new economic mechanism.

The contract groups have attracted several kinds of criticism. Some cannot either form or join such groups (for example, women with family responsibilities, and anyway many enterprises do not have such arrangements). The result is to introduce tension-creating income inequalities. The trade unions, in this instance genuinely representing the feelings of part of the membership, do not like this practice. Furthermore, since the contract groups work for themselves, they work harder and better, and it is suspected that their performance might well cause the management to raise the work norms for the regular ('first economy') hours. On the other hand, some find attractive the notion of the totally genuine self-management of the work groups. A modified form of workers' participation is in the process of being introduced, under the name of the Enterprise Council, 50 per cent of the membership being elected by the workforce, the rest representing management, the idea being that all large decisions must be referred to this body. We will see in due course how it will work in practice. It might be surmised that the strictness of control over incomes will lessen workers' interest in participating. A 10 per cent tax was recently introduced on orders placed with these various contract work groups (payable by the enterprises placing them), and taxes were also raised on second-economy earnings. This has been seen by some as a sign of party disapproval of private and contract activities, but against this it was said that, given the fall in real earnings in the first economy, rendered necessary by the recent economic difficulties, a gesture was necessary in the direction of taxing these other incomes more, though it was not the intention to reverse the policy of encouraging the second economy, as it is plainly essential. However, politics has played a role, and one quite senior and experienced man quipped: 'I am afraid we do have a few Tony Benns in the leadership group.' These began a mini-campaign against 'profiteers' in the second economy during 1984.

Several critical references were made to party officials' interference in town and village: this subverts the responsibility of management. One of my colleagues expressed strongly the view that the one-party state as at present conceived is inherently inconsistent with thoroughgoing market-type reforms. Yes, he agreed, the party can and should have political functions, the political organs can have broad economic policies; he does not advocate laissez-faire, but repeated intervention in the process of purely economic decision-making is bad and requires a self-denying ordinance. It is stressed that shortages have become more prevalent in all spheres except food, where agriculture and retail trade still perform satisfactorily (but it was pointed out that agricultural costs have risen, and the subsidy bill continues to be a burden, notably that linked to agricultural exports). Items not found anywhere included woollen gloves and two-way electric sockets. Management has had problems too, usually linked with shortages of foreign exchange and so to import restrictions and their consequences. This is another source of informal influence and control by the administration. Shortages have complicated life in the second economy too. For example, having gathered enough cash and found private builders is not enough to ensure that one can build, there may have to be recourse to a black market to get certain materials, or hire a building crane. One sensible economist contrasted the multitude of spasmodic party and state interference, often uncoordinated, with the more traditional ministerial controls. The latter, he agreed, were excessive and were rightly abandoned, but at least they were exercised with some consistency by competent people. Yes, said another one, 1982 was a very difficult year indeed, but reform was moving then, though slowly. Counter-offensives by opponents of the market are actually stronger now than in 1982, thus showing that politics too is a determinant, independently of economic and social pressures, though of course both exist.

Capital Market and Bond Sales

Several economists felt that the absence of any real capital market was a source of inefficiency, and that the monopolist State Bank as a source of credit was far from sufficient. Therefore the decision to allow the issue of interest-bearing bonds represents an important 'ideological' step in the direction of allowing a capital market, though it is at present still very limited. The idea is to mobilise private savings and also to allow enterprises of various kinds to invest a part of their reserves in other enterprises. Interest rates are high (about 11 per cent) and are guaranteed by the state, a guarantee which seems to some of my colleagues to be an error: enterprises that issue bonds should take full responsibility for the consequences. Savings bank deposits have a much lower interest rate, but there is the convenience of drawing money out quickly as needed. The bonds are saleable, and the going rate for purchase and sale sometimes appears in the press, setting another significant precedent. Their numbers are limited, and demand at present exceeds supply. Some more regular and convenient method for productive investment is still needed. There is even talk of state companies issuing shares, though this will probably not happen. Some private fortunes run to millions of forints, so there is capital to be mobilised. Its use in the private sector is limited not so much by any formal rules but by a widespread lack of confidence: that rules will be changed, that business success will attract some sort of hostility, restriction, new high taxes, and so on.

Housing

This is a major subject of conversation, and understandably so, since prices range from extremely high to incredible, for anyone not already in possession of their own or state/municipal flat. A three-room flat near the centre has a free-market rent of roughly 14 000 forints a month, which is well over double the average monthly wages, and so people with money find it worth investing in buying flats and renting them, especially as prices rise fairly fast. A very small and modest place to live requires at least a month's salary as rent. Purchase prices run to millions, several people saying that to buy (or to get a house or flat built) can amount to *twenty years'* salary. Limited loans are available sometimes from one's own employer or from other official sources, but more probable is *private* borrowing, with or without a high rate of interest. Thus one person mentioned owing a friend 300 000 forints, this being part of a purchase price. There are complex provisions for exchanging private for municipal accommodation by way of a legal exchange. That is, one cannot *buy* a municipal flat, but if the possessor of such a flat wishes to buy your private flat or house, then you (the seller) can move into the municipal flat as part of the transaction. Housing costs are one important reason why people have to do two or more jobs, *and* why all adults have to work, which also contributes to the very low birth-rate. I expressed incredulity about the huge free-market prices. Can there be so many people who can raise so much money? Apparently – yes.

Energy Problems, and Cars

It is clearly very important for Hungary to save energy, so much of which has to be imported at high prices. But it is hard to obtain energy-saving machinery and vehicles from Comecon countries. This applies to both tractors and cars. Budapest has a great many 'eastern cars': Dacia (Romania), Wartburg and the two-stroke Trabant (GDR), Skoda (Czechoslovakia), and Lada (USSR). The Lada is popular, the waiting list is long, efforts to persuade the Soviets to sell more of these to the Hungarians have been unsuccessful. I saw exhibited in a store in Budapest a price list with delivery dates, looking more or less like this (figures purely from memory): Trabant 38 000, 38 000 1986, Lada 55 000, 65 000 1990. It seems that the first figure is the deposit you pay, the second when delivery takes place. It was said that the Japanese offered to build a factory making small and fuel-efficient cars in Hungary, but they had to be turned down, because there is a Comecon agreement about who is to make cars – and Hungary makes Ikarus buses. Some calculations made in Budapest show that socialist countries are world champions in wasting energy and metal (in relation to their respective GNPs), with Hungary the least bad among them.

Nationalisms

There is much feeling about the treatment of Hungarians living in Transylvania and Slovakia, and some grassroots criticism of the lack of action on the part of the government on this issue. Much was said about the strength of nationalism in neighbouring 'socialist' countries, and the obstacle this poses to economic and political cooperation. 'It was easier to collaborate with these countries in previous days, despite the fact that the Little Entente was partially directed against Hungary.' Odd to see, in the Apostolok restaurant (recommended) one room decorated with portraits of apostles, the other (the 'irridenta' room) with pictures of towns lost to Hungary (Arad, Kassa, and so on).

Comecon and All That

Here pessimism and gloom were universal. The recent summit achieved nothing. The smaller countries seem to have fought a rearguard action to limit the effects on them of Soviet demands. Of course future Soviet deliveries of fuel and raw materials are constrained by availability, of course the Soviets wish to charge full prices and to acquire better quality manufactures (especially machinery) in exchange. It was also said that the Soviets were fairly generous in negotiating prices of machines imported from Comecon countries while the terms of trade of the latter were rapidly deteriorating, but they have become tougher now in respect of both quality and price. But there was and is no sign of any change in the methods of trade (bilateral quotas, and so on), though these are very inconvenient for Hungary – and will become very inconvenient for Poland also if the Polish economic reform (which has foreign-trade liberalisation as one of its aims) actually comes to fruition. (Whether it will or not – on this opinions differed.) Summarising prospects, one colleague expressed the view that no positive changes can be expected, but negative changes are to be feared. The need in recent years to cut back on hard-currency exports has highlighted the shortage of goods of the needed type and quality available from within Comecon countries. When goods do appear that are in real demand (example: four-year queues for Lada cars), efforts to secure higher deliveries usually fail. Of course some trade liberalisation is a precondition of effective competition in the home market, and without such competition the logic of the 'New economic mechanism' cannot operate. But – vicious circle. Shortage of currency inhibits imports, notably from the West, and the slowness of technological reconstruction of Hungarian industry inhibits the expansion of exports to the West.

Miscellany

Why, it was asked, introduce a large increase in heating prices in the middle of a cold winter? So much less painful, psychologically, to do so in July! One reason given was to finish with unpopular measures before the party congress. Interesting discussion, some of it in print, about reliability of statistics. Scepticism expressed both about the consumers' goods index (understates real price rise) and overall volume index, especially in some years. Something very odd, yet to be explained, happens to national income figures in 1974 (see, for example, A. Brody's article in *Acta Oeconomica*, 1980, Nos 1–2; he says that a rise of 4.7 per cent in 'comparable prices' became 7 per cent in 'unchanged prices', which, he claims, is beyond belief. The real figure he estimates as 1 or 2 per cent!).

Private and semi-private, legal and semi-legal, the rules and tolerance are complex, and fears that they may vary inhibit investment and long-term planning in such activities. Thus there is a limit today on number of rooms in a private boarding-house, or of employees in a private workshop, quite favourable terms of trade for the lease of a state restaurant for private operation, but what happens tomorrow, especially after Kadar? Reform in 1981–82 legalised a wider range of private activity, but a sort of press campaign against private profiteers began at the end of 1984. Increased taxes on private and semi-private groups is interpreted as a sign of a harder and more negative policy though this has been denied. It is justified by some as a necessary gesture to calm opinion which resents high private incomes at a time of falling living standards. Question I was asked: since virtually all the institutions suggested in my book on *Feasible Socialism* exist in Hungary, and since they do not work very well, is this not a basis for criticising my model of socialism? The questioners seemed partially satisfied with the answer (of which, of course, they were well aware) to the effect that various restrictions – listed above – substantially reduce the true competitive market element in the system. Also relevant is the relative weakness of Hungary's industrial traditions, contrasting in this respect unfavourably with both East Germany and the Czech lands.

Gloom caused by a general sense of frustration and aimlessness. Nothing really better in prospect, except a halt to decline in living standards. Party congress speeches and resolutions will seem unreal, and drafts have already been sharply criticised at some party meetings. No perspective, no policy aims, that can mobilise or inspire. Some writers (for example, an article by Nyers and Tardos) urge taking the public more fully into the leadership's confidence, greater democratisation. Other critics advocate a clearer and more limited definition of the role of the party, with some real protection from arbitrary interference in current economic (and political) decision-making. There should be 'legal regularisation', effective protection of property and other rights, an end to the virtually extra-legal power of party officials. But would such a self-denying ordinance actually work, or happen, without an unlikely degree of change in the *political* system?

One critic spoke of a sort of 'war economy' with low wages and sub-sidised necessities. A common guess was that 20 per cent of national income in the Soviet sphere is diverted to military purposes. The celebration of the 40th anniversary of the liberation of Hungary and of the 1945 victory are seen, in present circumstances, as something of an irritant. It was stressed that, although management is often paralysed by the multitude of orders and restrictions, the actual achievement of the economy in coping with the acute balance of payments crisis of 1982 was creditable. Exports rose, imports fell, a $600 million surplus replaced the trading deficit. This cannot be called a failure. One estimate is that imports from hard currency areas might rise by 5 per cent per annum in the course of the next five years. This would relieve shortage and provide a little limited competition, which cannot be provided adequately by CMEA goods, few of which people want to buy. The point was well made that the fact that 25 per cent of GDP enters into Comecon trade, which is conducted in the 'traditional' bilateral way, is among the main obstacles to coherent economic reform. It is said that the size of the second economy is understated in official estimates, because so much of its activities are invisible (mainly not because the activity is illegal, but to avoid tax and drawing unnecessary attention). Including private agriculture, some estimates put it at around 15 per cent of GDP. 'Soviet tractors seem to be by-products of tank production, and are heavy fuel-users. Soviet combine-harvesters are incapable of coping with a crop which exceeds 3 tons per hectare. So some Soviet farm machinery is unsuitable for Hungary.' Discussed Polish reform prospects. Opinions varied. Polish government's intentions do seem to be to travel the Hungarian road. But there is the problem of Soviet attitudes (which *may* be favourable), also of the Polish government's own determination to act, in a difficult economic situation.

The Hungarian plan for 1985 envisages, at last, a halt to the decline in domestically used GDP, in investments, and in real wages, 'which have been going on since 1979.' There should be a small rise (by 1 per cent) during this year. Real wages should not fall. The inflation rate of 8 per cent is high by CMEA (and Austrian) standards. If prices were freed and subsidies greatly cut, the increase would be much larger. To avoid too much hardship, subsidies are being phased out slowly, by stages. Interest rates charged by the Bank for credits have been increased substantially. Wage controls will remain tight. Some criticism directed at enterprises for not devising more effective forms of incentive wage-differentiation within the permitted total. Low wages, lack of incentives, are a vicious circle (chicken-and-egg problem). Price controls are maybe illogical but necessary. 'Marriage between water and fire' required as part of the battle to contain inflation. Tax rates on private incomes now rise to a maximum of

65 per cent, which is charged on revenues in excess of 200 000 forints. Kornai's *Economics of Shortage* applies in Hungary too, but less than in other socialist countries.

Finally: A most stimulating experience. Much enjoyed discussions and hospitality. Budapest is among the most intellectually stimulating cities. May this long continue.

Prague: May 1991

Plenty of food. Shops reasonably stocked. But many problems are crowding in. First is the external-trade crisis, now looming. By far the largest trade partners were the USSR and East Germany. Trade with both is collapsing. The Soviets failed to deliver all the oil promised last year, and the lower volume promised for 1991 will in all probability not materialise. Trade negotiations with Moscow have been held, but the Soviet importers are often unable to pay, and Soviet regulations stand in the way of international barter deals. How can Czecho-Slovak industry restructure to switch its products to other markets? Fortunately the debt inherited from the past is relatively modest, but is now rapidly increasing. This is the immediate problem No. 1. The official exchange rate for the Czech crown was devalued from 17.0 to the dollar to 28.0 in January 1991 and about 30.0 today. Meanwhile, the 'black' rate has *fallen* from 36.0 in January to 30.0 in March–April, a result of severe deflationary monetary policy. Joint ventures are impressively numerous: 2800 now, but only three of them are large, the biggest being the Volkswagen investment in Skoda.

Information received from the excellent economist Karel Kouba shows a startling fall in industrial production: –3.7 per cent in the year 1990, –6.5 per cent in January 1991, –6.7 per cent in February and –25.3 per cent (!!) in March. This is connected with the accumulation of unsaleable formerly-exported products, but even more with the deflationary measures (which include a large budget surplus in the first quarter of 1991). So far unemployment has not been a major disaster (under 2.5 per cent overall, though over 3 per cent in Slovakia), but it is rising, and the government expects it to reach 5 per cent by the end of the year – though Kouba and others consider this to be very overoptimistic, as and when bankruptcies are allowed to occur. The rapid rise in unemployment may generate a political crisis. For example, the miners in the Ostrava coal-basin would not accept mass redundancies lying down, especially as they were favoured under the communist regime.

Consumer prices in March 1991 were 40.9 per cent above the level of a year ago, though the rise in March was only 4.7. (The big increase was in January, when most prices were totally freed). Wages have been strictly controlled (as also in Poland), and rose only by 3.5 per cent in the past *year*. The average wage is now 3300 Czech crowns (KCs) a month, and a minimum wage law has also been adopted (despite initial opposition from finance minister Klaus) at 2000 KCs. At an exchange rate of 30 to the dollar, 3300 crowns is $110 a month. At such a rate, holidays outside Czechoslovakia become prohibitively expensive. So do many imported products, the more so because the government charges importers an extra 20 per cent levy over and above the exchange rate, plus an import duty. Imported products of all kinds are therefore very expensive, given that former Comecon countries now all expect to be paid in hard currency. (Imported) petrol now costs 18 crowns a litre, which makes ten gallons equal to the average *weekly* wage. No wonder I saw modest weekend traffic to and from Prague: people hesitate even to travel to their country cottages, if they have them. True, many consumer items are still fairly cheap, for example, public transport, but this too has gone up very sharply (trams in Prague now charge 4 crowns, four times the former fare, though this is still only about 12 cents). However, the harsh policies pursued by Klaus aim at demolishing most of the former welfare-state; charges for kindergartens, medicines, rents, utilities, are rising sharply, and even the concept of a 'safety-net' is regarded as dangerously left-wing. As Klacek put it in a conference paper, 'there is deliberately no adjective, such as e.g. a 'social' market economy.' Friedmanite–Thatcherite ideology rises high, though modified in practice by political considerations (as when Klaus had to concede a minimum wage). All this will be under severe social strain when unemployment rises, and when formerly favoured groups such as the coal miners at Ostrava find themselves sacked. Particularly as consideration of any investment *strategy* designed to deal with structural distortions of the economy is also ill-regarded, as it smells of 'planning'. Some of my Czech colleagues fear that excesses of neo-liberal ideological enthusiasm will impose such disproportionate sacrifices on the workers that there will be a political backlash. As one of them put it, 'the government seems unaware of the danger, but basks in the approval of the IMF.'

It has been pointed out that privatisation in Czecho-Slovakia is still at the beginning of a long process. Unlike in Hungary, Poland and even East Germany, the Czech regime was very rigidly opposed to all forms of private enterprise, so that the public sector covered close to 100 per cent of all activity. Small-scale privatisation is now taking off. Private shops, workshops and restaurants are appearing, and in a small Bohemian town I saw posted a list of what is currently being sold off: one hotel went for 4 million crowns. But state property remains dominant, and there is lack of private capital with which to purchase larger enterprises. Some speak of bureaucratic obstructions too, touching also the much-desired foreign investment. The vast majority of the new enterprises are in services and trade; there are said to be several hundred private travel agents in Prague alone. Material production so far benefits little, but one must recall that the whole process only started five months ago. Had a very interesting two hours with Jan Klacek, director of the Institute of Economics. He is clearly as worried as I am about the consequences of the neo-liberal policy pursued by Vaclav Klaus and his fellow-ideologists. Far too little thought has gone into the consequences of high unemployment and on the needed safety-net. The notion of any sort of long-term strategy, or even medium-term programme, is rejected. There is the naive belief that the market will take care of all problems, that with low wages 'the labour market will clear', when quite obviously it will not. Indeed, if employment and output fall through lack of demand, it is an odd 'remedy' to cut demand even more by lowering both wages and government expenditures. With interest rates at 24 per cent, though below the level of inflation, few feel able to borrow for productive investment. As also in Poland, nearly every new private business is in services or commerce, hardly any in manufacturing.

The right of former owners to reclaim their property has had a deplorable effect on the privatisation process, since the claims raise a multitude of legal and valuation problems ('they will keep lawyers busy for ten years'), while others fear that their efforts to buy may at any time be challenged by relatives of former owners. Klacek said that Klaus anticipated this and did not favour the restitution law, but his own party overruled him. Investment vouchers, *bought* for 1000 or 2000 crowns (worth much more, the charge is to cover the cost of issue) will be available from 1 January 1992 to every citizen aged 18 and over. These will contain 'investment points', with which to purchase shares. The points will be non-transferable, but the shares, once bought, can be sold. 'The best 10 per cent of Czech enterprises' will be offered to foreign capital (!?). Land ownership is still a subject of dispute. Some advocate total speedy privatisation, others want to go slow and confine sale of farmland to those who wish to farm. 80 per cent of the existing peasantry have expressed opposition to privatisation, which could disrupt the successful collective farms to no evident purpose. Speed here is not of the essence. The uncertainty can only discourage existing farms from investing. Disaster faces formerly subsidised culture. Playwrights and publishers have sent a petition to President Havel!

Finally, the very steep decline in industrial production in March, which is continuing, Klacek attributed primarily to the collapse of demand at home, though frustrated exports (formerly to the USSR and the GDR) is an important contributory factor. He considers the Czech crown to be vastly undervalued in terms of real purchasing power. At present the crown is fully convertible for trade transactions, but citizens are limited to 5000 crowns-worth of foreign currency a year for private use. It may be worth recalling that West European countries after the war took many decades to reach full convertibility and to free capital movements. Indeed some restrictions exist today, for example, it is all but impossible for foreigners to acquire companies or land in Switzerland and Austria. Klacek expressed concern about the consequences of a too rapid currency deregulation, while others (for example, Jan Kavan) were worried about foreign interests, largely German, acquiring a high proportion of capital assets, and at low prices.

It was a most interesting and rewarding trip. One leaves this beautiful country with a sense that, as an article in the *Boston Globe* once put it, 'in rejecting Lenin it is not necessary to embrace Milton Friedman', and it is time that some Western economists who do not reflect extreme laissez-faire views made their voices heard. It is understandable that, in rejecting the extremes of centralised state planning, they might go too far in the opposite direction. Understandable, but I hope, preventable, as the social –political consequences would be disagreeable for all concerned. Odd, in a country which coined the term 'socialism with a human face', that we now find such a loud advocacy of capitalism with an *inhuman* face.

Ukraine (Kiev): June 1991

10 June

Discussion in Kiev municipality, with M. Pogrebinsky, chairman of committee on reform (and a non-communist) and Kryukov (a deputy and a reform economist). The political position in the municipality is finely balanced, with communists and opposition with almost equal portion of the 300 deputies, but the communists have a majority on the 13-strong executive committee. But they, and the opposition, are divided. Most retail purchases in Kiev are made with money plus coupons, issued with wages. There is talk of overstamping rouble-notes with a Ukrainian emblem, and using them to replace coupons (outsiders will then be unable to buy with ordinary roubles in the Ukraine). It is intended to go ahead as quickly as possible with the privatisation of services, such as shops, cafes, hairdressers, and so on, *but* the legal position is not clear: they are *not* the property of the Kiev municipality, so it cannot sell them. There are hopes of the new republican minister dealing with these matters, Lanovoi, who is said to be favourable to the needed changes in property law. Meanwhile Kiev is going ahead with valuation and 'inventorisation', so as to be able to dispose of these properties when the time comes. Pogrebinsky is not too keen on employee buy-outs or employee control through dominance in shareholding. He prefers limited sales to employees to about 30 per cent of the capital, which would be offered to them on favourable terms. A great problem is shortage of qualified staff in the municipal offices. Now that *nomenklatura* privileges have gone, public servants seem poorly paid. Also in very short supply are persons qualified to act in the market, for example, as brokers. *Izvestiya* (8 June 1991) reported without comment that the Ukrainian Supreme Soviet passed by a huge majority a resolution to the effect that all-union enterprises on Ukrainian territory are henceforth under Ukrainian ownership. One reason given is to exert control over any form of privatisation. But the centre may wish to *sell* 'their' properties.

Kryukov (who, incidentally, is a Russian) began by making parallels (which *are* close) between the negotiation with Moscow today on Ukrainian sovereignty and the remarkably similar negotiations between

Kiev and the Provisional Government in Petrograd in 1917. He also noted the tendency for privatisation to take the form of making the existing management the *de facto* owners of state enterprises. This did not greatly worry him, in that they would then carry real responsibility. Others did not agree. He agreed that there was an impossible situation today with the 'war of laws', but insisted that the only way out is the priority of *republican* decision-making. As a deputy he attended the (all-union) 'congress of democratic parties', and found that the *Russian* democratic parties tended to support the preservation of the Union, unlike nearly all the others, who urged not *soyuznoye gosudarstvo* (a union state) but a *soyuz gosudarstv* (an alliance of states). The present ideas on a Union treaty involving the '9 + 1' formula (the nine republics plus the Union, with six outside) is just papering over the cracks and will not work, he said. The old ideology served as a uniting cement; its collapse means the *inevitable* disintegration of the Union. Yes, the several parts are at present acting separately, erecting barriers, beggaring their neighbours. But the Union in its present form, he insisted, is finished, cannot remedy the situation. What is needed is a speedy divorce, if possible an amicable one, and then economic necessity will cause voluntary economic collaboration, hopefully within a free market. Though also possible is an association with other countries, for example, the Ukraine joining Hungary, Poland, Czechoslovakia, also the separate existence of a Central Asian federation. He suspects 'democratic Russia', even Yeltsin, of traditional-Russian attitudes, a reluctance to recognise that Moscow domination is finished. He argued strongly against the granting of credits to Gorbachev, and against inviting him to London. To provide him with money will temporarily strengthen the centre but will simply prolong the process of divorce, and make it more hostile. Anyhow, he pointed out, it will be hard enough to divide the responsibility of honouring existing debt commitments between (reluctant) republics. (Indeed, it would seem that default is looming on the horizon, as and when the centre loses even more power, A.N.) As for any new debt, a proposal is before the Supreme Soviets of several of the republics *that any credits offered to, and debts incurred by, the Union after 1 September 1991 will not be recognised by the republics unless their prior agreement is sought.* A declaration to that effect, if adopted, would be a most serious matter. Kryukov spoke feelingly about the republic's representatives not being invited to the London meeting: 'Why is Kravchuk [the Ukrainian leader] not to be there, if Gorbachev is?' Even though there is a strong communist contingent in the Ukrainian Supreme Soviet, the majority will vote for sovereignty (as they voted, with only one against, for Ukrainian ownership of all-union enterprises), because there would soon be another election and they want to be elected.

If all this is so, two consequences seem to follow. First, the West's commercial and diplomatic links with the republics, and particularly with the Ukraine, need to be very considerably strengthened. And, second, our view of Gorbachev's position as the Union President should be looked at again. I had myself taken the view that he should be supported because there seems to be no tolerable alternative to him at the all-union level. Also because the necessary minimum of monetary order and stability, and a balanced budget, require strength in the centre. But if Kryukov's view is correct, the centre is in process of collapse anyhow, and power shifts to the republics, with all sorts of consequences, affecting foreign debt, trade, currency and (last but not least) the military–industrial complex. Gorbachev and his image of a loose Union federation has then been overtaken by events which are either irreversible, or only reversible by mailed-fist methods and the shedding of blood. Such a view as this cannot be rejected out of hand. The position of Yeltsin on such questions looks good in words. In a *Pravda* interview (published on 10 June) he expressed support for the 9 + 1 formula and said:

> The centre will be that which corresponds to the desires of the republics which enter it. This relates to powers, structures, and so on. As the functions will diminish, so the central structures will be significantly simpler and cheaper. But we are for the effective carrying out by the centre of those functions which the republics will grant it, and so we favour a strong centre, but strong only in the sphere of its competence and prerogatives. Otherwise it will simply not be needed.

What, in practice, will this mean? Can one conceive of powers delegated upwards (unanimously?) being effective powers? It is still very much unclear. I asked Kryukov about the claims of Tatarstan and other national subdivisions of the RSFSR for sovereignty. He expressed support for their claims. But where would this leave Yeltsin and his colleagues, if (as is expected) he wins the election for President of 'Russia'? Interestingly, the intelligent observer Kseniya Myalo (*Moscow News*, No. 22, 1991) points to 'Russia losing the consolidating role in relation to other republics because the drive towards greater independence for the autonomous states within the Russian federation undermines the Russian government's strongest support and main attraction: control over the sources of raw materials . . .'. Indeed, according to *Kommersant* (No. 22, 1991), the Tatar republic has refused to allow balloting for the RSFSR presidency on its territory.

The supply situation remains grim. In *Moscow News* (No. 22, 1991) Andrei Vavilov noted the halving of oil exports, the 'draconian' cut in imports, and the resultant sharp decline in production of consumers' goods (−15 to −20 per cent by the year's end). He expressed the view that the sharp rise in prices has in fact only been 'compensated' to the extent of 50 per cent, so that demand has fallen, and there would have been more goods in the shops had it been possible to maintain output.

11 June

Lecture in Management Institute. Discussions. Very keen on links with the UK. This is a non-state institute, which rents lecture-rooms and so on, on a commercial basis from the Higher Party School! (Marx should turn in his grave?) Lively discussion. Then a discussion in 'Republican Commercial Centre INCOMAC', director Vassily Titov. This is a joint stock company formed on the basis of the former republican office of *Gossnab* (that is, of the material–technical supply committee), which had 25 sub-offices in various parts of the Ukraine. He 'broke with Gossnab' in September 1990, registered as a joint stock company in January 1991. It has agreements with about 2000 enterprises, buying and selling materials and machines, while also acting as an 'information bank', organiser of publicity and exhibitions, of barter deals. It is licensed to sell some items abroad, sells some without a licence. It is the Kiev agent for the sale of Citroen cars (three such cars with Kiev registration plates were in the forecourt). They publish a periodical *Ukraine Business* in 50 000 copies (in Ukrainian). His office is co-founder of the Kiev commodity exchange. Answering questions, director Titov said that his turnover, though growing, is limited by the 'state orders' (*goszakazy*) which are still imposed on most industrial enterprises. They get better prices through his office, but the ministries still issue orders, and have some clout because they can still allocate some of the materials or fuel the enterprise needs. Parts of the command system function, though unreliably. Furthermore, the ministries and the financial organs try to cream off to the budget any extra profit gained from selling at higher prices. He said that trade barriers between republics obstruct his activities, sometimes contracts entered into are arbitrarily blocked by republican or local authorities. Prices are often fixed by republics at levels that differ from those of their neighbours. There would, he hoped, be better order in a sovereign Ukraine. He welcomed the recent takeover of all-union enterprises by Ukrainian authorities. They have collaborated with a Canadian firm in the production of a truly excellent and comprehensive business directory for the Ukraine, in English, with a huge list of firms of all kinds and what they do. It is published by Accent Publishing Inc. They have just received an advance copy, which I perused. It is worth ordering.

Conversation next with V. Chernyak, well known (Kiev) deputy in USSR Supreme Soviet. He is a 'Ukrainian-sovereignty' supporter, but no extremist. He stressed the one-sided development of Ukrainian industry: about 50 per cent energy (coal, electricity, and so on), 28 per cent 'directly military', leaving little else. Consumer goods and food processing industries as well as the metallurgical industry, are in a poor state due to obsolete and worn-out equipment. He too supported the notion of an agreement with and freer trade between sovereign states, replacing the Union in any form similar to the present one. Asked about the military–industrial complex, he expressed the view, first, that the present military budget (96 billion) is much too high; second, that real expenditure is higher still, since the 96 is the budget of the Ministry of Defence and not total military expenditure. It was not clear to me how he and others who think like him conceive of the future of the all-union military force, if there is to be one, or of who will be responsible for servicing debts incurred in the past. Titov suggested that the republics might agree on such a shareout, but clearly they could argue endlessly about who should pay and find good reasons for minimising their contribution.

Interesting conversation followed with M. Bidzilla, chairman of a *rai-iskolkom* (district executive committee). He is a native of Carpathian Rus, and spoke with a noticeable Hungarian accent. His attempts to privatise local services (for example, hairdressing, foods shops, cafes) are resisted by city bureaucrats, whose interest in keeping control he attributes to widespread corruption – they have a customary 'take' which they would lose if either the district or the free market took over. He expressed the view that Gorbachev *does* need support at his level, because the alternative could be the military, but that any Western aid should be shared out by agreement between republics.

12 June

Fascinating meeting with M.A. Shvaika, deputy-chairman of commission on economic reform of the Supreme Soviet of the Ukrainian republic. He was quite emphatic. 'The Union is a corpse.' Aid to the Union prolongs the agony and cannot have any useful effect. He was dismayed by an article in that day's *Izvestiya* (by M. Berger) which cites the view in Moscow that the Ukraine and other republics should *buy out* the all-union enterprises located there. No, he argued, the centre has been robbing the Ukraine for years, through unfair prices, through appropriating savings banks deposits, through taking over amortisation payments. He claimed that deliveries to other republics of cheap coal (at prices *far* below cost) and agricultural products ('pork at 1.80 a kilo') required subsidies from the *republican* budget. He not only argued for the speedy creation of Ukrainian currency, but showed me some samples ready to be printed, of banknotes (100 *griven*').

Together with my chief host, Veniamin Sikora (for whose energetic organisational activities I was most grateful), we met again for lunch with the USSR deputy Vladimir Chernyak. He was particularly interesting about the aims and personality of Kravchuk, who is the effective leader today in his capacity as chairman of the Ukrainian Supreme Soviet. He aims to be president of the Ukraine, and, according to Chernyak, manoeuvres skilfully, presenting himself as a moderate in Moscow and as a nationalist in Kiev. He did, however, clash in Moscow with Lukyanov, described as a 'Russian imperialist'. Kravchuk's own ambitions have driven him rapidly in the direction of seeking sovereignty, but perhaps within a Union. A couple of years ago he was publicly opposed to *Rukh*. Now, in alliance with *Rukh* moderates, he might settle for 'real autonomy within the empire'. His ambiguous position is typical of important elements of the Ukrainian Communist party. He is able (so far) to mobilise mass support, especially as the radical and democratic parties are numerous, fragmented, often fighting each other. (But there is talk of creating a Ukrainian *Solidarnosc*.) Chernyak said he thought seriously that the speedy destruction of the all-Union centre is desirable ('why prolong the agony'), but inclines to the view that, for the present, 'Gorbachev should be helped. He should be granted credits so that we all gain time for the necessary changes. We are doomed to support him, because right now *we* would otherwise be doomed.' He expressed favourable sentiments about Yeltsin. His election would, he thought, help the process of negotiating a workable treaty between sovereign republics. Economically and culturally, 'Russia and the Ukraine need each other, but relations must be on a new basis of real equality and fair exchange'. Chernyak also said that, a few months ago, he said directly to Gorbachev: out with the general secretary, but up with the president.

After lunch, visit to the economic faculty of Kiev University. Pleasant discussion with the dean, V. Nesterenko, and several of his staff. Subject: what sort of economics to teach, and the possibility of mutual visits and collaboration. We could do much to facilitate visits from their young economists to Britain. It is a valuable and inexpensive form of aid. After that, a visit to publishers, who produce the widely-read *Ukrainska Mladezh*, and who may translate the new edition of my *Feasible Socialism*. Night train to Lvov.

13 June

Day in Lvov. Impressive old town. Fine opera-house. Elegant old university building. Austrian–Polish architecture. Ukrainian spoken everywhere. Rector of economics faculty, Zinovi Batamanyuk, and director of institute of management, V.M. Penzenyuk, organised a lecture at the university, gave a (very good) lunch and showed me the town. Again, clear desire for contacts with us. Is the western Ukraine so distinct that, in the .event of an attempt at real independence, the east and the south would split off? This was the view expressed to me last year by Aleksander Tsipko, himself of Ukrainian origin, and was restated in a recent *Izvestiya* article, which even spoke of a five-way split. I asked about this both in Kiev and Lvov. The consensus was that things have changed fairly radically, that Kiev is now seen as a national centre by them all. Kiev too has changed. Even this casual observer who had been in the city before could not help noticing the *much* more widespread use of Ukrainian language and national symbols (including the yellow-and-blue traditional flag). However, an 'unknown' element in the equation is the still-strong Ukrainian Communist party. Its leaders are going along with the national-sovereignty trend, and could hardly do otherwise without massive loss of support. Also Moscow's relative powerlessness forces the authorities in Kiev to take responsibility. But there is a basic ambiguity in the attitudes of Kravchuk and co.

Food supplies in Lvov quite good, better than Kiev, far better than Moscow. The trains do still run, though on the return journey we were an hour late. The fare for a twelve-hour journey, in a two-berth sleeper, comes to 40 roubles, that is, well below £1 at the present slightly crazy rate of exchange.

14 June

Back to Kiev and the hotel Ukraina. (No hot water for three days. Very limited supplies in the buffet. TV set did not work. Service reasonably friendly but apt not to happen.) International conference in Kiev, on privatisation. Its American collaborators were such naive 'marketeers' that it was embarrassing. One of them said quite seriously that the fact that his luggage had not arrived proved that 'governments cannot run airlines' – as if only Aeroflot (and Air France? And Lufthansa?) misdirected luggage. *Everything* should be privatised, and all will be well. The 'missionary position' . . . Presented a paper myself, which was well received. Again there were a number of proposals for collaboration. Convinced that there is much to be done also by Britain to make contacts with Ukrainian institutions, business schools, universities, not to mention the nascent commodity exchanges and other economic–financial and banking institutions. This is a large country with impressive potential. With the decline of central power it must, willy-nilly, find its own way forward. Even under communist leadership, it must speed up its own move towards a market economy.

Jewish–Ukrainian Relations

During my stay I also attended a three-day conference on this theme, jointly organised by Ukrainian cultural societies and Jewish associations. Several hundred came, some from the Ukrainian diaspora in Canada, a few Americans. I seem to have been alone from Britain. Many émigrés came from Israel, and spoke Ukrainian at the conference. In the corridors were photo-exhibitions – of Jewish wartime heroes of the Soviet Union (over a hundred), plus victims of the Bayi Yar massacre (the fifth anniversary of this is in September this year). Among the Ukrainian organisers is the important cultural figure of Ivan Dzuba, while Ivan Drach, leader of *Rukh*, also attended some sessions. There was no attempt to evade the tragic past: the massacres by Bohdan Khmelnitsky in the 1650s, the pogroms that began in 1881 and continued on and off until worse befell during the Civil War, the help given by Ukrainians to the Germans during the Holocaust – but also (with photographs) a list of Ukrainian families, who hid Jews at great personal risk. Many provincial Jewish organisations were represented; I met people from Donetsk, Kharkov, Vinnitsa, Chernigov, Odessa. Interestingly, they too without exception spoke Ukrainian and clearly wished to be identified with the Ukrainian national movement, which, in its turn, wished to make a clean break with the past. One Jewish woman turned to me during a session and whispered (in Russian): 'Yes, but are they sincere?' I think the organisers were. As for the ordinary folk, how can one tell? In days gone by, Jews in the Ukraine either lived their own traditional (Yiddish) lives, or, if active in politics or culture, tended to be Russianised, and so were ill-regarded by Ukrainian nationalists. Times seem to be changing on both sides. A leading Ukrainian-language poet bears the name of Abram Katznelson (he gave a paper at the conference). I saw a Ukrainian version of Sholom Aleichem's *Tevye* (the basis of *Fiddler on the Roof*), with a fine performance in the title role by a leading Ukrainian actor, B.S. Stupka. The large (Ukrainian) audience showed their approval.

So – finally, some basic impressions, in brief. With over 50 million population and with large industrial and agricultural production (and greater potential), Ukraine is surely a key element in the political–economic jigsaw. Will it go its own way, with its own genuinely sovereign government, its own currency, its own armed forces? In what relationship with Moscow? How should the West react, politically and commercially?

Politics first. Local opinion seems strongly inclined to real sovereignty, and is expected to vote accordingly. The old divisions between west, east and south are diminishing. Kiev is seen as the capital, even by Russian miners in the Donets coal basin. Ukrainian nationalists are very careful to stress that they wish to collaborate with all other nationalities. *But*, though there is a dozen active political parties, some with similar names, the Communist party of the Ukraine has a hold on the levers of power. Its effective leader is said to be Kravchuk, the chairman of the Supreme Soviet who wishes to be president. In pursuit of this he takes the nationalist line, works closely with such organisations as *Rukh* (which he previously criticised), is publicly committed to sovereignty, but is also suspected of wishing to preserve the Union in some form. All speak of past colonialism, Russianisation, unfair terms of trade. Moscow is blamed for imposing a distorted capital structure, with mining, electricity, steel and arms factories dominating, with the consumers goods and food industries in a particularly poor state. The steel industry too needs modernisation urgently. Kravchuk plays on all these sentiments, either because he shares these views or because he wants to be elected president by popular vote. But he is not Landsbergis; he proceeds slowly, participates in discussions on a new union treaty, would go along with emergency measures to deal with the economic crisis – but the Ukrainian government controls the movement of goods out of the republic, and on 8 June the republican Supreme Soviet almost unanimously adopted a decision to transfer all the all-union enterprises to the property and jurisdiction of the republic. Moscow can (in *Izvestiya* did) respond by proposing that the republics *buy* these enterprises, but clearly that is very unlikely to happen. Yeltsin's election (welcomed by everyone here) still further weakens Gorbachev's and the centre's powers over events. This leaves a number of unanswered questions.

1. Whatever may be the attraction of Gorbachev as a leader at all-union level, can anything now be decided at that level? Yeltsin is unpredictable. He may well try for an inter-republican agreement (with Ukraine, Belorussia, Kazakhstan) bypassing the centre, in effect creating a new loose centre. He is already threatening to impose a very large increase in prices of oil, gas, timber, of which his republic is a key supplier, and to keep most of the export proceeds too. A *very* strong bargaining position.

2. Will Ukraine and other republics put an end to beggar-my-neighbour policies, which interfere with inter-republican trade? If they all go for separate currencies of their own, can they be made convertible into each other? Where does all this leave the centre, the all-union rouble, the central bank?

3. And where does this leave the debt to the West? If the centre has no independent source of revenue, and can live only on what the republics voluntarily provide, what hope is there of avoiding default on past debts, let alone the repayment of any credits which the 'seven' may grant to the centre? Contrary to my own previously expressed opinion, I now see substantial risks in any major financial support for the centre unless this is with the consent of key republics, or we will never see the money again.

4. The future of the military–industrial complex could likewise be under very serious threat. How is it to be financed? How will it react to being in effect throttled?

5. Can the hard-liners stage an effective counterattack? I believe that history will show that their last chance was in January this year, when they killed people in Vilnius and Riga. Gorbachev then called a halt. I am convinced that Gorbachev will not now unleash the military. They could restore the empire only at the cost of much bloodshed, and every month that passes makes it less feasible for them to impose their will. This said, a coup, based politically on such as Lukyanov and Polozkov, is not excluded. But then civil war really would begin, in the Ukraine too.

6. Given that the next steps in economic reform would be taken by each republic (or at the very least they would be able to veto any decision taken at the centre), what will the Ukrainian communist-led government actually do? Privatisation is making slow progress so far, but pressures are building-up in the republic's Supreme Soviet, and new elections could change the political balance. A separate currency, direct trade and payment relations with the West, may develop quickly. What is most urgently needed is privatisation of small workshops, retail trade, miscellaneous services, cafes, hotels, and so on, plus effective encouragement of family farming (which involves forcing *kolkhozy* and *sovkhozy* to part with land at reasonable leases). The heavy industry plants, which are very large and in urgent need of substantial modernisation investments, would have to be left in some sort of public hands (though there are schemes for a sort of *nomenklatura* takeover, that is, management and high officials take control). The decision last week to 'Ukrainise' enterprises under all-union control is of great importance.

7. The Ukrainian claims that they were unfairly exploited through unfair prices needs to be checked. Yes, the zonal price for grain was lower than for the less-favoured centre and north, and it is also true that Donbas deep-mined coal cost more than the price at which it was sold. But the Ukraine received oil, gas and timber from the RSFSR at far below world prices. The efforts of the RSFSR to put these prices up further will have negative effects, and the Donbas coal may prove uneconomic to produce, since costs in these old mines are far higher than the all-union average. But what do rouble prices mean when there is so little to buy? In the short run we will be dealing literally with barter terms of trade. Another unknown is the competitiveness in foreign markets. The potential is there, especially given the *very* low cost of labour. And there could be some exports of grain, though this would mean depriving deficit areas of the Union.

The Ukraine may now be on the point of emerging as a major sovereign state. It therefore seems highly desirable to establish contacts with Ukrainian organisations, at all levels, bearing in mind the commercial opportunities that will most certainly exist. They exist today, but while some highly profitable deals are possible, the problem is that they are closely linked with some highly unstable exchange rates and process, as well as legal uncertainties. There is supposed to be 'internal convertibility' by January 1992, there already is a legal currency market, but what calculations can meaningfully be made when the average wage (at the legal free rate) is somewhere around $12.00 a *month*? The goods that can be bought for roubles are often ludicrously cheap at this exchange rate. Beef in the Kiev market at 10 roubles a kilo works out at 10p a pound. Tolerable ornaments, combs, razor-blades, soap, light-bulbs all cost a few pence. People are currently making fortunes buying goods for roubles, taking them to Poland, selling them for zloty, changing the zloty in Poland into dollars and then reselling the dollars for a vastly greater number of roubles. Too many 'entrepreneurs' find a way to make money while producing nothing. But this will not last. Keep an eye on Kiev. The future is being decided, and the potential is vast. The Japanese are not idle. Prominent advertisers for their goods (for example, Canon) appear in the press. (A point of importance: someone should be taking seriously the study of the Ukrainian language and history, at presently sadly neglected, except in Canada.) Finally, the evidence points to a very substantial cut in real wages this year, both in 'statistical' and in real terms. I had anticipated that the big rise in prices this April would be matched or even exceeded by 'compensatory' higher incomes. But, according to Ukrainian colleagues, and also a published interview with Russian vice-president

Khazbulatov, this did not happen. Prices have risen by much more than anticipated (by a sum equivalent to 360 billion roubles, instead of the expected 120), affecting particularly prices of essentials (*Literaturnaya gazeta*, 5 June 1991), while average incomes have risen only to half this extent. The problem is that enterprises in many instances cannot find the money to pay even the 'compensation' provided for in the price decree of April. Meanwhile output continues to fall, so that, unlike in Poland, the price increases have not led to any marked improvement in supply of goods in the shops. Big rises in canteen meal prices have meant (according to my colleagues) that the student stipend which now stands at 60R a month enables them to eat once a day and leaves nothing over. The poor have got poorer. There could be disorders of a purely 'economic' kind.

To repeat, contacts with Kiev are highly desirable: academic (including management studies), financial, plus exploration of trade opportunities. Britain did run a trade-fair in Kiev last year, and a consulate is opening. But, apart from one oil man, I saw or heard nothing British during my stay. Opportunities may be being missed. I think that within two years at most a Ukrainian request will be made to set up embassies in London and elsewhere, and there will be a Ukrainian team in the 1996 Olympics.

Moscow diary: November 1992

Arrived punctually at Sheremetievo. All formalities smooth. Met by a colleague from the Academy of National Economy. Good discussion on car journey and over dinner. The radio gives the latest rouble–dollar rate as 416, with hyperinflationary expectations pushing it further down. The latest outburst of inflation is the effect of a political–economic decision. First, it was a consequence of the lancing of the boil of the 3000 billions of inter-enterprise debt, which threatened total financial paralysis and/or mass bankruptcies. Opinions differ whether these involuntary credits should be counted as a form of expansion of the total money supply. In a sense these were substitutes for the high level of credit that would have been required to enable enterprises to pay the vastly higher prices for their inputs. Second, sums have now been deliberately targeted at critical areas, such as agriculture, to ensure the minimum requirements of the cities, albeit at higher prices. Various kinds of subsidies amount to 15 per cent or so of the budget. Third, pressure from the Supreme Soviet led to very considerable rises in public-sector pay ('public sector' is what is called here 'pay of those employed in budget organisations', that is, civil service, health, education, and also the military). Their pay had fallen well behind the rate of inflation. Also the pay rose of those employed in productive enterprises, which had financed higher wages out of much higher prices.

There are two very divergent interpretations of the change of policy, which may be dated some time in June. One sees the first half-year as basically a correct attempt at shock therapy, which, despite some errors, was achieving its objective of a tolerable rate of inflation (it fell to 10 per cent a month in May–June). While output fell, goods did appear in the shops, market structures were beginning to emerge, the people showed patience; in a word they were on the way. But the opposition, consisting of a variety of critics, from the industrial lobby to the ex-communists and nationalists, succeeded in knocking the government off-course. Hyperinflation is now unavoidable, and, in the words of Aganbegyan, they are back to where they started: 'it is all to do again, but in a yet more difficult situation.' Such a hyperinflation threatens to destroy society and the economy and makes a stable government impossible. This line was taken eloquently by Anders Aslund, of Stockholm, in a recent *Financial*

Times conference in Moscow. His 'villains' are Gerashchenko, appointed to head the State Bank, and Arkadi Volsky, self-proclaimed head of the industrial lobby. (According to Bunich, his influence is exaggerated: see below.) The other view accepts that the dangers of hyperinflation are real and deplorable, but writes the history of 1992 somewhat differently. In the first six months top priority was given to macroeconomic stabilisation, and far too little attention was paid to the needs of production. This was a time of temporary domination of naive marketeers, advised by such as Aslund and Sachs. The programme was not succeeding. By mid-year the leadership realised that the stabilisation programme had to be modified to take account of reality, to prevent the further collapse of production. This was politically reflected in a series of appointments of industry-related 'moderates', and the appointment of Gerashchenko to head the State Bank. No more free-market euphoria; there had to be compromises not just with political reality but with common sense. Aslund is seen as a rather extreme neo-liberal critic. However, true enough, the cost of the policy turn has been a speed-up in inflation. Contributory factors were: a larger budget deficit, uncontrollable movement of roubles from other republics (for example, 'capital' outflow from Ukraine was huge, as I duly noted in Ukraine), plus political pressure to spend more on cash-starved social services, pensions, and keeping alive lame ducks in industry for political–social reasons. Also many firms have taken advantage of the loosening of credit restrictions to borrow to stock up with material inputs, insuring themselves against the expected price rises. So a necessary relaxation of strict credit restrictions did get somewhat out of hand, even according to those who regarded the relaxation as absolutely necessary. In September the budget deficit became a (small) surplus. The Ministry of Finance achieved this truly remarkable result by not paying its bills for a month. By the end of the year, however, the deficit will have greatly exceeded earlier expectations. It could rise to 15 per cent of GNP (Bunich says no: not more than 10 per cent).

One result of the series of compromise policies is the possible defusing of the political crisis, set for the December meeting of the Congress of Soviets. Gaidar has been touring the provinces, holding meetings with leaders of the large industrial complexes. He has been promising them support, assuring management that they would be given greater powers to manage, in effect putting them in charge – provided they can cover their costs. They were assured that privatisation procedures would not threaten them, and/or that they could take advantage of them. This leaves the chronic loss-makers in an uncertain position. Examples of the latter include not only some of the military–industrial complex, but also such civilian white elephants as Rostselmash, the big farm machinery complex at Rostov, which employs tens of thousands and whose combine-harvesters (and so on) have become unsaleable. The policy seems to be to let them fade away slowly, avoiding the political–social chaos which mass unemployment would cause. Gaidar's tactics have divided the 'managerial' lobby, largely neutralised Volsky and his group, weakening their links with the nationalist-and-ex-communist opposition. This makes possible (not certain, *possible*) the survival of the broad market-based strategy under Gaidar, with Yeltsin still President with powers, carrying out a more interventionist and targeted policy. We have been publicly promised a development plan for the next six months, with priority for energy, agriculture, transport, but with no return to centralised material allocation. In my view (unlike Aslund, who denounced sector targeting in his speech), this is a necessary policy in the increasingly difficult circumstances of output decline and accelerating inflation. But the problem is not so much that the government intends to proceed with priority investment projects, but rather how it can finance them without printing yet more money. But if it does not, decline will accelerate. Both sides of the controversy agree that the inflation rate must now be around 25 per cent a month, *and* that the fall in output has speeded up since August. And all also agree that political uncertainties combine with inflationary expectations to paralyse or distort economic activity. There is still no functioning constitution, and the balance of authority between the centre and the provinces (and the autonomous national republics) is still a source of confusion. All agree that there is massive corruption and little legal order.

Interestingly there is some hope of a revival of the CIS, that is, of an economic agreement with some of the republics of the former USSR. Kuchma, the Ukraine's new premier, had advocated closer economic ties with Russia, since otherwise the Ukraine's collapse is ever nearer. True, Kravchuk has just announced the departure of Ukraine from the rouble zone, the end of the use of the rouble in their republic. This, however, is welcomed by Russia, and there are trade-and-payments negotiations in progress, in which both sides hold some cards: the Russians have oil and gas and timber (Ukraine cannot possibly pay the world price without instant ruin), and Ukraine has reminded Russia of its power over the pipelines that transit its territory. There is much industrial interdependence. Good sense *might* prevail. Lithuania too, under a less intransigent government following elections, seeks an agreement. But will the Russians play? A complication is the power of the separate oil-producing territorial administrations, who may simply ignore agreements negotiated by Moscow. Still another is the continuing *fall in oil output*, estimated to continue through 1993 ('by at least 50 million more tons, and that is optimistic'). My Russian colleagues confirm that there is a barely controllable

tendency to sell oil direct to hard-currency customers and not to repatri-
ate the dollars, despite decrees to the contrary. Asked if any new decrees,
for example, on export licences, would be obeyed, the typical response is a
shrug of shoulders. All this is vitally important for the centre's ability to
dispose of hard-currency earnings, to service debt, to make meaningful
promises to the IMF, and so on. Aslund's solution is full trade liberalisation, with the raising of energy prices to world levels. How he squares this
with his anti-inflationary domestic strategy passes my comprehension:
world prices for oil and gas at 450 roubles to the dollar would have a huge
knock-on effect on industrial and farm costs, and living costs too. Could
this be controlled by a 'hard' monetary and credit policy?

Yeltsin addresses a conference of managers, state and private, and
Volsky declared himself satisfied with the government's willingness to work
closely with them to restore production. Yeltsin sounded an optimistic
note: prices may be stabilising as it becomes increasingly difficult to find
customers. Given a harder line on credits (to quote him: 'We know you
want another trillion, and we promise firmly not to give them to you'),
some prices may even start falling, he said. Asked about this at another
meeting, Gaidar was more cautious. Russian TV quoted him as warning of
hyperinflationary times ahead. The line on credits is unlikely to hold.

There are plenty of signs of business activity, reflected in radio and TV
advertising, and lots of street sellers. But the impression is closer to the
third-world: people in all walks of life standing in the pedestrian subways
selling anything from sex manuals to Samuelson's *Economics*, from
Tampax to tea. On a main street close to Red Square a line of 30 middle-
aged women sell packets of imported perfume and cosmetics. 'Commercial'
stalls sell many kinds of imported goods. But also, to the annoyance of the
public, there is large-scale resale of foodstuffs bought in shops, in the street
at a higher price. Yeltsin apparently issued a decree banning the establishment of limits on retail sales to any one person. So, for instance, when she
waited to buy *kefir* (buttermilk), a colleague found that two men in front of
her in the same queue had bought the entire stock (30 cartons). Another
motive for buying all that can be found is anticipated inflation and fear of
shortages. Indeed shortage is still real. A suburban food store had meat, *but*
it was either a hunk of frozen beef of most dubious quality (450 roubles)
or reasonable-looking steak (800 roubles, that is, a week's wages for
many!!). Butter has vanished. Sour-cream appears only occasionally. Under
these conditions, even privatised shops do not have to care for customers. A
complainant was told: 'We are privatised now, so we have no duties
towards you. Get out!' Not quite what the market was supposed to do for
supplier–customer relations. But this is a most imperfect market, in a
transitional phase.

Serious military trouble threatens in the Caucasus, where Russian troops are involved in a Georgian naval base (Poti) and in a complex struggle involving the Chechen, Ingush and Ossetians. Some tribesmen seem to be considering a holy war against the Russians, and with each other too, though latest reports suggest that sense will prevail. A TV interview with the leader of the Tartar republic, which has still not signed any constitutional agreement with Russia, underlines continued problems with the definition of the powers of the federal centre. He stressed sovereignty and the right to make direct deals of every kind with foreign countries, though geography (and the large Russian population, and the fact that many Tartars live in Russia) complicates his case. Others too are following the line of bypassing Moscow. Thus representatives of the Komi autonomous republic are establishing relations with the UK and opening an office in London. Like the Tartars, they have some oil to sell or barter. Moscow authorises them to dispose legally of a quota, but these limits may prove unenforceable. Meanwhile barter deals continue: thus the provisional government of Nizhni-Novgorod has signed an agreement with Kazakhstan, providing for the exchange of machine-tools. At the moment while Ukraine and Belorus are setting up their own currencies, the situation is confusing for the citizenry. A colleague said that the post office refuses to accept any parcels, however small, to addresses in Ukraine. Yet they all have relatives and friends in these neighbouring republics. Trade with Ukraine is being disrupted by complete uncertainty over payments.

The investment voucher scheme may or may not succeed. It depends to whom one talks, or what paper one reads. Some citizens are prepared to sell their vouchers now at a discount to anyone willing to buy them. A 10 000 rouble voucher sells for 4000 or so in Moscow and St. Petersburg last week. But one hears of Chinese and other businessmen in the Russian Far East paying a large premium (70 000 roubles!) to acquire vouchers which they hope to use in purchasing land and houses. There are daily radio and TV advertisements urging citizens to hold on to their vouchers until they can consider what stocks and shares in what company or mutual-fund to invest, and also in buying flats and a plot of land. But of course this would in effect be with money given to them by the government, and the issue of the vouchers has begun ahead of creating the mechanism by which to invest them.

Discussions with Goland (government adviser on currency), Tsipko (a key member of the 'Gorbachev foundation'), Migranyan (leading political journalist), and A. Belkin (Ministry of Health). The following are some relevant impressions gleaned from these conversations. First, the extent and depth of official corruption are deplorable. Thus when the

Marriott hotel wished to build in Moscow and ignored a broad hint that a bribe was needed (they offered instead to build a swimming pool for Muscovites), no agreement was signed. The 'democrats' have discredited themselves. The public is deeply perplexed, cynical, demoralised and, for the time being, apathetic. Political manoeuvres have ceased to interest them. Nothing has made life more tolerable, though queues are few. Tales are told of mafiosi who ensure high prices by keeping competitors and food supplies out of the big cities. Anger may take irrational forms, such as attacks on salesmen from the Caucasus, who are blamed for a variety of rackets. Medical services really are in total disarray. The few medical drugs which reach the hospitals often end up in the possession of street salesmen. Western charitable aid also gets stolen. Those who cannot afford to pay the (grossly underpaid) medical staffs may get no treatment, and the real death rate is said to have risen faster than the statistics allow. Dangers of epidemics are growing. The ecological mess remains untackled.

It seems probable that Yeltsin and his government will survive the 'crisis' of 1 December. True, some (including foreign-minister Kozyrev) advise Yeltsin to dissolve the Supreme Soviet. There *may* be a majority there to limit presidential power to issue decrees. But the opposition has been split, no clear alternative policy is emerging, though a full-page statement of the 'economic platform of the united opposition' fills a large page of the newspaper *Sovetskaya Rossiya* of 19 November (measures include strict price control). Gaidar has come to an agreement with part of the industrial lobby. A real danger, however, is disintegration into 'regional fiefdoms', whose leaders will make deals with abroad and with each other and ignore Moscow altogether.

Goland presented a very clear picture of the 'enterprise payments crisis'. As I had frequently reported, mutual debts grew to enormous proportions. One reason for the failure to cope with the problem was that Central Bank credits intended for enterprises were unused by commercial banks 'for highly profitable operations on the financial market', that is, for speculation. In July steps were taken to cancel (or rather to set off against each other) most inter-enterprise debt, with the remaining debt taking the form of bills of exchange (*vekselya*), which, however, carry little creditworthiness. In practice, because prices of materials and energy rose much faster than the wholesale prices of end-products, much of the debt has accumulated at the latter end of the production chain. Anyhow, in mid-July the central bank issued credits of 150 billion roubles to cover the immediate needs for working capital, though the need for such credits has been estimated at 1 trillion roubles. The latter sum may in the end be close to what actually occurs, despite Yeltsin's statement quoted above. Interest on these latest credits (issued through the Ministry of Finance) was fixed at 10 per cent (against the commercial-bank interest rate of upwards of 80 per cent) *but* the rate would rise up to 80 per cent if prices charged by the recipient enterprise rise by 70 per cent or more above the levels of 1 July 1992. Goland is critical of these and similar arrangements. There is still no bankruptcy procedure. Oddly enough, while there is still a (reduced) debt mountain, on paper 96 per cent of industrial enterprises show a profit, and even pay profits tax into the budget. But the 'profit' is measured in relation to goods disposed of, not goods paid for. This suggests that a sizeable part of the state budget revenue is fictional, that is, has to be covered by ministerial or bank credits. (What a mess! A.N.)

On the same theme there was a major article by the head of the State Bank, V. Gerashchenko. He attributed the payments crisis to the fact that cash and credit supply fell well behind the rise in prices, causing a famine in working capital – while the financial organs taxed away the bulk of the profits. He argued that the government should have appreciated earlier the need for more credits, instead of criticising the Bank for doing what was essential. He presented the following figures (1992, in billions of roubles):

	1 Jan	1 April	1 July	1 November
Cash in circulation	173.5	255.4	457.6	998.4
Total money supply	951.4	1359.0	2082.3	4381.6
Credits to the economy	439.4	918.1	1393.0	2731.0

Source: *Ekonomika i zhizn'*, No. 46, 1992.

Note how the increases were far less than the rise in prices. Gerashchenko estimates that by the end of 1992 the purchasing power of 100 roubles on 1 January is to fall to 4 roubles. He agrees that the present credit policy may be supporting 'inefficient production'. Another problem is that the commercial banks grant only short-term credits, so investment finance is neglected. Asked about the hard currency holdings illegally kept abroad, he mentioned estimates varying from 5 to 15 billion dollars for the single year 1992, 'but we lack currency control structures capable of changing the situation'.

Comic interlude: six Bangladeshis are reported as having arrived in Germany with Russian passports all in the name of Ivanov. They purchased the passports in Moscow from suitably bribed officials, at $400 per passport. (The Germans did not believe they were all Ivanovs!)

N.B. Valuable discussion with members of the young 'Gaidar' team (notably his assistants) in the government offices (the former Central

Committee building). Discussion also with Pavel Bunich, well-connected economist and Aganbegyan's deputy. He supports the idea of 'voucheri-sation', as to some extent returning to the people the property which the Soviet regime created with their money. The process of revaluing enter-prise capital assets is proceeding, though certainly in a rough-and-ready way. He is not sure about the outcome of the Congress due to meet on 1 December. He expressed strong antipathy towards Volsky ('unprin-cipled intriguer who knows little'), a smooth talker, he said, who pretends to represent management and does not really do so. While he and his kind could not reverse the reform process, they could greatly slow it down. He expressed the hope that a new and more competent govern-ment can be formed, with Gaidar and his group still in charge of policy. There are two few competent ministers. It is no longer necessary to follow IMF guidelines, because (he said) 'they don't give us money anyhow'. In July the change of financial and credit policy was forced, since the alter-native was the collapse of production and a 'social explosion', and so Gerashchenko was right to choose a speed-up in inflation as the lesser of two evils. Bunich thinks that Gaidar only pretended to complain: he too could see no alternative. The budget deficit will be between 8–10 per cent of GNP. (I queried this: is that optimistic? No, replied Bunich, it is realis-tic.) Asked about the slowness of privatisation and retail trade and other services in Moscow, Bunich advanced several reasons: first, Moscow city charges high rents for premises. Second, there is a shortage of affordable credits, some banks now charge 120 per cent, and the needed work and equipment is very expensive. Third, racketeers demand protection money, and will burn you out if you do not pay. Fourth, there is a high (60 per cent) profits tax. Fifth there are bribes to pay. (Oy weh, as my ancestors used to say . . . .) Yes, Bunich agreed, investments are minimal and are urgently needed. But with living standards down, and medical services collapsing, priorities are elsewhere.

The radio has reported a $600 million loan from the World Bank, to be used for priority purposes (oil industry, transport, medical drugs). Good. No more 'ideology' about auctioning it all to the highest bidder. Newspaper reports speak of major Chinese penetration in Khabarovsk, and probably elsewhere in the Russian Far East. Visas have been abol-ished, there is a Chinese consulate at Khabarovsk, and trade in both directions is unofficial and lively. Chinese have been purchasing vouchers and property, and some Chinese workers have been hired by Russian con-tractors. The Chinese 'import' blond and blue-eyed Russians to serve in restaurants in China ('clients like to be served by Europeans'). Various rackets have been reported, as might be expected. Aganbegyan tells me that his salary, equal to that of a minister, is 14 800 roubles a month. At the present exchange rate his son, who works for Price Waterhouse, earns 30 times more than he does! Both Aganbegyan and Bunich point out that people still save a sizeable amount in cash, despite an inflation rate of 20–25 per cent a month, simply for fear of being left with nothing, and having no alternative they can trust into which to put their money. The journal *Kommersant* anticipated a short-term stabilisation of the free rate for the dollar, at around 420–440 roubles. Within four days they were proved wrong; the rate rose to 450.

My lunch at the Academy hotel costs me roughly 60 roubles (soup, mutton chop, potato, tea). At today's exchange rate that is 11 pence. The train ticket from Moscow to St. Petersburg is 280 roubles, 48 pence! A two-volume biography of Trotsky by Volkogonov costs 85 roubles, 15 pence. A metro ride is now 1 rouble, but there are no rouble coins, and because prices are expected to go up the booking office sells one token at a time, causing long queues. The public telephones need a 15-kopeck coin to operate them, but there are no such coins, except occasionally in the hands of clever old women who will sell them to you for several roubles, so few can use the public phones!

TV programme devotes space to re-equipment of river and lake steamships for use at sea. Russia has lost not only most European ports of the old USSR, but most seagoing ships too. The *oil trade* is worried. 'The break-up of the all-union oilpipe system' makes it difficult to identify whose crude is which, and output of crude has fallen this year by 16 per cent, against a fall in products of only 9 per cent, this being made possible by a cutback in exports of crude. Pressure to export more crude is expected to lead to a shortage (and higher prices) of petrol, diesel-fuel and fuel-oil. 'Oil equipment is extremely worn out, investments in the fuel and energy complex are inadequate' (*Kommersant*, No. 41). As mentioned earlier, oil output is expected to fall by at least another 50 million tons in 1993. The internal price of oil has been supposedly 'freed', but this is only apparent. A price in excess of 4000 roubles can be charged, but there is a rapidly progressive tax on the excess. A very wide difference with the world price is thus maintained. There are (as already mentioned) some solid reasons for this. A sevenfold rise in energy prices would stoke up hyper-inflation. The *balance of payments has* benefited from the introduction of a 100 per cent import tariff on hard liquors. (!! Yes, there was plenty of imported Smirnoff vodka in Moscow!) *A new decree on 'licences and quotas for exports and imports'* was adopted on 6 November, which applies also to trade with the former USSR republics. Some quotas will be auctioned by the government and/or local authorities. This contradicts (cancels) the decision taken earlier in the year to control imports and exports only through tariffs. Export licenses will be applied to materials which have a high world-market price, to ensure domestic supplies (for example, energy, some chemicals, some foodstuffs, medical drugs), also military goods, precious metals, narcotics. But joint enterprises with more than 30 per cent of foreign capital will be left free to sell own produce.

(*18 November*) Despite confident forecast of *Kommersant* of only a few days ago that the dollar rate will not go above 440 roubles, today it is reported to be 446 roubles. Government decrees about selling to those who leave the rouble zone only in hard currency threaten dire consequences for Ukraine, and also for Moldova, Georgia . . . and payments agreements there surely must be, to avoid much damage to all concerned. Vice-president Rutskoi has publicly raised territorial issues: the Crimea, which can cause more nervousness in Kiev. And finally a very sad and vivid article from Riga tells the sad tale of Latvian nationalist extremism and the deplorable situation there of the very large (42 per cent!) Russian minority (*Moskovskie novosti*, No. 47). Trouble likely! The Russians are raising this and similar actions of Estonia in the Security Council. Meanwhile Yeltsin is in Seoul. Interestingly, Volsky is with him. And Gaidar is visiting the huge heavy-industry complex of the Urals, and promising them credits (the great Uralmash combine has little work and reports having lost its best specialists because of low pay). Government policy looks increasingly like handing over effective control of state enterprises (the larger ones) to management, with some employee share ownership. How vouchers will be used remains unclear, at least to me.

Important event: V. Gerashchenko, head of the Bank of Russia, has become a member of the government this day – although nominally the Bank is subordinate to parliament and not to the executive. Khazbulatov, oppositionist speaker, has naturally complained. The papers comment that this continues the line of 'diluting' Gaidar's team with practical managers such as Shumeyko and Chernomyrdin. Gerashchenko will give priority to 'preserving industrial capacity through specific monetary injections into priority sectors'. Taken together, these appointments, and promised policy changes (including more social security spending) suggest that the aim is a 'government of national agreement', according to the well-informed *Nezavisimaya gazeta* (18 November). This would checkmate the critics of the Congress of Soviets. Meanwhile V. Gurevich, of *Moskovskie novosti* (No. 47), reports that a trillion of credits, refused to industry by Yeltsin in his recent speech, is bound to be forthcoming all the same. In the same issue Yeltsin is cited as accusing ex-Soviet republics of in effect smuggling out Russian materials for hard currency. Thus 'Estonia produces no aluminium, but has become a major exporter' (!).

Dramatic story in *Moskovskie novosti* of mafia-like gangsters in charge of the docks at major ports. Thus in Odessa nothing gets loaded without large pay-offs. Ports are jammed with goods, including Nakhodka, deliveries are delayed, contracts broken, corruption flourishes exceedingly. Desperate civil-war-and-anarchy situation reported from Tadzhikistan. There are Russian troops there, but they try to stand aside while the natives kill each other, and Russian residents complain bitterly about lack of protection.

Literaturnaya gazeta (18 November) publishes long interview with Anatoli Chubais, minister in charge of privatisation. Asked whether the sale by citizens of their vouchers will not act to speed up inflation, he agreed that it would do so, 'but since in September and October we managed an inflation rate of 28 per cent a month' (!!) an extra 10–16 per cent would not be disastrous. And, he added, some would be able to buy meat, which is in excess supply at today's very high prices. Chubais pointed out that the vouchers become usable for purchasing shares and other property only from 1 December, and those recipients that now sell them at half-price make a mistake, but have full rights of disposal as they see fit. Prices of shares will depend on the market. Initially they are using net valuation in old (pre-1992) prices, but that is just to start the process. There will begin very soon 'Voucher auctions', i.e., sales of shares through voucher-cheques. He expects the face value of the 10 000 rouble cheque 'to rise high above its nominal sum.' Asked whether in the end vouchers and the state firms will be 'bought by the rich', he answered 'Yes', he welcomes it. He is quoted as saying: anyone who is not a socialist at 20 has no heart, anyone who is still a socialist at 30 has no head. He agreed that where there is danger of an undesirable change of use, auctioning can be replaced by conditional sales (*konkurs*); thus if a bakery switches to selling cognac, the contract of the sale would become invalid. Chubais insists that some 80 per cent of all privatised state property will be sold via voucher-cheques. (That suggests a remarkable degree of under-valuation! A.N.) But he agreed that the whole scheme's future hangs in the balance.

More evidence of chaos: in the North Caucasus (Russian republic), there is a major oil-pipe which carries *benzine* and other products from Grozny refinery to various petrochemical and other plants. This has been breached by entrepreneurs armed with guns and drills, and petrol sold off. Some of the petrochemical plants have stopped: nothing reached them! The gangs have modern vehicles, tanker-lorries, machine-guns . . . The trouble is that Grozny is controlled by the Chechens, who ignore Moscow. More evidence, written and verbal, about the new '*government programme of anti-crisis measures*', which runs to 180 pages. Its key elements are: 'stabilisation of production and stimulation of investment'. The period covered runs through June 1993. There will be a growth of centralised purchases through the 'contract corporation Goskomtrakt'. To provide investment funds there will be a sharp rise in depreciation allowances to reflect inflation (inflation-indexation every six months), with rules to prevent the use of depreciation fund for other purposes. There will also be a centrally-financed investment programme. The budget deficit is to be limited to 5.5 per cent (of GNP?), to be financed by high-interest short-term bonds, not money creation. Any ex-Soviet republic remaining in the rouble zone will be subject to closer financial control through agreements to be negotiated, others will be charged hard-currency world prices for energy. The programme envisages what are called 'critically-vital imports' in 1993, equal to $15–$20 billion. To help pay for this there will be centrally-determined export deliveries, while imports for 'the needs of the state' will be freed of customs duty. The volume of foreign credits expected in 1993 amounts to $7.4 billion (*Kommersant-daily*, 18 November). Vladimir Mau, one of Gaidar's assistants, confirmed that such a policy statement had been prepared, but considers that it could well have little practical significance. One hears of steps to enlarge the autonomy of management, with the spread of managerial buy-outs or leasing, with or without workforce participation, though it is not clear how this will relate to sales via vouchers.

Moscow–St. Petersburg in good and punctual sleeper train, at the absurd cost – including supplement for bed-linen, of about 65 pence, repeat pence. Smart hotel. Hospitable colleagues from the St. Petersburg Economic and Financial University, which has 10 000 students (it was known formerly as the Financial–Economic Institute), and claims to be a leader in this field. Its rector, Leonid S. Tarasevich, is developing links with Western institutions. Gave lecture to a large and sympathetic audience. Also interviewed by St. Petersburg TV. TV reports speech by Kuchma, Ukrainian premier. He repeated the words: 'this is not a crisis, this is a catastrophe'. The coupons are rapidly depreciating. Shortages are worse than ever. He said that the budget deficit has reached 40 per cent of GNP. (I doubt it, he must have meant 40 per cent of the budget. But he *said* GNP twice, in his speech, which was televised.) Two British tourists at this hotel told me that they had air tickets to Odessa, but that lack of fuel had caused plane cancellations, so they had a 48-hour train journey instead. 'No sugar in Siberia'. So an academic-entrepreneur has negotiated a $1 million deal with Israel to supply some sort of saccharine. Long TV interview last night (19 November) given by Nazarbaev, president of Kazakhstan. He sounded most sensible and impressive, and popular also among Russians, as opinion polls show. He spoke out vigorously for breathing life into inter-republican collaboration agreements. He cited examples where Kazakh producers, for example, of iron ore and coal, cannot get paid by their Russian customers, and so are about to cut supplies, and this in turn will cause production bottlenecks affecting Russian steel and electricity. Similarly, it is absurd, he said, that there is no joint management of the rouble zone, and no real life in so-called Commonwealth institutions. (How right he is: but what action will follow?)

Excellent session with colleagues from the Economic and Financial University and the Engineering–Economics Institute, also with the editorial board of a new economic journal (circulation: 100 000). Warm reception, generous hospitality. These people need and deserve far closer links with Western institutions. The British contribution has hitherto been too small. Problem in St. Petersburg: drunken Finns at weekends. There were plenty in my hotel – which, by the way, is good, as is the food in its restaurant. The city seems to have had a facelift since I was last there three years ago. One of my reasons for visiting it was to find out what progress had been made in creating a free trade zone in and around the city. (I had met some of the 'architects' of the scheme in Stockholm last year.) Answer: a non-starter. St. Petersburg's big problem is that its most famous and largest factories were mostly working for the military. Their conversion requires large and unavailable sums. I wish I could see grounds for optimism.

PART II

The USSR and Post-Soviet Union

The new Soviet five-year plan and the 26th Congress, 1981

The Soviet economic system is in a period of serious difficulties. So, of course, is ours! In our assessment of the performance of the Soviet economy we rightly emphasise the marked slowdown in growth, the failure to fulfil various output plans. But even a growth rate of 2 or 3 per cent per annum is preferable to an absolute decline, accompanied by mass unemployment, and this should be borne in mind. The table shows that the previous (the tenth) five-year plan was greatly under-fulfilled, both in aggregate and by industrial sector. In fact I have only been able to find two products for which the target for 1980 was reached: gas and passenger cars. All the other identifiable items are behind schedule, and the shortfall affects both producers' goods and consumers' goods. Output of coal fell absolutely in both 1979 and 1980, and this must cause alarm, especially as it is becoming so difficult to increase the supply of oil. The figures also show a very substantial shortfall in the output of steel and of the chemical industry. There are serious imbalances, transport bottlenecks, shortages of building materials (and long delays in completing investment projects), serious shortages of food in many parts of the country. Very large investments in agriculture, substantial improvements in the incomes of the peasantry, have produced only modest results – though the weather has also been unfavourable in the last two years. Far from being a source of income for the rest of the economy, agriculture has become a burden, a ball-and-chain. Directly and indirectly it absorbs 33 per cent of all investments, and the subsidy which covers losses in livestock-raising is now at least 23 milliard roubles, more than the officially-declared level of Soviet defence spending, the highest agricultural subsidy known to human history. At the low retail price of food, unchanged since 1962, demand substantially exceeds supply, and, as also in Poland, shortage of meat is particularly severe. The one sector which has done relatively well is foreign trade: the high price of oil and of gold have helped to reduce the deficit with hard-currency countries, and the terms of trade have moved favourably for the USSR also in its exchanges with her Comecon partners.

The new five-year plan is more modest than the previous plan, but exceeds the rate of growth actually achieved in 1976–80. It is clear that the plan can only be fulfilled if there is a significant improvement in efficiency. This is spelled out in the following table, which formed part of Tikhonov's speech to the Congress.

Labour productivity (per cent increases in five years)

	1976–80 (actual)	1981–85 (plan)
Industry	+17	+24
Agriculture (state and collective)	+15	+23
Construction	+11	+16
Rail transport	+0.5	+11

Source: *Pravda*, 28 February 1981.

This is to be achieved although the volume of investment is to rise much more slowly (by 14 per cent over the previous five years, against 29 per cent in 1976–80), *and* despite a marked slowdown in the growth of energy supply. If my calculations are correct, energy supply rose by over 4.2 per cent per annum in 1976–80, but the new plan provides for a growth of only 3.2 per cent per annum in 1981–85, and even this depends on the overcoming of formidable obstacles which face the oil and coal industries. There is to be a drive to economise energy, and also metal, but even so the plan looks decidedly over-optimistic – *unless* major changes bring about a sharp decline in waste and a substantial improvement in productivity. Sure enough, the leaders know this and say so: there must be a shift from extensive to intensive growth, the diffusion of technical progress must be speeded up, plans should be rational, balanced and stable, capital investments deployed to maximum effect, production must accord more closely to the requirements of industry and of the consumer. The higher status of the consumer is symbolised in the new plan by a slightly higher rate of increase for consumers' goods as against producers' goods. However, similar speeches and resolutions have been heard before, and the higher rate of increase for consumers' goods is not totally new: it formed part of the ninth five-year plan (1971–75), but the traditional priorities reasserted themselves in the course of its fulfilment. Nor is this surprising. If serious shortages and delays are encountered, it is understandable that planners pay more attention to (say) energy than to footwear, given the consequences to all of industry (including even the footwear industry) of energy shortage. The key point is to identify the principal causes of inefficiency and waste, and then to see whether some new strategy has been adopted which could overcome these malfunctions.

In my view, shared by a number of 'reforming' Soviet economists, most of the problems are in some way related to *diseconomies of scale*. Every productive unit has to be given instructions as to what to produce, its output and its inputs are allocated administratively, there are also plan-instructions on labour, wages, material utilisation norms, profits, and so on. In a highly interdependent economy, this lays upon the central planning mechanism a truly impossible burden. Inevitably there are inconsistencies, failure to coordinate, since the huge task must be divided between many departments, ministries, committees. Fertiliser is produced, which then cannot be bagged, stored, transported or spread, because the decisions on bags, storage space, lorries and fertiliser-spreaders belong to different departments. Managers receive instructions on production which do not match the supply plan, or the wages plan. Managerial initiatives are stifled by the need to apply for allocation of materials and for a change in plan-instructions. To make their task manageable the planners have to aggregate, to issue plan-orders in tons, square metres, roubles, and production adapts itself to these plan-indicators instead of to the specific needs of the customer. All this is rendered worse by the prevailing sellers' market for producers' goods and for consumers' goods: though in both instances the customer has some redress, he cannot use his formal rights, when it is so often a matter of 'take it or leave it'. Prices do not serve as economic signals, since they do not reflect demand, scarcity or utility, being based (very roughly) on cost. This means that profitability cannot serve as a basis for decentralised decision-making. In the face of all this, it is evident that good resolutions and exhortation are not enough. Major changes are essential. The negative attitude of a part of the labour force, the widespread absenteeism, petty thievery, indiscipline, are also connected with diseconomies of scale. Top management is remote, everyone's property is no one's property, the sense of alienation is strong.

Were these issues debated at the Congress? Brezhnev and Tikhonov made some critical remarks, but in fact there was no debate. With hardly any exception, the speeches were unrelated to one another, save that everyone had fulsome words of praise for the wisdom of comrade Brezhnev. The 5000 delegates unanimously adopted the text of the five-year plan, identical in virtually all respects to the draft published before the Congress. Efficiency is to be achieved not by decentralisation but by greater centralisation, the emphasis being on discipline at all levels, on better planning, better machines, more emphasis on final results. Reference was made to the reform adopted in July 1979, and to new prices which are now being determined. However, one can say with confidence that the reform will not succeed. There is being introduced a 'normed value-added' indicator, to replace the value of gross output, since the use of the latter penalised economy of materials (the dearer the planned inputs, the higher the price, the

larger the value of output and the faster your 'growth'). While on the face
of it net output is a better measure than gross output, *normed* value-added
now has to be determined for each of literally millions of products,
together with their prices; this will represent not the actual net output
(wages bill plus profits) but a theoretical norm, that is, what it *should* be.
This complicated and confusing change has been the subject of numerous
explanatory articles in the specialised press. But this is only part of the
trouble. Alongside the normed value-added indicator there will be an
extended list of items planned in physical units, plus specific delivery obligations imposed by the planners, plus tighter material utilisation norms.
Efforts will be made to impose better quality and technological standards,
by devising appropriate plan indicators. Typically, the urgent need to produce for the customers' requirements is recognised, but the remedy sought
is by attempting to incorporate them in the plan-instructions to produce
and to deliver. As for the price reform, it is on traditional lines. Certain
prices will rise sharply to eliminate losses (this applies particularly to
energy), but prices will remain in theory and in practice unaffected by
scarcity, demand, utility. Furthermore, they are intended to be stable, and
so cannot be flexible. It is plain that proposals for radical reform of planning and of prices have been rejected, along with any extension of the
market mechanism. Similarly, the many complex problems of agriculture
are to be 'solved' primarily from above, by the creation of agro-industrial
complexes, with not a word about greater autonomy for farm management,
or the creation of autonomous units (*zvenya*) within state and collective
farms. The one step forward is the more positive attitude to the private
plot, especially to private livestock raising. On foreign trade the plan document confines itself to generalities and gives no figures. In the present
uncertain state of the world, this is not surprising. There may well be voices
raised against any further extension of interdependence, given the possibility of Western embargoes. For this reason it is doubtful if the new plan
implies any increase in imports of Western technology over present levels.

So we have an ageing conservative leadership, aware that much is amiss
but unable to imagine new ways of overcoming increasingly serious problems. Brezhnev's policy of stability was in many respects an improvement
over Khrushchev's unpredictable reorganisations and 'hare-brained
schemes', but stability has now become immobility, or even petrification.
What Brezhnev calls *vedomstvennost'* and *mestnichestvo*, departmentalism
and localism, is strengthened when the same officials hold the same
offices for many years. So are various forms of corruption. There seemed
to be little connection between the tone of the speeches at the Congress
and the real situation. While there is yet no catastrophe, the economy is
certainly in a mess. The evidence suggests that a further decline in growth
rates is inevitable, and that serious shortages will persist. Clearly the

power of those who resist any major change in the economic system is still very strong. Some would say that the decentralising 'market'-type reforms which are proposed by some economists have no chance whatever of being seriously considered. True, the existing system seems to suit the party machine best, and the probable increase in military spending will reinforce the attraction of centralisation, the influence of the defence sector. However, economic inefficiency also has adverse effects on power, the power of the USSR in the world, and also the power-position of any individual leader in charge of a section of the economy. Would not Gorbachev gain political strength if agriculture did well? So, while agreeing with those who consider major reform of the economy unlikely, it does seem to me to be not impossible, when the new generation finally takes over the leadership, as soon it must.

The tenth and eleventh five-year plans

(a) Rates of increase, per cent	1980 Plan	1980 Actual	1985 Plan
National income	+26	+20	+19
Industrial production	+37	+24	+27
Producers' goods	+40	+26	+27
Consumers' goods	+31	+21	+28
Agricultural production*	+15.5	+ 9	+13
Labour productivity (industry)	+30.6	+17	+24

(b) Physical output	1975	1980(p)	1980(a)	1985(p)
Electricity (mlrd kWh)	1039	1380	1290	1575
Oil (mill. tons)	491	640	604	632
Gas (mlrd. cub. met.)	289	435	435	620
Coal (mill. tons)	701	805	719	785
Rolled steel (mill. tons)	99	117.5	103	118.5
Fertiliser (mill. tons)	90	143	104	152.5
Resins and plastics (mill. tons)	2.84	5.5	3.64	6.12
Cement (mill. tons)	122	144	125	141
Fabrics (mill. sq. met.)	9965	12750	10700	12700
Grain*	181.6	215	205	240
Meat	15.0	15.3	14.8	18.2

Notes: Some 1985 plan figures are midpoints of ranges (for example, '610–630' is given here as 620)
* Five-year averages, including previous four years.

The reformability of the Soviet economic system (memorandum for Prime Minister Margaret Thatcher, Chequers, 1983)

I have sketched out below the text (imaginary, but, I believe plausibly realistic) of a position paper prepared for a sub-committee of the Soviet politburo chaired by Yuri Andropov.

REFORM OF THE SYSTEM

Comrades will be aware of the many difficulties in which we find ourselves. Growth has slowed to 1.5–2 per cent per annum, that is, to a per capita growth of just about zero (our statistics say 3 per cent, but they are inflated). Bottlenecks in transport, shortages of metal, increasing difficulties in food supply, a growing gap between people's incomes and the goods and services available, an accelerated growth in money supply (especially in the form of bank credit), the slow diffusion of new technology, intolerable delays in completing investment projects, equally intolerable growth of indiscipline, corruption, alcoholism, these matters cannot but cause us the gravest concern. The more so as we are being pushed against our will into an accelerated arms race. Of course we are not in a state of collapse, as some of the US President's advisers seem to imagine, but one of the major objectives of our economic strategy is, and has long been, to catch up and overtake the West. Yet here we are in a condition bordering on stagnation, and the technology gap is actually growing wider. What are the causes of this slowdown? Let us briefly list some of them.

1. *Demography*: the working population is not increasing (except in Central Asia but they are immobile). Growth now depends on higher labour productivity.
2. *Agriculture's demands*: This sector has become a ball-and-chain, a burden. Far from providing labour and resources for the rest of the economy, it absorbs about a third of total investments (which give a

very low return) and we have annually to mobilise 15 million workers, students, soldiers, to help bring the harvest in. (Despite which we have food shortages). Farm subsidies have reached astronomical levels.

3. *Armaments*: Our effort to achieve parity has meant diverting into weapons production the best technology, managerial talent, productive capacity.

4. *Siberia*: In the long run this rich storehouse of energy and minerals will be of immense value, but in the short run the investment costs are huge.

5. *Foreign aid*: Poland, Cuba, other Comecon countries and foreign commitments are a burden.

Therefore growth could only be maintained if we increased efficiency. But this has not happened. The late comrade Brezhnev ten years ago said that we must radically change our methods of planning and management 'in the age of technological revolution'. Yet the system itself generates inefficiency and waste, and the chronic shortages generate corruption and weaken discipline and labour incentives. *What are the 'systemic' causes of inefficiency?* The key is surely to be found in Academician Fedorenko's quip, that a fully balanced and articulated plan for next year would, with the help of computers, be ready in 30000 years . . . The centre – the party's central committee, the government, Gosplan, the economic ministries – *cannot* plan the whole economy. The multiple millions of interdependent plan decisions are necessarily divided between different offices. It is neither lack of skill nor lack of commitment which is to blame if plans are *not ready in time*, or are *unbalanced* and *contradictory*. Repeatedly, *production plans are out of line with supply plans*, and/or in conflict with plans for labour productivity, costs, profits, contractual obligations to customers, investment finance, railway capacity and so on almost ad infinitum. Lack of knowledge of 'micro' requirements, and sheer lack of time and information, compels the issuance of *plan targets in aggregate terms*: roubles, tons, pairs, and so on, with the familiar result that management *produce for plan-fulfilment statistics* and not for the customer. Quantity takes precedence over quality. As the economic editor of *Pravda* correctly put it, 'use values do not count.' Shortages weaken the customer's position still further ('take it or leave it'). Economy of materials is actually penalised, if it leads to non-fulfilment of plans in tons. *Technological innovation is frustrated* by strict central control over investment expenditure and overallocation of materials and equipment, as well as by management's risk-aversion. We suffer from *creeping price inflation*, as management tries to increase the value of output by shifting towards dearer product variants. Particularly is this true in the case of machinery. Escalating costs in agriculture and industry have led to a big increase in subsidies and unplanned credits. Our so-called budget surplus is actually a deficit, as comrade Belkin has pointed out.

The 'reforms' we introduced in 1979–81 cannot be an effective remedy, if only because they still further overburden the already overburdened centre. It must now not only compute 'normed value added' for millions of products, but also impose norms of material utilisation and economy of materials (*and* cost reduction targets too) on hundreds of thousands of production units. Far from being relaxed, administrative material allocation has been reinforced, managerial powers further restricted. Though new prices have been introduced in 1981, they still quite fail to reflect supply and demand, relative scarcity, use-value, and thus prices and profitabilities are no guide to action (or a misleading one) at any level. A drive against corruption and indiscipline are clearly desirable, but by itself it cannot be enough. Comrades, the necessity for fundamental reforms must be faced, and therefore . . .

Therefore *what*? Gertrude Schroeder, in the recent 'green book' of the US Congress, correctly states that 'planning is more centralised, rigid and detailed than ever', yet precisely this *is* at the heart of the malaise, precisely this inhibits inefficiency of enterprise. Can the leadership be brought to recognise the futility of detailed centralised current planning – outside of some key sectors, such as energy or armaments, where the centre does in fact possess the information as to needs, and the means to issue unambiguous orders, and where achievements are indeed impressive. *The so-called 'Hungarian' solution* seems to be the only alternative to futile tinkering with the present overcentralised system. This would leave most current output, and therefore inputs too, to free negotiations. There would still be some state interference (as here with our nationalised industries!), but some real autonomy too. Realistic prices, the profit motive, competition, consumer choice, are all part of the same reform package. A precondition must be the elimination of excess demand (concealed inflation), which plagues the economy in both the producers' goods and consumers' goods sectors. *Pace* Milton Friedman, one could readily imagine a socialist monetarism. But the consensus of Western expert opinion is that if such a reform were proposed it would be rejected, or be so watered down as to be ineffective, and this for the following reasons:

1. *Power and vested interest*. Much of the party-state apparatus is engaged in planning, allocating, controlling, appointing, dismissing. Greater reliance on market forces must seem a threat to valued power and privilege.
2. *Nervous conservatism*. No one remembers any other system. Transition to a different one may seem too risky, a leap into the

unknown. Priority sectors, of which armaments are an obvious example, would fear the possible effect of weakening the central allocation of resources at a time of widespread shortages, particularly with Reagan seen as speeding up the arms race.

3. Timidity is further reinforced because *reform must be large-scale* to be effective. Otherwise systemic contradictions must cause partial reform to collapse, as happened in and after 1965 in the USSR. (A Chinese leader used in this context the image of a bird in the cage. 'The bird should be allowed to fly, but within the cage, otherwise it will fly away.' Not surprisingly, their industrial planning reforms of 1979–81 ran into difficulties!)

4. *Lack of pressure from below*. Few understand the logic of this kind of reform, even among managers. (We all like competition so long as it affects others!) Workers are accustomed to overmanning, featherbedding, stable prices, job security.

5. *Ideology* (or the Soviet equivalent of wanting to privatise the post office!) The very words 'market socialism' are contrary to Marxist holy writ.

Even the most fervent Soviet advocates of 'Hungarian' type reform would recognise that very real difficulties must be overcome. Markets are everywhere imperfect, futures markets especially. There *is* no capital market in the USSR, and it is hard to see how one can be created. Endemic shortages could lead to worse problems if the system of priority-allocation were eliminated. Also the present state of the Western economies must be seen by the Soviet leadership as a warning rather than as an advertisement for free markets as a solution to all problems. For all these reasons, the most probable outcome is: *no* major change. This view is reinforced by the latest 'reform' decree (24 July 1983), a timid and limited 'experiment' in very partial managerial autonomy. *However*, the possibility of more drastic action cannot be excluded, because:

1. Andropov and his less hidebound colleagues must realise that *economic inefficiency also threatens political power*. Power cannot be given *total* priority over efficiency. *If* the leadership finds the malfunctioning of the system intolerable, it *must* look seriously at alternatives. At present its own policies and plans are being frustrated.

2. In *agriculture*, because of the vital importance of feeding the people, *real changes have been introduced*, which may perhaps have positive effects. The huge collective and state farms are being broken up into small groups of peasants, who are to operate as a species of autonomous subcontractors. (In China, where techniques are still

mediaeval, a similar type of reform is based on the family ('the house-hold responsibility system'), a development which a few years ago seemed impossible, politically and ideologically.) Agricultural service agencies, and producers of industrial inputs for agriculture, have been ordered (in a decree announced on 22 July 1983) to produce for the customer and are to be judged by the actual increases achieved in agricultural production. Also private-plot production by peasants is being encouraged. A possible (likely?) successor to Andropov, Gorbachev, is in charge of all this at top level. This might 'infect' the rest of the economy, over the next few years.

3.   True, the middle grades of the party-state bureaucracy would be threatened by market-type reforms. But this does not apply to the apex of the power-pyramid: it is not there that one allocates sulphuric acid or women's blouses, or issues output targets for ball-bearings factories. Reform would in any case have to be enforced from above (it was so in Hungary). Besides, is it really true that the Communist party's political power would be threatened if 'socialist' firms or farms produced what their customers actually want?

4.   Ideology can be reinterpreted, if the leadership so wish.

To repeat, *the probabilities are against major reforms*. The arms-race may constitute a major obstacle, because it adds to strains and shortages. More likely are repeated attempts to improve the present system. There may be a wave of purely administrative reorganisations, including some revival of regional planning authorities (this is actually happening in formerly empty areas of Siberia). But despite all this we must not exclude the *possibility* of a major reform decree within the next two or three years. An American scholar, Joseph Berliner, has expressed the view that it might take the form of legalising small-scale private enterprise, rather than freeing state enterprises from central control. This seems unlikely in the USSR, though it may be happening in China. If major reforms are frustrated, the likely consequence will be not collapse but stagnation.

Does Gorbachev need a breathing space? (Luxembourg, December 1988)

If this title implies that Gorbachev should halt the reform process to consolidate what has already been achieved, then this would be quite the wrong thing to do. Economic reform has not yet had any serious effect. A series of radical resolutions have been adopted, laws passed, but as of now little has changed. There are three interlinked explanations for this lack of progress: *difficulties of transition*, *opposition*, and, finally, *ambiguities or contradictions* in the reform model itself.

Other papers at this conference have dealt with measures that have been adopted. That they have so far had little effect is not disputed by anyone, least of all by our Soviet colleagues. It is worth stressing that the more important measures date from 1987 and 1988, and so far have had little time to operate. Of course, the reforms were prepared earlier. Indeed they were already under discussion ten and more years ago. Thus in 1977 I wrote an article 'The economic problems of Brezhnev's successors', which was published in the *Washington Papers* in 1978. This article took the form of an imaginary report written by a committee of reforming economists appointed by the (unknown) successor of Brezhnev. Its 'chairman' was Aganbegyan. A comparison of this article with the reforms actually adopted in 1987–88 shows many similarities. This is not to be explained by any special far-sightedness on my part. Even in the 'stagnant' days of Brezhnev, reform-minded economists did put forward criticisms and proposals for change. What they could not do in published work was condemn the *system*, their proposals had to appear as aiming at 'further perfecting' it. Various reform measures that were adopted were half-hearted and ineffective, because they could not be 'systemic'. And partial measures could change nothing, as they did not tackle the basic problem: the incompatibility of centralised planning of the 'command' type with the needs of a modern economy and society.

The urgency with which Gorbachev is tackling the task of radical reform is due in large part to the realisation that there existed what he has repeatedly called a 'pre-crisis situation'. There were and are shortages, inflationary pressures, structural imbalances. Yet these very same factors represent major obstacles to a successful transition. For example, how can one abandon the system of material allocation, shift to 'trade in means of production', or relax price controls, when there is excess demand? A recent article in the journal *Kommunist* (No. 17, 1988) has referred to a budget deficit of close to 100 billion roubles, a deficit covered very largely by money creation, thereby fuelling inflation. Yet there are very urgent needs for higher expenditures on housing and health, and for raising the low pay of engineers, technologists, teachers, medical personnel, the service sector generally. The fall in the oil price has reduced export receipts, and to the high cost of the Chernobyl disaster has been added the tragedy of the Armenian earthquake. But even without these added complications the problems of transition would be immense. Few managers have any experience of marketing, they have been accustomed to supply customers designated by the planners. Market-type institutions, and personnel to work in them, are underdeveloped, and so are the needed information flows. Competition is advocated, but again there is lack of experience, and also fear that many suppliers would abuse their position under conditions of shortage (that is, a sellers' market). Measures intended to stimulate cooperative and private enterprise also become distorted when shortages enable those enterprises to make a great deal of money – or they fail to operate because they cannot obtain needed material inputs. Meanwhile there is much uncertainty and confusion. It can be illustrated with a story, trivial in itself, but symbolic, published last year in *Moskovskie novosti*: a film script writer asked in a big public library to consult the *Guinness Book of Records*. He was told: together with thousands of other books it had been transferred from the so-called *spetskhran* (closed section of the library) to the open shelves, an obviously desirable change. However – they could not find it! For analogous reasons many Western businessmen report that they find confusion among Soviet foreign trade officials; the old arrangements have been swept away, the new ones are not yet functioning.

So it would all be very difficult even if there were no opposition. But of course there *is* opposition. Nor does it come only from 'bureaucrats', who understandably defend their power and privileges. Party and state officials are not well paid. Thus a first secretary of an *obkom* (provincial party committee) has recently published his salary: 550 roubles a month, or (at the official exchange rate) a little less than half of my university pension after tax, and little more than the pay of an experienced Moscow bus driver! Less eminent party officials receive much less, and so they naturally value the legal and less legal 'perks' of office. Some Soviet sources speak of 'feudal principalities', sectoral and regional interest groups capable of defying Moscow and blocking or deforming reform measures.

But in addition there is ample evidence that many workers are unhappy: redeployment has to be, even unemployment could be, the consequence of a necessary and overdue restructuring of the economy. Millions are accustomed to being paid regularly regardless of the enterprise's economic performance, for little effort. Tightening of discipline, the new-quality-acceptance commission, the emphasis on financial results and the end of easy credit, cause concern among the labour force. Of course, as consumers they would benefit from higher productivity and improved quality, but meanwhile the shops are still poorly supplied and so there seems to be little reward for harder work.

Many have also noted the widespread belief in a kind of egalitarianism, and there is a long-established ideology-based belief in the unfairness and basically non-socialist nature of markets. As was recently pointed out by A. Sergeyev in a discussion on a draft of a new textbook of political economy, 'It is known that Marx and Engels held that socialism and commodity production were not only contradictory but incompatible. Lenin was of the same opinion. Even today no one has the "theoretical effrontery" to say that Lenin was the creator of the theory of commodity production under socialism. Was the theory of Marx, Engels and Lenin about socialism wrong; or was their theory on commodity production wrong? . . .' (*Voprosy ekonomiki*, No. 7, 1988). Similar thoughts, formerly regarded as heretical, can be found in the discussion, in No. 10 of the same journal, concerning the 110th anniversary of Engels's *Anti-Dühring*. Of course, 'ideology' is not easy to define, is adaptable to circumstances, indeed is being adapted. However, it does have some effect on genuinely held beliefs. It helps to explain the suspicion with which cooperative and private enterprise is regarded by ordinary people, not only by 'bureaucrats'.

The opposition is able to take advantage of the difficulties of transition. The necessary reforms are interlinked and require to be introduced together. Thus 'full *khozraschyot*', the enterprises' financial responsibility cannot be effective until prices are radically reformed, excess demand cannot be curbed unless and until enterprises can be made fully financially responsible, shortages are (in part) generated by the material allocation system, which cannot be abandoned while shortages remain serious, and so on. Meanwhile the five-year plan drafted in 1984 is still current, and enterprises are still judged in relation to various plans and fulfilment targets, despite the decision to abandon them. Nor have prices yet been reformed, but in their present form they are quite unsuitable for the economic calculations and incentives the reform requires. Partial, step-by-step reform frequently results in contradiction and confusion, which can be made use of by those who prefer to block radical changes.

Similarly, political and economic reforms are seen as depending on each other, yet hard to carry out simultaneously. The more so as political power at the centre is essential to push the process through against opposition. Here, for instance, is the view of E. Ambartsumov: 'I think that right now it is impossible to proceed to a democratic society, since we have never had one. It is difficult to imagine the transition without passing through a certain "authoritarian" stage' (*Voprosy ekonomiki*, No. 6, 1988). So the process of *demokratizatsiya*, under conditions in which public opinion is divided, when one sees 'the non-conformity of current and short-term interests of a sizeable part of the population with the strategic aims of *perestroika*' (S. Tolstikov, in ibid.), is itself contradictory. One needs a *reform strategy*. It is easier to say this than to devise one that works.

Then one must also consider the ambiguities of the reform model, due partly to necessary political compromises, and partly to differences of view among the reformers themselves. Thus exactly where *is* the line to be drawn between plan and market? What will be, should be, the content and targets of the next (thirteenth) five-year plan? What is to be the theoretical and practical basis of the reform of prices? What proportion can be, should be, freed of control altogether? If there is to be a capital market, then of what kind? How is wasteful duplication of investments to be avoided? Should wages be 'residual', that is, depend on the net revenues of each enterprise, or be based on a tariff rate plus bonus? What precisely is to be the role of the party in controlling appointments (and supervising elections), what (if anything) is to remain of the *nomenklatura* system by which party control over personnel has been exercised for 60 and more years? Are economic ministries to survive, if so in what form? What are to be the economic powers of republics and of local soviets? Problems linked with nationalism are clearly already present. How far should one go with family leasing, petty private enterprise, cooperatives? How can the rouble be made convertible? What should be the role of joint ventures of foreign capital? ('Will foreign capital in joint enterprises exploit our labour-power and create surplus value on our territory?' to cite a hypothetical question by V. Musatov (*Voprosy ekonomiki*, No. 7, 1988)). Some cautious reformers may resemble the Chinese 'moderate', Chen Yun, who is said to have expressed the moderate-reform view as follows: 'Our managers are in too small a cage, they cannot spread their wings. We must build them a bigger cage. But we must keep them in a cage, otherwise they will fly away.'

The reform process is supposed to move faster in 1989, it having been decided to cut back 'state orders' (*goszakazy*) and extend trade in means of production, so that a larger part of the output of enterprises will be subject to negotiation with customers. We shall see if this actually will happen. The reform must be pushed ahead, since little has yet changed, and a 'breathing-space' (*peredyshka*) is the last thing that is now needed. One cannot halt to consolidate when there is as yet so little to consolidate. However, a breathing-space may be helpful if by this is meant temporary relief from the balance of payments constraint. So we should now turn to the *external factor*. The fall in the oil price, problems with oil production, the continued need to import grain, have compelled the Soviets to cut back on hard-currency imports. The idea has been put forward, unofficially, that the USSR could borrow large sums in order to provide quickly some visible benefits for the consumer. N. Shmelev argued for the direct import of consumers' goods, but other alternatives are imports of machinery to make such goods (provided it can be effectively used), and, finally, the encouragement of joint ventures which aim to supply the home market. All three require borrowing.

Should we 'aid' the USSR? In my view, this is the wrong question. In the first place, no one doubts that the success or failure of the reform will be due primarily to internal factors. Second, the USSR is not asking for economic *aid*. Third, there is no good case for some sort of 'Marshall plan', or for making such a plan conditional upon changes in Soviet policy. In any case, there is ample evidence that policy *has* changed, whether in relation to human rights or to intervention abroad. The Soviet leadership is in any case conscious of the fact that too much foreign indebtedness is undesirable, and recalls the sad fate of Poland. No, the correct posture, in my view, is to join in *mutually* profitable exchanges, including the granting of credits, on a non-discriminatory basis. As a commercial risk, the USSR clearly is a more reliable creditor than, say, Mexico, where net debt is five times higher. Not to grant credits would be conscious discrimination against the USSR, based upon the supposition that it is our task to do them harm. This seems to me quite a wrong approach: we should prefer Gorbachev to succeed, given that any alternative leadership is likely to be both unstable and unpleasant. Some have urged that the Cocom list be pruned, and indeed it does contain items only remotely connected with military end-uses, so I would support this. However, Soviet needs also extend very much into the area of what could be called 'low technology', relatively simple items such as small-scale farm machinery, or moderate equipment for the clothing and food industries or for materials handling. The USSR is at present overdependent on exports of oil and gas, and her future export earnings should include a wider range of manufactures, though here there is bound to be severe competition from the newly-industrialising third-world countries. It is official policy to incorporate the USSR much more closely into the world market, and this too should be welcomed and facilitated. Closer contact, economic and cultural, cannot harm the West and can help a little in the internal evolution of the Soviet Union.

Is *perestroika* irreversible? No, not yet. To repeat, its progress does not depend primarily on us – though the reversing of the arms race can also help by enabling Gorbachev to devote more resources to cope with the many internal claimants. Meanwhile, voices are heard in the West: a healthier Soviet Union could become a more powerful enemy. A leopard cannot change its spots. We spend too much time persuading the wolf to sign a document promising to be a vegetarian. A well-fed bear is dangerous – and a hungry bear even more dangerous. These analogies are, in my view, misleading. Whatever animal best represented the Stalinist Soviet Union, we now face something different, new, to which 'zoological' stereotypes are increasingly inappropriate (unless one views all of *glasnost*' and *perestroika* as an exercise of dressing the wolf in sheep's clothing, which seems to me contrary to all the evidence). Instead of or alongside MAD (Mutually Assured Destruction) I would advocate MAID (Mutually Advantageous Inter-dependence). That way lies hope.

The economy: its present state, problems and prospects (report to the British Embassy, December 1989)

'The financial situation in the country is extremely grave . . . The budget deficit, amounting to a fifth of its expenditures, has a destructive effect on the consumer market . . . Money emission grows rapidly. The purchasing power of the rouble is falling. Rising prices are accompanied by growing shortages of articles of mass consumption. Internal and external debt exceeds permissible bounds.' This is an extract from a Supreme Soviet economic committee's report, circulated at the end of October 1989. 'The food situation is becoming ever more threatening. I am convinced that, unless there are radical changes in farming already this year, then next year we may face real hunger.' This from Academician V. Tikhonov (*Voprosy eonomiki*, No. 9, 1989). Finally, from a list that could cover many pages, the view of Academician S. Shatalin: 'The situation could hardly be worse . . . Our deplorable finances and the catastrophic condition of the consumer market are but the visible part of the iceberg.' 'Shall we freeze this winter?', asks *Izvestiya* (29 October 1989). Coal strikes, a decline in oil output, the closing on ecological grounds of some nuclear power stations, bottlenecks on the railways, can add up to a fuel crisis. All agree that shortages have grown worse, and, in the words of the well-known columnist V. Selyunin, 'the bony hand of product-famine is well able to throttle *perestroika*'. The same gloomy picture of the present situation is presented by virtually every Soviet economist of any and every political persuasion, though there is widespread disagreement as to the remedies to be adopted, and also on the aims and purposes of the entire reform programme. How did matters reach this pass in the fifth year of the Gorbachev era? What remedial action is being taken? Will it have the desired effect? What is to happen next?

The reform process would have been complex and painful even if all had been agreed as to what to do, even if there were no opposition. This is because everyone had been accustomed to the old system, knew how to relate to it, work within it. A market economy was and is, to most of those called upon to introduce it, a thing unknown which they had read about in books. Managers are untrained in the art of marketing, of seeking out customers, are accustomed to manoeuvre and bargain with their ministerial bureaucrats. New commercial banks lack experienced managers. Market intermediaries, institutions, information flows, are rudimentary or non-existent. Furthermore, the very need for reform arises from the fact that the old system generated imbalances, distortions, shortages, but these make market-type reforms more difficult to introduce. There *is* opposition, of course, and not just from 'bureaucrats'. A recent (November 1989) protest meeting in Leningrad, called by conservative party officials led by the recently-appointed first secretary Gidaspov, which directly criticised the whole reform, was supported by managers of large industrial plants in the city; clearly some managers are not anxious to be exposed to competition and the uncertainties of the market. Hard-liners argue that market-type reforms represent the abandonment of socialism, that the reform programme announced by Abalkin (the vice-premier in charge) is 'a fig leaf to conceal the restoration of capitalism', to cite a speech I heard myself at an economists' discussion panel. Right-wing populist speakers denounce the recently legalised cooperatives and appeal to the egalitarian instincts of the masses. 'Democratisation', a real parliament, freedom to organise and to protest, can act as a brake on necessary reform measures, such as for instance the long-overdue increase in the highly-subsidised food prices. Workers demand job security, are able to strike if demands for higher wages and better conditions are not met, negotiate face-to-face with the prime minister, force humiliating concessions, ignore the official unions.

There is considerable unclarity as to the ultimate aim of the reforms and of the reformers. Gorbachev in effect argues for *socialism* with a human face, market *socialism*. Some leading reformers in private conversation regard socialism itself, Marx, even Lenin, as obsolete or irrelevant. Sweden is the ideal for some, 'Chicago' for others. But the majority (in my view) remain within the world-view of Marxism–Leninism, though they seek to reinterpret it. It is significant that the loudest applause at the November conference on economic reform followed a speech by Sergeyev, economic adviser to the right-wing-populist 'United Front of Working People' (the audience included party and ministerial bureaucrats, as well as numerous managers and academic economists). Meanwhile much remains unsettled. What *should* be the respective roles of plan and market? What proportion of prices should be settled by free negotiation? Should management be elected by the work force? Is a market-based economy compatible with the dominance of state ownership of the means of production? If not, what forms of ownership should be permissible? What meaning can be attached to draft laws on property and on leasing (*arenda*)? Should private entrepreneurs be allowed to employ labour (illegal today)? Should there be a capital market? The recognition of a labour market? Decollectivisation of agriculture? Plus the very important and indeed explosive issue of how to cope with the nationalisms, Russian and non-Russian, with the claims for economic independence of the republics, economic autonomy of regions. Many articles appear under the heading '*Kuda my idyom*?', where are we going? I for one would be hard put to find an answer.

All these problems, bad enough in themselves, have been vastly exacerbated by a grave error in financial and monetary policy. There was a (hidden) budget deficit for 20 years, covered by bank money. Under Gorbachev revenue dropped because of the effects of the fall in world oil prices (which directly reduced revenue, and also led to a cut in imports of consumers' goods), and the effect on the budget of the cutback in vodka sales. Expenditure rose because of soaring food subsidies, the consequences of the Chernobyl disaster and the Armenian earthquake, and higher expenditures on housing, medical services (grossly underfunded) and education. In 1988 all this led to a huge rise in the budget deficit, and in money creation. A relaxation in income controls led to a sharp rise in money wages. While some prices did rise, the gap between demand and supply widened; the exacerbation of shortages stimulated hoarding and petty corruption, lengthened queues, strengthened discontent, so disenchantment with *perestroika* naturally deepened. Incentives became less effective when there was little to buy. Savings bank deposits rose rapidly, creating a dangerous overhang of purchasing power which has little power to purchase. Similarly, enterprises accumulated large sums in profits which they could not spend because of shortage of the required machinery and materials. Clearly, all this was not the appropriate setting for a *market* type reform. In so far as enterprises, regions, republics, acquired the right to dispose of part of their production (that is, in excess of the still-compulsory plan), they tended not to sell for roubles, but to make barter deals, thereby disrupting supply links with those who happen not to have the desired barter counterpart. This is the logical consequence of not having confidence in being able to obtain the needed inputs (or imports) for roubles. Those who can export for hard currency, or do a barter deal with (for instance) Japan or Sweden, make such deals in preference to selling to a Soviet customer. This has led to a decree, in November 1989, requiring licences for export of some items which are particularly scarce in the home market. Ministers and their advisers do now recognise that it is extremely urgent to restore real purchasing power to the rouble, and the reform can make no headway unless this is done. Otherwise the disintegration of the supply system into a multitude of ad hoc barter deals can result in intolerable bottlenecks and a fall in output. So a series of remedial measures have been taken or promulgated. Thus: (a) Cuts in the defence budget and in the size of the armed forces, the 'conversion' of part of defence industries to produce consumers' goods and equipment for their production; (b) some major investment projects are being abandoned or halted; (c) more is being spent on imports of consumers' goods (and also pharmaceuticals), to relieve shortages and to provide budget revenue; (d) more vodka is being sold, an important revenue item; (e) a new tax law is to be introduced, affecting personal incomes and also enterprise profits; (f) ideas are mooted to raise revenue by sales of council houses, advance payments for scarce consumer durables (for example, cars), bonds, life insurance, pension-fund contributions (these are not yet operational); (g) an unusually large increase in consumers' goods production (7.6 per cent) is planned for 1990, filling gaps in the shops and providing more turnover-tax revenue.

As a result, the budget deficit is supposed to fall from the 100 milliards originally planned for 1988, or the 120 milliard anticipated at mid-year, or 92 milliard (the 'actual' for 1988), to 60 milliard roubles in 1990. It is to be financed very largely by the sale of interest-bearing bonds, which it is hoped will be voluntarily bought by enterprises and financial institutions, though the interest rate (5 per cent) is well below the estimated rate of inflation (8–9 per cent). However, this plan has been greeted with suspicion by such intelligent economists as Aganbegyan, Popov, Petrakov. Both publicly and privately they point to the fragility of the assumptions on which it is based. Consumers' goods output is planned to rise at a rate which is very unlikely to be attained, and so turnover tax revenue will be below expectations. 'Conversion' of defence industries to civilian production necessarily takes time. The new laws on pensions and on paid vacations will push up expenditures. So would the proposed increase in agricultural procurement prices, unless accompanied by a rise in the highly-subsidised retail prices of basic foodstuffs – so Abalkin told us that farms are holding back from selling grain to the state in anticipation of a higher price. True, Abalkin also told us that he considers the plans for 1990 to be fulfillable, though with difficulty, and then only if there are no more major strikes. (In conversation, Petrakov forecast that when the 1990 plans will be seen to be beyond the possibility of fulfilment, premier Ryzhkov and vice-premier Abalkin would be greatly relieved if the Congress of Soviets will reject the entire package, which in his heart of hearts he knows to be unreal.)

Aganbegyan strongly expressed the view that the whole reform programme is proceeding with insufficient sense of urgency (indeed of emergency) and he has apparently bombarded Gorbachev and Ryzhkov with suggestions for much more decisive action to 'tie up' surplus money, by measures similar to those listed under (f) above (sales of houses, payments in advance for durables, and so on), but more ambitious and far-reaching. His plan includes an ingenious idea of selling attractive goods, including imports, via mail-order catalogue, with each citizen entitled to order up to 1000 roubles-worth of goods. He claimed that this would be preferable to selling them through normal trade channels, since the latter are corrupt and often controlled by local mafias. Aganbegyan told me that he ended a memorandum to Gorbachev with the words, taken from Danton, 'delay means death'. Yet, he claimed, his proposals for instant action were not taken up – and he himself set out on a journey to Argentina . . . I imagine that Aganbegyan has personal reasons for disapproving of Abalkin (though he claims to have had no ambitions to take up political posts, and says he is happy to be rector of the Academy of the National Economy). (He has been replaced as Academician-secretary for economics by S.S. Shatalin). However, his view of the over-optimism of the government is shared by many other economists. Continued printing of money, directly and via the credit system (many new commercial banks have been created), a looming energy crisis, the likelihood of more strikes, regional maldistribution of food supplies, possible paralysis on the railways, unpredictable clashes between nationalities, all these point to a possible, or even likely, decline in output, to disruption of industrial supplies, leading to disorders and riots, possibly in major centres of industry. Given these immediate dangers, the Ryzhkov–Abalkin plan for stage-by-stage movement towards a market economy, and the three-day discussions at the economic conference (15–17 November 1989), may well turn out to be largely irrelevant.

The conference itself brought to the surface a mounting opposition to the entire reform package. Abalkin said that he had expected criticism from the 'left', that is, from those who thought he was too slow and cautious, not radical enough. In fact, as we have seen, the audience (which included many party officials and senior managers) reserved the loudest applause for speakers from the 'right'. The words 'right' and 'left' are misleading in the present context, so a few words of explanation are called for. The so-called 'Right' can be said to consist of three elements. One is comprised of Party functionaries, deeply worried about loss of power and privilege, and no doubt genuinely concerned about the social and economic disorders they see around them – a rising crime rate, the disruption of economic life, political opposition (many expect to be defeated in the forthcoming republican and local elections). A Soviet journalist said that one provincial secretary said to him: 'What is going on in Moscow? Is Gorbachev betraying us?' A second group is composed of those who have taught, or still believe in, the old official ideology: they stand in defence of state property against cooperatives, leasing, capital markets, private enterprise, against anything that smells of capitalism. The conservative party functionaries find such ideas convenient. The third group is Russian nationalists. These are split between neo-Stalinists, one of whom told me in all seriousness that the economy was properly planned in 1948–53, and those who believe that the Stalin regime had a disastrous impact on the Russian nation and especially on the Russian peasantry. Some believe that the revolution itself was a disaster, and wave the old Russian tricolour flag at unofficial demonstrations. Among them are many who express a neo-Slavphil ideology and, like Dostoyevsky and Solzhenitsyn, have no time for Western 'bourgeois' ideas. Some denounce the sale of irreplaceable natural resources such as oil to the West, dislike joint ventures, oppose the inroads of Western pop culture, are economic and political isolationists, and are heavily tainted with militant anti-semitism. They also urged decisive action against 'the mafia', and the freezing or confiscation of large savings-bank deposits. The three groups are in some respects strange bedfellows, but together they represent a growing threat to the whole reform movement. On certain issues they are supported by those who are customarily labelled 'left': for instance on ecology, and in opposition to price increases and to the toleration of unemployment. I have even met a semi-Trotskyist sociologist who expressed the hope that the coming collapse of the economy would herald 'a true proletarian revolution'. However, as Abalkin and others have noted, the real danger is from the Right, and from the fact that the 'marketeers' lack an adequate support base in society.

Also lacking are both the determination and the means to implement the new policies. Laws are drafted, discussed, amended: on the enterprise, on leasing, on land, on cooperatives, on foreign trade. But it is a most important fact of life that the old lines of authority are breaking down. To take several examples of different kinds: there was, first, that Leningrad mass meeting at which the Leningrad first secretary, Gidaspov, launched a direct attack on reform and on the party leadership, soon after his own appointment ('election') to that post to replace a known hard-liner, and he is still very much there. A second example is Gorbachev's request that the editor of *Argumenty i fakty* (a weekly with a world-record circulation of nearly 30 million) should resign. As of now (December 1989) he has refused to do so, with the backing of his colleagues. A third is the support of party members, local officials, Soviet deputies, for the strikes in the coalfields, where authority passed from the party-soviet apparatus to the strike committee in several instances. A fourth is the evident impossibility to impose party discipline in the

Supreme Soviet itself; nearly 90 per cent are members of the one party, yet they feel free to vote against the government. It is a paradox that party discipline is far tighter in the *British* parliament, where there is an opposition. As matters stand, it is by no means certain that essential features of the reform programme will be adopted by the Soviet parliament; our old (and well-founded!) concepts about the nature of Soviet political life are in need of drastic amendment.

Politics as such is not the subject of the present paper, but all this has profound significance in the context of the implementation of economic reform. The situation in certain republics must also be seen in this context. The Supreme Soviet, after acrimonious debate, passed a law on 'economic independence of Lithuania, Latvia and Estonia' (published on 2 December 1989). Both Abalkin and Gerashchenko (head of the State Bank) expressed the view, in conversation, that supply links will not be disrupted, that these republics cannot do without Russian fuel and materials, and that the central bank will be able to control or limit the republican banking and credit institutions. But suppose they ignore such controls and limits and do their own thing? After all, the Lithuanian *communist* party has publicly announced its intention to be independent of Moscow, and has borne Moscow's disapproval of such ideas with equanimity, while Moscow sent Medvedev to appeal to the Lithuanian comrades not to go as far as this (*Pravda*, 2 December 1989). The Azerbaijani blockade of Armenia continued for months despite Moscow's orders to desist. Nagorno-Karabakh proves no simpler a problem to resolve than is Northern Ireland. Events in Central Asia may take a dramatic turn before long. Moldavia could also erupt at any time. The dangers of destabilisation are compounded by a sort of power vacuum. This is in part a consequence of the (welcome) process of democratisation, but, in a country lacking political culture and beset by many urgent problems, the effects could be a slide towards chaos, which many speak of with real apprehension. All this may sound excessively alarmist, and I sincerely hope that this is indeed so, since what has happened under Gorbachev can only be welcomed, and this people has suffered enough in this century and deserved better than to go through yet more convulsions. But I would be less than honest if I were to exclude the possibility of catastrophe. Indeed I have yet to meet a Soviet citizen, economist or no, who would regard such an outcome as impossible. The optimists would regard it as improbable. On Soviet TV a member of the Supreme Soviet remarked, in an interview: 'after a visit to my constituents, I have to say that if we do not deal decisively and quickly with the economic crisis, we will not be meeting here in a year's time.'

So to turn to prognosis. *Can* they, *will* they, find a way to 'deal decisively with the economic crisis'? Abalkin is well aware of risks and difficulties. He says that his plan will (or rather may) succeed. But, to coin a phrase, he would, wouldn't he? One of his colleagues thought that Abalkin the economist knows that it will not work, but vice-premier Abalkin has to say that it will.

I attended (as an observer) a meeting of Supreme Soviet deputies belonging to the inter-regional group – led by Popov, Afanasyev, Yeltsin, Sakharov, a mere five days before Sakharov died. They met on 9 December to discuss tactics for the Congress of Soviets session due to begin the next week. Afanasyev spoke of the 'rotting-away of the parto-cratic regime', the 'wonderful' example of Eastern Europe; the so-called advance-guard party is now 'the rearguard party'. He called for constitu-tional amendment to remove its so-called leading role. Meanwhile 'the crisis grows worse', and while those to the left of Gorbachev are disor-ganised, the Right is on the march. Gavriil Popov, who chaired the meeting, also spoke of 'the united front of the enemies of *perestroika*; the main danger is from the Right, which has managed to mobilise part of the working-class.' In conversation over lunch he told me that Abalkin's plans have no hope of getting anywhere. To get things moving 'we need a little chaos' (*nuzhen nebolshoi khaos*). Several deputies demanded a multi-party system. Criticising Gorbachev's tendency to compromise, one (Kazannik) proposed that state organs from highest to lowest should 'refuse to implement party directives'; the reform had not freed the means of production, indeed that men control nothing but their personal means of reproduction (this raised a laugh!). The deputies split on the issue of the appropriateness of a 2-hour 'warning strike', called by some individ-ual leaders of the group, but expressed alarm at the activities of the Leningrad 'conservative' party leader Gidaspov and his (and others') links with the populist-right United Workers' Front. In Kiev I was told that the republican and city party organs have decided to back Gidaspov. Other sources speak of the possibility that regional party secretaries will support conservative positions at the forthcoming extended plenum of the central committee.

All this is highly relevant to one's estimate of what will emerge from the coming crisis. That it will come is – almost – a consensus, the only question is – when? Much depends on how cold the winter will be, whether fuel stocks can be moved, whether strikes will hit the railways, whether serious food shortages will cause trouble in some major indus-trial centres, whether nationality issues will come to the boil and where. The publicist Selyunin, in the course of a long talk, described his experi-ences in Vorkuta and the Kuzbas, talking with striking miners. He, and also the socialist Boris Kagarlitsky, stressed that the miners have not been seriously influenced by the right-wing populists, and expressed the hope that the liberal-and-left forces will get their act together before the crisis breaks and stop the new right from utilising it for their purposes: 'Otherwise blood will flow.' However, again one must stress the potential disunity of the so-called 'left'. Selyunin clearly wants a free-market economy and believes that the miners want it too (so they do, for themselves, since they have a product that sells for hard currency in world markets!). Kagarlitsky, though he recognised the need for markets, is much more concerned about social services, mass unemployment, workers' rights, keeping control over prices of basic foodstuffs. As was also the case with Solidarity in Poland, it is hard to see such ill-assorted bedfellows emerging with a coherent reform programme. Kagarlitsky is attempting to be a founder of a new Socialist Party. Selyunin (and such men as Lisichkin and Strelyany) are not, I believe, socialists of any kind. So the 'little chaos' desired by Gavriil Popov seems to me more likely to provide an opportunity for the hard-liners, led by such men as Gidaspov, with the support of many trade-union officials and of a part of the working-class, plus the Russian nationalists and the remnants of the ideologists. Yes, as already pointed out, they too are divided. Nor do they have a coherent economic programme, other than a negative gut-reaction to the market, to cooperatives, to any private enterprise. Furthermore, the Russian-nationalist aspect of their programme is an irritant to other nationalities in a multi-national state. So, what *could* happen if, say in a few months' time, disintegration reaches a point at which a state of emergency requires to be declared?

Scenario one: Gorbachev does the declaring, takes emergency powers, sacks the remaining conservatives, but uses MVD troops and, where necessary, the army to restore order, with the KGB enforcing tough anti-strike measures. Recentralisation of economic decision-making would be virtually forced as a short-term remedy for the crisis, under the slogan of 'reculer pour mieux sauter', though, as Popov wrote in his memorandum to the Congress of Soviets, the danger is that such measures will not be temporary. It seems that the military have been pleased by recent (and long overdue) improvements in pay and allowances for officers. An actual military coup seems very improbable, even though the name of General Gromov (former C-in-C in Afghanistan) comes up from time to time, and it is said that those who served in Afghanistan ('Afghantsy') are potential storm-troopers. (Incidentally, at a meeting organised by (pro-reform) young managers and cooperators and held at the 'Plekhanov' economic institute, a lieutenant in uniform told the audience that the army would not act against *perestroika* (probably he is right, but it is not insignificant that he chose to say so publicly and received a round of applause).)

Scenario two: party functionaries succeed in removing Gorbachev. Their law-and-order campaign would be harsher. Their immediate economic steps would be similar, but we would have a reaffirmation of a largely anti-market ideology. There may be more trouble in some of the republics. A variant of scenario two has been sketched out by Tatiana Koryagina, in a Russian-language newspaper published in Riga (*Sovetskaya molodezh*, 18 October 1989). Uncontrollable wage demands will fuel 'colossal inflation', leading to more strikes.

> This will lead to a severe fall in living standards, many times worse than in Yugoslavia and Poland. It will prove very hard to emerge from this crisis because the people and the apparatus are ignorant of economics, have only the false theory of the political economy of socialism. And there will be people interested in furthering a speedy and explosive disintegration of the economy, to cause the masses to hate Gorbachev, so as to have a right-wing coup . . . More strikes will be followed by the use of military force, leading to collapse, hunger and, in the case of strikes in the energy sector, also cold.

Her scenario goes on to envisage forced labour, shooting of alleged saboteurs, sharpened national conflicts, and so on. I hope that this is a nightmare vision. As Koryagina herself would certainly stress, this is just a possible scenario, not a forecast, and she expresses the hope that 'if Gorbachev shows strength', forces through the needed radical changes, such an outcome can yet be avoided. The bad thing is that I met few who consider such an outcome outside the bounds of possibility.

Scenario three: the free-marketeers win, with or without Gorbachev (without him they seem to have no hope). This is the programme recommended by the most radical of the economic 'liberals': raise prices to the level at which supply and demand get into balance, even if this does mean high inflation rates in the short term and much public protest. This is the painful but necessary way to a market economy. It is the road now being travelled by Poland. But there is another example, which I happened to see for myself when, from Moscow, I travelled to Vietnam (Hanoi) to attend a symposium held on 12–15 December. The Vietnamese leadership faced a similar dilemma, took a risk, allowed prices to rise (the inflation rate in 1988 was enormous), allowed petty and even not-so-petty private enterprise in town and village, fixed a realistic exchange rate and tolerated free convertibility. The result was an economic miracle. Empty shops filled, queues disappeared, the dollar circulates alongside the dong, private traders are everywhere, of scarcity in the market there is no sign. Yes, there is poverty, yes, prices are high in relation to incomes. Of course Vietnam is not Russia. Yet what we see around us is a living advertisement for this radical–liberal scenario. Visiting Russians were most impressed. Yet this scenario is emphatically rejected, as politically far too risky, by almost everyone from Gorbachev down.

Scenario 3A: Same objective, different tactic. This is the scheme advocated by Gavriil Popov and a few others: a temporary basic ration at low prices, while all other goods (including the rationed ones, over the ration) sell at free prices. Abalkin and most other economists with whom I discussed this idea have opposed it, partly at least because he believes that such powers should be transferred to the republics ('One ration scheme to cover the whole country from Vladivostok to Lvov? No!'). To operate such a proposal would require the dismantling of literally hundreds of thousands of ad hoc distribution and rationing schemes based on factories, offices, connections. Though the idea seems to me the only quick way to move towards real market prices, it looks like a non-starter. So do various schemes for parallel currencies, inspired by the 'hard rouble' (*chervonets*) of 1923–24, which circulated along with the rapidly depreciating *sovznak*, though some believe that this could be a road to convertibility.

Lastly, there is the least dramatic scenario, one of 'muddling through'. The Russian people are patient; they have seen worse than this, enough of the old arrangements will function to prevent total breakdown, a new price system will be operational by 1991, the inflationary creation of money will slow down, savings banks deposits could be partially frozen, the republics will realise that they all depend on Russia as a supplier and a market and will see that their dreams of total independence are a chimera. A substitute supply system can be improvised, such as a recently-published (in *Izvestiya*) 'white market', in which hundreds of enterprises enter a sort of multilateral-barter club, in which the material inputs they can offer are valued on a points system to their relative scarcity. Then, gradually, as shortages diminish, the reform process, now stalled, can take off. This is not an impossible outcome, but very few of my Soviet colleagues consider it to be probable.

The people's patience would last longer if food supplies could be improved, and much more spent on imports of consumers' goods. More *is* being spent, but the goods disappear at once, so great is excess demand, and there is much talk of an efficient mafia and also unorganised thievery. Shmelev's well-publicised proposal to borrow massively in the West (or sell much of the gold reserve) is widely rejected as too risky; they see the debt to the West as excessive already. As for agriculture, despite some good laws about family leases and genuine small cooperatives, little has yet changed. In Academician Tikhonov's view the only solution is to pass a law *entitling* every peasant family that wished to do so to leave state and collective farms *with* an allotment of land. Otherwise, as he put it, the 'landlords' (*pomeshchiki*), that is, the farm directors or chairmen, will cling to the land and the power this gives them over the peasantry, who are dependent on them for supplies, fuel, transport, and whom some still see as semi-serfs. Indeed, a leading member of the farm lobby, Starodubtsev (a *kolkhoz* chairman), told a TV interviewer that the most he was prepared for was to allow peasant families to cultivate 10 per cent of that farm's arable land (probably the least fertile!). Needless to say, those of the existing state and collective farms that are efficient should be allowed, indeed encouraged, to continue. However, it is the unanimous view of my Soviet colleagues that no real change has yet occurred, and so no immediate improvement in food supply is expected. The greater power that regions and farms have acquired over the disposal of their output could lead to major inequalities between areas, with some in serious trouble, even while agricultural output shows no sign of diminishing.

So far I have perhaps paid insufficient attention to the nationality issue. The Baltic republics, and also Belorussia, have acquired a considerable degree of economic autonomy, and may in fact become genuinely independent, passing their own laws (for example, on private enterprise and on peasant farming), and ignoring those all-union laws that do not suit them. The Georgians, in the presence of their party secretary, put up demands which include the right to secede from the USSR if any laws or orders are imposed on them against their wishes, a recognition that they had been invaded and forcibly annexed in 1921 (by Lenin!), the right to their own military formations . . . Azerbaijan and Armenia will make or are making their own demands, when not fighting each other. Antisemitic outbreaks in some Russian cities could occur. Relatively quiet, so far, is the most populous non-Russian republic, the Ukraine. I visited Kiev and spoke with two leaders of *Rukh*, the national movement. They proved more moderate than I had expected. Strongly against the party 'establishment', strongly for the revival of Ukrainian culture, and much greater economic autonomy, Ivan Drach thought that economic ties with Russia were too close to be broken, though the terms needed renegotiating. In the *Rukh* offices (in the Union of Ukrainian Writers) I saw proclamations addressed to Ukrainians who speak Russian, to the 15 million Russians who live in the Ukraine, to the Jews, to the Crimean Tartars, telling them that *Rukh* poses no threat to them, promising full cultural autonomy and full political rights. The most explosive issue – that of the Uniat church – affects only the Western Ukraine, and there appears to have been police brutality in Lvov on 1 October, in reaction to Uniat demands for recognition. However, Gorbachev's meeting with the Pope is likely to be followed by their legalisation (against the protests of the Orthodox church!). Interestingly, neither Drach nor his more radical colleague Shevchenko expected a nationalist majority in the forthcoming republican elections. Some party functionaries in big cities will be defeated, but, they said, apathy plus the still-effective control over the peasants will probably ensure a majority for the party's nominees. However, several well-informed Russians spoke of the forthcoming *raspad imperii* (disintegration of empire), and made no exception for the Ukraine. Others drew attention to the big differences between the west and east of the Ukraine, the latter long semi-Russianised. In cities like Kharkov and Odessa, in the Donets coal basin, most workers are Russian. It may turn out that Ukrainian nationalism will prove less disruptive than many supposed.

So, finally, what *is* likely to happen next? An acute crisis in 1990 seems probable. Who will seek to find a solution to the emergency and in the name of what? The émigré novelist Vladimir Voinovich recently paid a visit to his homeland. Asked by the journal *Teatr* for his opinion on the present situation, he replied: 'The country reminds me of a bus on a steep mountain road: of its four cylinders one is functioning, someone has put water in the petrol, the brakes work intermittently, so it cannot reverse or even stop. And some of the passengers try from time to time to grab the steering-wheel, crying: "I'll drive"'. This may seem a little 'unacademic', but presents a fair picture. Will the 'bus' stay on the road? What happens to it and to its passengers if it does not? Will the present leadership remain at the wheel, and be able to repair the brakes? Or, as some of my Soviet colleagues seem to think, a crash down the mountain-side as the least probable outcome? I told my Russian friends that I was trying to find an optimist, and they sadly agreed that they were very hard to find in today's Moscow.

I have not so far mentioned the contribution, positive or negative, of Western policies. In my view, we should not hinder, and could marginally help, the reform process. But success or failure must depend overwhelmingly on internal factors, and the Soviet leaders themselves take this view, and are reluctant to increase the level of their indebtedness. We could remove remaining discriminatory restrictions on Soviet exports, and prune the 'Cocom' list, but this will make little difference in practice. The essential constraint on greater Soviet participation in the international division of labour is the ability to compete in world markets, other than in energy and materials – and oil output has begun to decline. Joint ventures could make a positive contribution, especially if they can produce consumers' goods for the home market. Though this raises the question of profit remittances and currency convertibility, the *Soviet* leadership may see this as less burdensome than importing consumer goods for hard currency, and more effective than buying the equipment to make them in Soviet enterprises, where low quality remains the rule. Also to be considered is the possible economic effect of the break-up of Comecon (CMEA), which must be envisaged as a consequence of the momentous events in Eastern Europe. Of course Comecon integration has not really worked, but the USSR did rely heavily on its more developed partners for suppliers of machinery and equipment. Comecon *could* be replaced by a genuine common *market*, which indeed is a possible outcome of republican and regional autonomy within the USSR itself, as is advocated by the radical reformers: they argue not that Moscow bureaucrats be replaced by Lithuanian bureaucrats in controlling Lithuanian enterprises, but that the latter be free to sell where and to whom it is most advantageous to do so. This, too, would be the spirit underlying the reforms in Hungary, Poland, Czechoslovakia, and the GDR. But progress along such lines, while clearly desirable, depends on the successful 'marketisation' of the *Soviet* economy. The present state of the rouble, and the chronic shortages, may in fact drive the Soviet republics and regions to erect barriers, just as (for example) Estonians refuse to sell many items to non-residents of Estonia, and the Czechs prevent Russian and Polish tourists from acquiring consumer-goods. Unless the Soviets can get their act together soon, such practices may even be extended, in the USSR itself and within Comecon, contributing further to the downward path of the economy. (Apparently Hungary intends to cut its exports to the USSR.)

All this leaves a would-be prophet facing a dilemma. No one knows what will happen next, and it would be foolish indeed to pretend otherwise. I hope most sincerely that the feelings of alarm which have found expression in this paper will prove to be exaggerated. We should wish Gorbachev well. In terms of political freedom, cultural liberation, a true assessment of their own history, the gains have far exceeded expectations. Yet even the gains have had some side-effects. Thus the necessarily unpopular measures required to correct economic distortions are rendered much more difficult by the real advances in democratisation: public opinion cannot be ignored. And when a man who was then employed in an institute of the Central Committee (Tsipko) can write that the Stalinist terror and despotism was 'the responsibility, tragedy and pain of Bolshevism' (*Nauka i zhizn'*, No. 2, 1989), and *Novy mir* serialises the *Gulag Archipelago*, what is left of the legitimacy of party rule? Yet the painful measures that require to be taken can only be taken in the name of some set of principles by legitimate authority – what principles? There is no longer a promised land. Jokes abound around the theme 'socialism is the longest road from feudalism to capitalism'. Where *are* they going? Clear answer comes there none. All the scenarios sketched out in the preceding pages could be within the bounds of possibility. The sovietologist lives in interesting times, but there could hardly have been a period in Soviet history in which it was more hazardous to attempt any forecast or prognosis.

Letter to Neil Kinnock, 2 January 1990

Dear Mr Kinnock,

At the request of Charles Clark, I enclose a copy of a report on the USSR which I wrote three months ago for the merchant bank, Morgan Stanley, which contains some ideas which you may find of interest. Since then I have spent nearly six weeks in Moscow, 'borrowed' by the British Embassy and wearing a (very) temporary diplomatic hat. The following impressions expand and/or modify what I wrote in that bank report.

The crisis has become more serious. The government recognises the need for drastic measures to restore health to the currency, since quite clearly no advance towards any sort of market economy is possible in the face of disequilibria, both macro and micro, the disruption (too kind a word) in both retail and wholesale trade. Demand exceeds supply both for consumers' goods and for industrial materials and equipment. Managers and ordinary citizens have lost faith in the rouble. As they say, 'it is not a currency, it is a lottery ticket'. There is a vast overhang of purchasing power in savings bank deposits, in cash, in the bank accounts held by enterprises. In such a situation, the freeing of prices from control could fuel a runaway hyperinflation. The freeing of management from control over the disposal of their output can lead (is leading already) to bilateral barter. ('I will sell you this sheet metal only if you supply me with bricks, timber', or whatever.)

The plan for 1990 envisages a sharp reduction in the budget deficit, which is a major cause of the monetary mess: cuts in defence, higher vodka sales, more imports of consumer goods for resale at high prices, increased domestic output of consumer goods, some of it through the 'conversion' of defence-industries. These and other measures do point in the right direction, but I agree with those Soviet economists who say that it is all too little and too late. Price reform has been postponed until 1991, and the gigantic (100-billion-plus) subsidy bill keeps on growing. More money will be printed. The gap between official and free-market prices will rise still higher. Control over wages has been weakened, partly as a result of enlarging the financial autonomy of enterprises, partly as a byproduct of the series of strikes. There are fears of an energy crisis if the weather is cold this winter, the railways are facing great difficulties, this in a country decisively dependent on rail transport. Add to this the many troubles over issues of nationality and nationalisms, which can further disrupt industrial supplies, with cumulative effects on production, *and* the effects of recent changes in Eastern Europe on deliveries to the Soviet Union, and one can see why Soviet pessimists (alas, very numerous) are predicting serious trouble in the near future.

Food supplies could be one cause of trouble. This is because, despite many fair words and good decrees on family contract and leasing, nothing much has yet changed, due to local obstruction and lack of farmers willing to take risks. And the greater powers now possessed both by the state and collective farms and by the regional authorities over sale of farms produce could well result in serious food shortages in particular localities. Much has been said and written about the role of cooperatives in production of goods and services and in retail distribution, catering, etc. However, given the prevailing shortages they can and often do charge high prices, and so are unpopular. Supreme Soviet deputies are under pressure from below to take restrictive measures. This is but one example of the fact that large segments of public opinion are out of sympathy with the logic of market-type reform (which means higher prices, harder work, reduced job security, etc.), and so it can be said that the welcome progress of *demokratizatsiya* is an obstacle to reform, since public opinion and the now-real 'parliament' now matter. Indeed, one has the impression that the power of the centre to enforce *any* solution to the economic crisis has been seriously weakened. A test case is Lithuania, where the *party* has gone for independence. Gorbachev has expressed his disapproval in no uncertain terms. What will he do, what can he *do*? The whole political power-system is in grave danger of unravelling. Furthermore, one must note (and deplore) the rise of a right wing populist movement, supported by a whole number of provincial party secretaries plus the so-called 'United working-peoples' front'. Abalkin, the vice-premier in charge of economic reform, expressed surprise and some dismay at the degree of opposition from the 'right'. Let me add at once that 'left' and 'right' may be misleading labels in the Soviet context. The 'right' quotes Marx and Lenin against marketisation, leasing of enterprises, freedom for private enterprise, while the so-called 'left' includes not only the would-be founders of an independent socialist party (Boris Kagarlitsky, a confident young man who speaks English well), but also the Russian equivalents of Thatcherites, who think that Abalkin is advancing too slowly towards total marketisation.

I am sure that everyone, from Gorbachev down, would agree that solutions to the crisis depend overwhelmingly on internal factors. Western help would be marginal, but of course we should render some help, or at the very least not hinder. Arms reduction agreements, the pruning of the Cocom list, the elimination of any discrimination against Soviet exports, encouragement of joint ventures, offers to provide training (few Russians really know how a real market actually works – and some have exaggerated belief in its magic powers), all this could help. So would credits. However, the Soviet side is anxious to avoid getting deeper into debt. The present leadership is anxious to include the USSR much more into the international division of labour, to join various international organisations, e.g., GATT. But the immediate snag is the inadequate capacity to export. There is overwhelming dependence on oil as a hard-currency earner, and oil output has started to fall. Soviet manufactures are not, as a rule, competitive.

So the short-term outlook is stormy. I wish this were not so. The progress achieved in terms of freedom of speech, the press, real elections, not to mention attitudes to changes in Eastern Europe, would all have appeared incredible a few years ago. So if what we are witnessing is in fact a stage in the process of disintegration, I would be very sorry. On questions of nationalisms it is not only Lithuania and Estonia. Serious trouble must be expected in Moldavia now that Ceausescu has gone. Azerbaijan is a tinderbox. And quite recently (reported in *Izvestiya*, 20 Nov., 1989) the Georgians, in the presence of *their* party secretary, passed a resolution to the effect that no Soviet laws should apply to Georgia unless the Georgians agree, reaffirming the right to secession, demanding that Georgians do their military service in Georgian military units (in Georgia), and demanding also that it be officially recognised that Georgia was improperly conquered in 1921 in breach of the non-aggression treaty. (LENIN did that!!) So where do we go from there? Action must be taken, urgent and drastic, in the name of some principle or purpose. What principle or purpose? Leninism has little mobilising power these days. Russian nationalism has, and it has been underpinning the right-wing populist backlash (if I may mix metaphors). It has its unpleasant manifestations in an alarming growth of militant anti-semitism. It also serves to strengthen other nationalisms. I wish I could be an optimist. There are not many in Moscow today.

Hoping these few remarks are of some interest to you, and wishing you a happy and successful 1990.

Sincerely yours.

Baltic republics – agriculture

Before World War I, all three republics had large landed estates, and in what later became Latvia and Estonia the landlords were mainly German 'Baltic barons'. With independence came land reform and the dominance of the peasant proprietors. By the standards of the time agriculture performed well, and much food, especially meat and butter, were exported to Great Britain and to Germany. When the Bolsheviks first came to power in 1939–40, and again when they returned in 1944–45, they assured the peasant smallholders that their interests and rights would be respected. (The same line was followed at first in Czechoslovakia, Hungary, and so on). However, in 1949–50 such promises were forgotten, and collectivisation was imposed. Direct resistance seems to have been strongest in Lithuania, where the 'forest brothers' remained in being in the first years of Soviet occupation. But there, as in Latvia and Estonia, selective deportations, arrests, threats, compelled the acceptance of the inevitable. So from 1950 until the most recent times Balt agriculture was organised on standard Soviet lines.

There were three categories of producers, distinguished by their property relations: *kolkhozy* (collective farms, nominally a cooperative with elected management), *sovkhozy* (state farms, with an appointed management), plus the household plots and private livestock in the possession of rural and suburban families. Members of these families were in the main also working for *kolkhozy* and *sovkhozy*. The size of the plots and numbers of private animals were, until recently, strictly limited (for example, one cow, one sow, no horse). In practice the *kolkhoz* manager ('chairman') was a party nominee, and the farm had to fulfil plans, as did the state farm. It is now accepted even by the official media that *kolkhozy* were pseudo-cooperatives. Until the late 1960s the peasant members (unlike the state-employed *sovkhoz* workers) had no guaranteed minimum income, their pay depending on what was left over after all other financial and delivery obligations had been met. First priority was delivery of a quota of produce to the state, at prices which were for many years far below production costs. After Stalin's death, policy changed. Procurement prices were several times increased, much more was spent on investment in agriculture and in industries serving agriculture.

Performance improved, but at quite disproportionate cost. No longer could inefficiency be blamed on low prices and neglect (in Stalin's time the aim was to extract resources from agriculture for the benefit of heavy industry; but from at least the early 1970s higher procurement prices, with unchanged retail food prices, plus much higher state investments, led to the emergence of even-higher net subsidies to agriculture). What were the basic defects of the system, which could not be remedied by throwing money at them?

First, the negative attitude of the peasantry within these very large farms. Alienated from the soil, ordered about by officials, treated as day labourers, with little visible connection between effort and result, it proved all but impossible to devise effective labour incentives. As a Soviet observer remarked: 'In the old days the peasants reasoned: "why should we work, we will not be paid." Now they reason: "why should we work, we will be paid anyway".' Quite different was their attitude to work on the household plot. Incidentally, it is a common error to contrast two figures: household plots account for just over 2 per cent of sown area, but account for 25 per cent of agricultural output. It does *not* follow that productivity in the private sector was ten times that of the state and collective sectors. Two thirds of private production consists of livestock products, and livestock is not pastured on the family holdings, and in any case on a small plot of land one naturally plants high value crops. For the same crop 'private' yields are usually higher, but not ten times higher. However, given the part-time nature of most private activity, and the absence of mechanical tools, the performance of this, the most important private sector of the Soviet economy, was very credible. *Kolkhozy* and *sovkhozy* suffer from the poor quality of machinery and equipment, the frequent non-availability of machines which relate to the special needs of the region, a chronic shortage of spare parts. E. Gaidar, who was at that time economic editor of the party's journal *Kommunist*, referred colourfully to 'painted scrap-iron proudly mis-named "agricultural machinery".' While much more fertiliser came to be available, it was often of the wrong kind.

In all these respects agriculture was the victim of the failure of industry to respond to demand. Another notorious 'lack' is infrastructure. Insufficient storage space and packaging materials, far too few hard-surface roads, refrigeration, specialised transport, and so on. There has also been severe criticism of deficiencies of social infrastructure: lack of amenities, poor schools, deficient housing, cause the energetic to migrate to town. Finally there has been much damage done by bureaucratic interference. Farms have received orders about what to grow, when to sow, what animals to keep. They have been ordered to build huge uneconomic livestock complexes. Various service agencies (for example, for repairs, supplies, 'chemicalisation', drainage) tried to fulfil their own plans in roubles instead of serving the needs of farms. To overcome this deficiency, in 1982 a new agro-industrial hierarchy was created. Though modified in 1985, the so-called AGROPROM proved to be a clumsy and bureaucratic coordinating agency, and was finally eliminated in 1989. Jokes circulated in Moscow to the effect that it was the creation of the CIA!

All the above weaknesses and defects have been known for decades, and freely criticised in the official press. Remedies included the encouragement of small-group contract and (after 1987) of family leases. Many farms undertook joint processing activities, or set up construction brigades. Limitation on numbers of private animals were relaxed. But change was slow, and *kolkhozy* and *sovkhozy* were able to retain the bulk of cultivable land, despite pressures to allow family farms to develop. Within this unpromising institutional environment, the Baltic republics did better than most. Recovering from the damage done by compulsory and brutal collectivisation, already in the 1970s they (especially Estonia) out-performed all the other republics. The same was true in the 1980s (with the exception, for grain, of 1988, when weather was very unfavourable). The grain harvest figures (centners per ha) are shown in the table.

	1981–85	1987
USSR average	14.9	18.3
Estonia	26.1	32.3
Latvia	21.5	29.9
Lithuania	23.6	31.7

The same picture emerges for milk yields per cow (figures are for 1987): USSR average (2682), Estonia (4103), Latvia (3525), Lithuania (3632). Peasants, especially *kolkhozniki*, were much better paid, again especially in Estonia. Per pay month (in roubles): USSR (161.8), Estonia (304.9), Latvia (243.1), Lithuania (223.9). The question arises: why did the Balts do better? The answer appears to be as follows.

First, the peasant spirit survived, since they were collectivised in 1950, not 1930. Also most continued to live in farmsteads (*khutora*), despite orders from Moscow that they should move to compact village settlements. Compared to Russia, fewer young people abandoned the countryside. Commitment to honest work survived. Second, all three republics inherited from the days of independence a network of hard-surface roads, in contrast with their neighbours to the east. Third, the local party chiefs, especially in Estonia, were able to protect the farms from an excessive number of stupid orders and excessive delivery plans. After all, agricultural success can help one's career in the party hierarchy (or there could have been genuine commitment to minimise damage to one's fellow-countrymen). Anyhow, we were told that the Estonian party leader also persuaded Moscow to allocate more material inputs to that republic, since it was frequently visited by Finns and other Baltic foreigners and therefore should be a showpiece. (We were also told that the former Latvian party secretary was much less helpful.) Finally, success was both a cause and an effect of the much higher-than-average rates of pay. In Estonia indeed *kolkhoz* peasants earned much more than the average industrial worker, and this excluding income from family plots.

WHAT PROBLEMS FACE BALT AGRICULTURE TODAY?

First, what should be its future organisational shape? Should there be a return to peasant smallholdings, and if so, how small or how large should the farms be? Should the more efficient of the *kolkhozy* and *sovkhozy* be dismantled, privatised, and, if so, how fast? What of the claim of former owners and their descendants to return the land to them? Perhaps the efficient farms should be kept in being, especially if their comparatively well-paid peasants prefer this. Or some of the excessively large *kolkhozy* and *sovkhozy* could be sub-divided into smaller and genuine cooperatives? Then also there are ideas to keep the existing collective or state farms' workshops and machinery and make them available to farms on hire. Also we were reminded that farmers in the independence years often farmed cooperatives, for example, for processing meat and dairy produce. Such cooperatives were destroyed (statified) in 1949–50, and could be revived. The restoration of private farming is making progress. Thus in Estonia there are now 4119 farmsteads, averaging 26 hectares, while a year previously there were only 1053. In Latvia the numbers exceed 7500, with holdings of 30–40 hectares. But all this is but a fraction of cultivated land. Thus in Latvia in 1939 there were 120 000 farmsteads. Land commissions have been set up to determine who should get what land, a process complicated by claims from former owners, some of whom have no intention of undertaking serious farming. Some of the claimants may have part-time 'hobby' farming in mind. There is concern about holdings being too small to be economical under modern conditions. We were told that the biggest private farm in Estonia covers 182 ha., of which 86 ha. is cultivated (the rest is forest, meadow, and so on), but this is quite exceptional.

The privatisation process seems to have slowed down in the most recent months, because of serious shortages – of credit, of building materials and of suitable machinery and equipment. To set up as a private farmer, even if one has an actual homestead (*khutor*) to work from, requires considerable initial expenditure, and the republican budget and banks cannot quickly provide the large sums that are needed. But more frustrating still is the fact that the money, even if obtained, cannot buy what is needed. Most kinds of building materials are 'imported' from Russia, and are in very short supply. As for machinery, it has long been notorious that Soviet quality is inadequate, and also that the equipment that is produced tends to be large, and quite unsuitable for family farming under 'Baltic' conditions. The simpler kinds of farm implements used to be produced in all three republics, but under the Soviets most of these workshops were closed. Very little farm machinery is produced by the Balts at present. Attempts were made to fill the gaps by improvisation, for example, using the workshops of the former *Sel'khoztekhnika* (equipment supply and repair bases). The Swedes have helped by sending some second-hand equipment. But the needs are great, supplies clearly inadequate. There is also mixed reaction on the part of the peasants themselves. Some do certainly wish to undertake the hard work and accept the risks of family farming. But many have been earning quite well in *kolkhozy* and *sovkhozy* and have no great wish to change. The more so because of uncertainty about supplies and prices of inputs, of access to markets (of which more below), and the still-present basic political uncertainty. Clearly in the immediate future the bulk of output will still originate in the collective and state sector. But here the management operates under great uncertainty and short time horizon: at any time some of their land could be taken for private farming, the farms themselves divided, perhaps turned into jointstock companies . . . What sort of forward planning can a manager attempt under such conditions? Among the greatest of these unknowns is: markets.

As already mentioned, all three republics exported food and some raw materials to the west, first and foremost to Great Britain and Germany. Now the EEC's agricultural policy is an obstacle. The Soviet Union is close, is accessible, needs more meat and dairy produce, which indeed the Baltic republics – especially Estonia and Latvia – have been specialising on. The grain crops sown were predominantly feed grains, notably barley, but Russia and Ukraine supplied a large part of the feed grain and concentrates, as well as grain for human consumption. Deliveries in both directions were part of the compulsory 'command' plan. However, the three republics now became the victims of the breakdown of the command structure, without it being replaced by either a market or by a rouble with real power to purchase. What has happened can be illustrated with the example of Estonia. The Leningrad conurbation is close, its need for meat and dairy products intense, it has the roubles with which to pay. But Leningrad is not a grain-growing region, and its roubles cannot be 'converted' into grain from other parts of the Union. Grain deliveries to Estonia are being drastically cut, the most probable reason being not badwill but the inability of the centre to procure enough grain for inter-republican distribution, while each republic operates its own export-licensing-and-barter schemes. Estonia relies on imports for half of its feed grain. Also imported from the rest of the USSR, and now very scarce, are pesticides, herbicides and some kinds of fertiliser (and for what there is the price has multiplied). Already in 1990 grain deliveries were severely curtailed, and worse is expected in 1991. The result: a sharp fall in agricultural output, especially of livestock products, plus the need to slaughter many cows and pigs that cannot be fed. This finds its reflection in Estonia's forecast for 1991 (the figures that follow in the table are cited from *Ekonomika Estonii v 1991 godu*, published in Tallin in November 1990). It should be borne in mind that state organs still purchase the bulk of marketed farm output. The story is the same for dairy produce. We were told that total agricultural output fell in 1990 by 7.5 per cent. The immediate future thus depends greatly on whether and when Moscow gets its house in order.

Agricultural purchase prices are fixed by the republics, as are retail prices (as we have seen, republics differ, with Lithuania still adhering to low and highly subsidised retail prices of food). There continues to be a legal free market in the towns, where (in Estonia and Latvia) prices differ little from the now much higher official ones. Sales outside the republic, including by private peasants, require a license. Naturally, the question of agricultural prices is a subject of controversy, as is the case also in Western Europe. Totally free prices are seldom found in the real world, west or east (except possibly in Poland, where pure laissez-faire rules). The state has raised the prices it pays, apparently disregarding whatever prices have been fixed by Moscow (though these too have risen). A further rise in procurement prices in January 1991 was rendered necessary

Meat	1989	1990	1991	
State procurements				
(000 tons)	182.7	169.4	133.6	
Marketed internally	123.8	126.5	101	
Centralised exports	59	39.5	30	(i.e., to Russia etc.)

by the very large increases in prices of inputs (fertilisers, equipment, building materials, and so on) received from the rest of the Soviet Union. For example, fertiliser prices were raised three- to fourfold, and so would have to be used much more sparingly. Retail prices in Latvia and Estonia had already been very substantially increased, towards the end of 1990, with the object of eliminating subsidies. Even in Estonia it was felt to be politically too dangerous to put retail prices up so soon after the huge increase of October last, so, as also in Latvia, they feel compelled to subsidise at least butter.

Supplies to farms of all categories are still mainly in the hands of AGROSNAB, which used to be an integral part of the Agroprom hierarchy. This is the channel through which purchase requests (*zayavki*) are channelled, from *kolkhozy*, *sovkhozy*, farmers' unions, to Moscow. Thus the head of AGROSNAB in Riga was about to leave for Moscow to 'vybivat' fondy', which can be rendered as 'to battle for allocations' – of equipment, materials, and so on. But this remnant of the old system is becoming ineffective. Apart from cuts in allocations, the designated suppliers may refuse to supply, or make barter-like conditions. Some of the machinery and equipment used to originate in Czechoslovakia and East Germany, and was of better quality than the Russian. This used not to need hard currency, but it does now, so, unless the republics can acquire independent hard-currency sources, no more may be available now. A visit to a *kolkhoz* near Riga showed the still high degree of dependence on government, now mostly the Latvian government. Apart from price-fixing the farm received sales plans from the Latvian ministry: for example, 500 tons of grain, specified quantities of milk and meat. This *kolkhoz* keeps large numbers of fur-bearing animals, and this too is subject to a delivery quota from the (Latvian) state, at prices well below market prices. (The farm uses over-quota furs as barter for grain with Ukraine, and exports some via the all-union fur trust, *Soyuzpushnina*.)

Shortages, the sorry state of the rouble, the need to feed the population, the need for the state to deliver to and barter with the Union and many of the republics, all combine to delay and to complicate the desired move to a market economy. The high degree of dependence on the USSR as a supplier of inputs forces the continuance of administered rationing of increasingly scarce inputs. This in turn is one factor inhibiting a swifter move towards private farming. In the short run, *the* problem, the bottleneck, is supplies: of feed grain, of building materials, of appropriate machinery, of equipment for processing produce (for example, that 'fur' *kolkhoz* desperately needs equipment for hides and skins). And, of course, they need markets, to supplement or even to replace Russia – unless, of course, Russia can get its house – and its currency – into order.

The ex-USSR: scenarios for 1992

WHERE ARE THEY NOW?

1991 ends on a dire note. Output is falling. Official figures for the first nine months show GNP down by 12 per cent, agricultural production down by 19 per cent, investment completions by 15 per cent, oil output down by 10 per cent, coal by 11 per cent, and the downward trend is accelerating. Money incomes are out of control, and according to V. Kozlov (*Ekonomika i zhizn'*, No. 46, 1991) they trebled in 1991, with an increase of 186 per cent in the third quarter! The budgets (union and republican) show a combined deficit of around 300 billion roubles, or close to 25 per cent of GNP. The grain harvest (160 million tons) is 25 per cent below 1990 levels. Particularly alarming is the breakdown in deliveries from agriculture to the (state-owned) food industry and trade network (grain procurements, already below requirements in 1990, fell by 41 per cent in 1991). Farms are reluctant to sell for worthless roubles, and prefer to hoard or engage in ad hoc barter deals. Production is limited not (as in Poland) by 'defaulted' demand, but by supply bottlenecks and breakdowns. Foreign trade and payments likewise show a disastrous trend. In the first nine months exports fell by 30.3 per cent, imports by 45.2 per cent, and the fall in imports has contributed to bottlenecks in industrial supplies and to shortages of many consumer goods (for example, a high proportion of medical drugs had been imported). The gold reserves have fallen to a mere 240 tons, according to a statement by Yavlinsky (though others have cited slightly higher figures). Yeltsin's decision to cut oil exports, so as to give priority to domestic energy needs, will further reduce hard-currency earnings, already insufficient to service the debt.

The acute nature of the crisis calls for coordinated action by a strong government. However, the centrifugal tendencies already apparent in 1990–91 have been greatly strengthened by the failure of the August coup. This has virtually destroyed what was left of the Union, politically, ideologically, organisationally. Gorbachev, prime minister Silayev, and economic adviser Yavlinsky (and now also foreign minister Shevarnadze) are operating in a void. Meetings between representatives of the republics – the numbers attending varies – lead to no result, other than on paper, although they all know how much damage they could do each other unless they collaborate, and pass resolutions saying so (the latest one, on jointly acting to deal with the food crisis, was signed by ten republics on 14 November). Schemes for a stabilised joint currency and an agreed credit policy, administered by a federal reserve bank, a customs union, are put forward and run into the sand. So do proposals for a coordinated strategy of marketisation and privatisation. Meanwhile elements of a market infrastructure are developing: commercial banks, commodity exchanges, the beginnings of a stock exchange. But much of this sustains purely speculative activities, taking advantage of multiple prices, exchange-rates and the presence or absence of trade barriers between republics and regions. Thus in November the dollar was 'worth' 0.58 roubles ('official'), 1.73 roubles ('commercial') and 47.0 roubles (free, tourist), with wide local variations of the free rate. Barter deals are (insufficiently) replacing the planned supply of inputs. All the republics have declared their sovereign independence, but most will surely be forced to make some sort of trade agreements with each other, and especially with the Russian Federation, since the latter supplies most of the others with energy, timber and other basic materials. Russia has formally adopted a radical reform package, drafted by Egor Gaidar. The package includes an invitation to other republics to join in a combined operation, but so far without tangible results – though the Ukraine's line may change after the elections due on 1 December. Until then its leadership (Kravchuk and Fokin) have to keep clean their nationalist credential and avoid signing anything in or with Moscow, though they know how necessary this is.

So – what can happen next? Especially in the two biggest republics, Russia and Ukraine? If what follows appears to be gloomy, this correctly reflects the views of virtually every Soviet economist. As one of the best of them, Evgeni Yasin, put it: 'I am an optimist . . . A pessimist is one who thinks that the situation is so bad that it cannot get worse. An optimist thinks it can.'

Scenario 1. An inter-republican trade agreement is signed, maintaining trade at existing levels. This could at least maintain output at existing levels, but such a scenario would require several conditions. One is an agreement on prices. Russia argues that, by supplying energy at levels far below world prices, she subsidised the others, so that according to an article in *Ekonomika i zhizn'*, No. 44, 1991, the balance of trade with the other fourteen republics was as follows in 1990 [see table on next page]:

If world prices are charged, the other republics would suffer severely, unless (like Kazakhstan and Azerbaijan) they too are energy producers. Another precondition is that the republics (or the enterprise management within them) will supply other parts of the former Soviet Union and

	In internal prices	In world prices
Russian exports	48.6	80.7
Russian imports	48.4	47.0

not divert to hard-currency markets anything that can be sold there. This temptation affects trade *within* republics too: thus if (when) St. Petersburg or Sakhalin become free-enterprise zones, they may do deals with abroad whenever they can, to acquire dollars, in preference to supplying Russian customers. So, finally, still another precondition for the maintenance (let alone expansion) of inter-republican trade is the replacement of the worthless rouble by some other unit of payment or account, or by some new form of multilateral clearing, or via 'dollarisa- tion', or a new hard rouble similar to the *chervonets* of 1924–26. But this in turn requires a degree of financial order of which, so far, there is no sign. In favour of this scenario is the fact that without it, worse will befall, and particularly in most of the non-Russian republics. This is doubtless why a number of them may sign up as members of a new (and ill-defined) Union of Sovereign States. Some well-known publicists (for instance Shakhnazarov) continue to urge the need to preserve the Union in some form. However, the political and monetary confusion that now reigns make a favourable outcome improbable, in my opinion.

Scenario 2. The 'Yeltsin–Gaidar' economic reform is introduced in the Russian Federation. Then we will have the predominance of uncontrolled prices, rapid strides towards privatisation of small and medium-sized enterprises, a tough monetary policy, the dissolution of unsuccessful state and collective farms, 'competitive sale of export and import licenses for roubles'. Russia takes over the Union's gold and currency reserves and debt obligations. Other republics are invited to join, but Russia expects to have to go it alone. The above is not so much a scenario as a statement of intention. Will it be carried out? If so, with what consequences?

The economic obstacles are formidable. A tough monetary policy requires eliminating that huge budget deficit and imposing stringent credit restrictions, resulting in much unemployment. Can the cuts in expenditure be made, and taxes raised, while maintaining a minimum of 'social guarantees'? Can a hard rouble be introduced? Without it the process of marketisation cannot take off, and the farms will continue to hold back food. It is hard to see how Russia could honour its debt obliga- tions in face of falling exports; the large payments deficit exceeds the available reserves. Yeltsin's recent visit to Bonn provided little hope of a large aid package being channelled via the Russian republic. But political obstacles are equally formidable. Has the Yeltsin administration any effective control over the territories of the federation? Can it even control the foreign trade and hard-currency payments and receipts of the autonomous republics, regions, enterprises, within its borders? What will be the consequences of the inevitably huge price rises of necessities (under conditions which already are those of hyperinflation) upon the sorely tried population? Will there not be strikes and disorders? Nor are matters helped by divisions within the Yeltsin team: the shareout of powers between Yeltsin himself, Rutskoi (vice president), Burbulis ('state secretary'), Khazbulatov (*de facto* chairman of the Supreme Soviet), Isakov (chairman of the 'Council of the Republic') and Gaidar (vice premier in charge of the reform package) seem to ensure confusion. This was illustrated in November by the fiasco over the revolt of the Chechen-Ingush autonomous republic: Yeltsin declared a state of emergency, and then had to cancel it when, by a huge majority, the Russian Supreme Soviet disowned him. (Incidentally, Khazbulatov happens to be a Chechen). So alongside the question of how effective the radical reform proposals would be if carried out, is the equally vital question: are there the political means to carry the proposals out? Thus the wage–price spiral may be unstoppable without some curb on wages, but this does not figure in the plans so far announced. Indeed, the republic's Soviet has legislated for a higher minimum wage.

Two major financial problems are a consequence of the death of the Union and the disappearance of its budget. One relates to debt service, not only the external but also the very large *internal* debt. According to Lyubimov (*Ekonomika i zhizn'*, No. 46, 1991) the republics are deliberately overspending their budgets, borrowing without limit since no one knows who, if anyone, will be responsible for repayment. The other is the defence budget: the same source anticipates that the Russian Federation's defence bill will come to 100–120 billion roubles, owing to soaring costs even if other republics maintain their own forces. He quotes illustrative price rises: a soldier's cap from 8.90 to 50 roubles, an officer's overcoat from 108 to 697 roubles. Then there is the heavy cost of bringing troops home from Eastern Europe. There is no sign of adequate provision for these expenses in the republic's budget for next year. What hope, then, of reducing the budget deficit and restoring real money? (Nikonov, the agricultural academician, heads an article: 'There will be no bread-grain so long as the rouble is worthless'.) And if there is ethnic violence there will be millions of Russian refugees from other republics to take care of. Where would the new taxes come from? And one must again stress that the power-structure in Russia rests on no constitution, and orders from

Moscow may or may not be obeyed even in the purely Russian provinces and cities – let alone in the autonomous republics.

My Soviet colleagues are not optimistic. But success is not ruled out. For Russia *not* to attempt to go it alone would have guaranteed disaster.

Scenario 2A. The Ukraine also adopts 'market' reforms. Although there have not yet been such spelt-out marketisation plans as those drafted by Gaidar, there is no doubt that similar policies are intended, though tough measures have been postponed until after the election due on 1 December, which will probably confirm in power the Kravchuk–Fokin team (but we must watch for the strength of the more extreme nationalists on the one hand, and a possible backlash of the large Russian-speaking minority on the other). Success (or the avoidance of disaster) is conditional upon several factors. The first is the negotiation of a tolerable trade agreement with Russia. The Ukraine imports nearly all its oil, gas, timber and non-ferrous metals from Russia, which is a major market for its manufactures. The second is monetary order. At present the Ukraine uses Soviet roubles, but either overprints them with Ukrainian symbols or requires Ukrainian coupons to validate their use in the shops. There is supposed to be a new Ukrainian currency, the *griven*, introduced perhaps in 1992. But gold and foreign-currency reserves are minimal, and a Russian sarcastically remarked that they are insufficient to pay for the printing-press on which to print the new currency (which may be printed in Canada). Anyhow, the Ukraine, like Russia, has a huge budget deficit (40 billion roubles is the current estimate). There is already a food crisis looming, because of the reluctance of Ukrainian farms to sell for roubles, and the leaders are forecasting the need to ration bread in the new year, even if they succeed in importing some grain. The intention to create a Ukrainian army is a further drain on highly limited financial resources.

The political problem of negotiating with Russia may be eased after the election, but Russia can afford to take a tough stance on prices: oil, gas and timber can be sold on world markets, while the Ukraine's manufactures are mostly uncompetitive outside the old Union. Then it may be politically difficult for the Ukrainian government to take on any share of the Union's foreign and domestic debt, though Russia will surely press for this. It is alarming to note that the complex negotiating process has not yet even started. The Ukraine may wish to negotiate trade agreements with its Western neighbours, for example, Poland, Hungary, Czechoslovakia, Romania. But it is hard to see how they could replace Russia, both as suppliers and as markets. While the Ukraine, unlike the Russian Federation, has no autonomous sub-units within its borders, it does have large groups of Russians, in cities such as Odessa and Kharkov, and in the Donets coal basin, and it faces a claim for sovereignty from the

Crimea, to which the Crimean Tartars are returning, having been deported by Stalin while there are also many Russians in the Crimea. The Ukrainians themselves are divided not only in the extent of their nation-alisms (many in the east do not even speak Ukrainian) but also by religion (Uniat-Catholics in the west, two competing orthodox churches in the east). Kravchuk and Fokin, the leaders, are former communist functionaries repainted in national yellow-blue colours.

The Ukraine has good agricultural and industrial potential. Much progress would be achieved *if* they establish monetary order and avoid political in-fighting. They would benefit from good business advice from the Ukrainian diaspora, especially from Canada. But there is not much expectation of significant foreign aid or major investments. The chances of maintaining order may be somewhat higher than in the Russian Federation: a smaller territory, different political traditions, perhaps less popular reluctance to accept the logic of a free market. There is some-what less pessimism in Kiev than in Moscow, though of course there too the scale of problems to be solved is seen as formidable.

Scenario 3. Russia and the Ukraine succeed in maintaining internal order, while progressing towards real marketisation. Then the smaller republics, from Belorussia to Uzbekistan, will gravitate towards them as would Kazakhstan. As already mentioned, a precondition for the Ukraine will be an agreement with Moscow, and so the stage may then be set for the most optimistic (least pessimistic) scenario of all: the signing of an agreement for economic collaboration and a customs union between (say) ten of the former fifteen republics, plus bilateral trade agreements with the remaining five. There has to be at least internal currency convertibility, which in turn requires financial and monetary order, at present so tragically lacking. This, in turn, requires progress towards a joint monetary and credit policy. So far there has been no such progress. But a small helpful note: in early November there was a 'Ukrainian–Russian businessmen's conference' in Kiev, which urged close collaboration, and president Kravchuk was able to say that 'the two republics cannot live apart from each other'. Which is true, but in no way guarantees that the nationalists will listen. An important 'unknown' is the possibility of significant Western investments, which could be attracted towards these republics once they set their internal houses in order. Russia especially could benefit quickly from investments in oil produc-tion, which could improve the balance of payments. However, both republics would have to devise a means of combining liberalisation of foreign trade (and limited convertibility) with ensuring that the govern-ments and their central banks acquire sufficient sums to service debt, old and new. The 'hunger' for foreign currency at lower levels is such that much of it could be dissipated on instant purchases of material inputs and consumers' goods. Gorbachev's attempt a year ago, to 'tax' enterprise foreign-currency receipts at the rate of 40 per cent was ineffective, though the object had been precisely to ensure the availability of sums needed for debt service. And in 1991 the Ukraine was reduced to begging enterprises to *lend* the government some *valuta* (hard currency) to enable it to pay for urgent imports of grain. Of course, once convertibility is achieved, these problems will disappear. But meanwhile the republics' credit standing, and the possibility of continuing or resuming debt service, does depend on what happens to current earnings of foreign currency.

Scenario 4. Chaos. This, unfortunately, is all too easy to imagine. Hyperinflation. Prices multiply. Wages do the same. Efforts to balance the budget conflict with the cost of even a minimum social safety-net, and the efforts fail. Strikes and riots disrupt production and normal life. Each area and city tries to save itself by beggar-my-neighbour policies. Taxes are not collected, money loses all value. Looting begins, directed first at the 'commercial' and hard-currency shops, in which almost anything can be bought by the new-rich and foreigners, while normal shops are empty. Separatism breaks out within the Russian Federation (in *Izvestiya* of 1 October 1991 the well-known publicist Alexander Tsipko forecast a 'Kuban republic, a Far-eastern republic, an independent Ossetian and Cherkess republic, not to mention the Tartars and the Yakuts, the last of these being the major diamond producer', and he did not even mention the Chechens, who have since rebelled). Ethnic strife in many republics leads to a flood of refugees. Islamic fundamentalism raises its head too. Some areas suffer acutely from hunger and cold. The nightmare of civil war looms. Nature abhors a vacuum. Such a disaster as this will call into being a strong man who would impose an authoritarian regime. It matters greatly who it would be, acting in the name of what principles? A Russian-nationalist neo-slavophil extremist? Then one can foresee conflict with the Ukraine and other republics with large Russian minorities. A Russian Pinochet with a radical 'market' programme? Or else will Yeltsin dissolve elected bodies and try to rule by decree, imposing his rule with the help of the Russian army? The mind boggles. Most unfortunately scenario 4 is *not* improbable. Some would even regard it as the least improbable of the four. Unfortunately, this tends also to be my view. I sincerely hope to be wrong, but the route to any sort of stabilisation is beset by so many obstacles that there is no basis for optimism. Western investment cannot be attracted if the danger of catastrophe is as real as it appears to be, and it is in any case not clear how, or to whom, Western aid should be channelled. Of course, some republics have better chances than others. The Baltic states have reasonably effective political structures and can maintain order, though even there, especially in Latvia, there could be problems with the Russian minority (which is a majority in the capital, Riga). Kazakhstan has a wise leader and considerable mineral resources which could attract Western capital – provided it also can avoid trouble with its large Russian minority, almost as numerous as the Kazakhs.

For Russia, anything is possible, from break-up to the return of the Romanov dynasty, with perhaps Solzhenitsyn as court philosopher. If only the democratic, market-orientated forces were better organised, with solid support among the public. But *Argumenty i fakty* (No. 44, 1991) reports that in St. Petersburg a public opinion survey had the following result: Should all goods be rationed? (32%); Should only necessities be rationed and other prices left free (39.4%); Should all prices be free of control? (17.8%); Don't know (10.8%). Uncertainties are overwhelming, the outlook stormy, and anyone who claims that he or she knows what happens next is a person I have yet to meet.

The Ukrainian crisis: September 1992

An independent Ukraine, with a population of 52 million, an area larger than that of France, must be seen as one of Europe's major states, and its industrial and agricultural potential should in the long run make it an attractive proposition for investors. However, the existing situation was characterised by the deputy-minister of the economy as critical and bordering on the catastrophic. Part of the crisis is political–governmental. The president (Kravchuk) and the prime minister (Fokin) are under attack from those who consider them to be insufficiently nationalistic and to be tainted by their past careers as communist party *apparatchiks*. There is (as in Russia) no functioning constitution, there is little of legal order, and many Ukrainian officials and economists stress the urgent need for the establishment of a clear line of authority, without which measures of economic stabilisation will remain on paper. In his speech, the deputy minister deplored the lack of legal protection for private enterprise, uncertainties facing foreign investors, confusion between legislative and executive powers, and between the centre and the periphery, widespread bribery and corruption. He and other ministers, and also an able Canadian–Ukrainian (Bohdan Kravchenko) who directs an administrative staff college in Kiev, speak of 'cadre hunger': far too few competent officials and bureaucrats. Thus the minister of finance stated that his entire ministry has 400 employees, with hundreds of unfilled vacancies (Kravchenko pointed out that the province of Alberta employs 4000 in *its* finance department!). Economic policy errors are closely linked with the 'crisis of authority'.

The economic inheritance was most unpromising. Half of all industry, and 70 per cent of R&D, worked directly or indirectly for the military, and now have to convert to civilian purposes, but this requires time and resources (the minister in charge of conversion, Antonov, spoke of his many difficulties; he was about to leave for the United States in the hope of securing a 'conversion' credit, and complained of lack of understanding in the West). At the same time the sizeable civilian machinery and engineering sector suffers from low demand because of the collapse of investment. The Ukraine had devised no strategy of its own when the Union broke up, and since last December has followed Russia's reforms 'six months late and with less competence', to cite the deputy minister of economics. The Ukrainian authorities felt unable to persist with 'shock therapy', and, to cite the deputy minister again, 'we have come to the end of the liberal–romantic period of reform, we will be combining market and administrative measures. If 90 per cent of production is still in the state sector, we must exercise some control, otherwise management is responsible to no one. Most enterprises are *de facto* monopolies. We have had a year of drift, we must establish elementary order and put an end to disgraceful chaos', and so on in the same vein. 'Disgraceful chaos' also effects statistics. Much of what is going on may be incorrectly recorded. Thus no one claims to have a reliable retail price index (the more so because provincial towns and districts have often imposed their own price controls). Foreign trade is a mystery: no record is kept of the origin of goods exported from Ukrainian ports, and the long frontier with Russia is only occasionally controlled, with large-scale unrecorded movement of goods in both directions at unknown prices or at no prices at all (that is, informal barter). There is said to be a flight of capital to Russia and to the West, of unknown magnitude. Dealers travel to Poland and even Turkey, and the 'fruits' of their journeys are on sale in the streets of Kiev.

Two reports on the present situation and on future policies were produced and discussed: one by an expert group nominated by committees of the legislature (principal authors Filipenko and Sikora), and another by a group of experts nominated by the cabinet of ministers. (I have copies of both reports in Ukrainian). Then for four hours the two groups had a joint meeting, which I attended. What follows is largely based on these reports and discussions.

THE PRESENT SITUATION AND CURRENT TRENDS

The decline in production began in 1991. (GNP fell by 11 per cent). It accelerated in 1992. The 'ministerial' expert report gives the following picture, which, for reasons already given, must be seen as somewhat approximate: *First half of 1992* (compared with same period in 1991): GNP –15 per cent, Industrial production –12.3 per cent (Food industry –25 per cent), Capital investment –41 per cent (another source –50 per cent), Retail sales volume –29.4 per cent, Services –34.1 per cent. As also in Russia there is a payments crisis: inter-enterprise debt rose 1.6 fold in June over the previous month, reaching the huge sum of 576 billion 'karbovantsi' roubles (see later note on currencies in circulation). Meanwhile in the first half-year bank credits increased in nominal value by 7.7 times, but since wholesale prices rose 23-fold in the first half of 1992, in real terms the volume of credits declined rapidly, thereby contributing to non-payment of debts. Currency emission in 1992 already exceeds that of 1991 twelve-fold. Control over wages was lost, and personal incomes increased 8.6-fold in the first half of 1992. Opinions differ as to what has happened to retail prices, which vary widely by area, with sometimes a large gap between officially-fixed and free market prices for food, though most prices have been, or are supposed to have been, freed. Statistics show that, despite widespread poverty, 26.4 per cent of the population's revenues remained unspent. This was partly due to still-existing shortages, but also (some say, in the main) due to the use of banknotes intended for use in retail trade for other purposes, for reasons to be explained below. Wages have risen extremely unevenly: I was told that the average is now 4900 karbovantsi a month, but some in heavy industry (as also in Russia) have succeeded in demanding over 10 000, while the ministerial expert committee proposed a minimum wage of only 1350 karb., and an old age pension of 1250 karb., which implies that today's minimum is lower. In the free market in Kiev a kilogram of pork costs 250–300 karbs., that is, a week's pension. There is understandable and probably irresistible pressure for income rises, especially by those (including civil servants, teachers, doctors) who have been left behind.

Wholesale prices have moved exceedingly unevenly. While before the reform the prices of basic materials and fuels were artificially kept low, these have now soared, thereby distorting the cost structure and greatly damaging the finances of industry and agriculture, as can be seen from the following figures (my source is the government's experts' report): *July 1992 over July 1991*: All wholesale prices (23.5 times), Electricity (47.3 times), Oil products (81.4 times), Coal (96.5 times), Ferrous metallurgy (46.2 times), Chemical industry (35.9 times). The report states that the price increases were faster than in any of the other ex-Soviet republics. Furthermore, while agricultural input prices rose 20-fold in the half-year, prices of agricultural products rose only 12.9 times (a similar pattern is observable in Russia). As also in other republics, farms and peasants are reluctant to sell to the state for rapidly devaluing paper money, especially after their sad experience in 1991, when they were paid in the old and much lower prices of that year, and faced enormous increases in costs soon after.

THE BUDGET AND THE CURRENCY (CURRENCIES . . .)

As in Russia, decisions were taken to reduce very severely and quickly the very large budget deficit, which was being financed by printing money (or borrowing from the state bank). As also in Russia, the decisions could not be implemented. The legislature (the 'Supreme Rada') passed a law limiting the deficit to a maximum of 26.7 billion karb. in the first half-year. The deficit in practice came to 69.6 billion (total revenue to 300 billion, this being the combined revenue of all public authorities. As a percentage of GNP such a deficit might be estimated at 11–12 per cent). The deputy minister of finance stated that the budget owed 176 billion karb. to the state bank, and that he and his colleagues could not possibly keep spending down to prescribed limits, given that there were no effective controls over local-authority spending, while large sums were voted to pay wage and pension increases for the state sector (for example, for teachers, medical staffs, officials at all levels). Internal debt was variously estimated as 738 or 1000 billion karbovantsi. By the end of the year the budget will need 875 billion, according to the deputy minister of finance. It is far from clear where these sums will come from. All agree that tax collection is weak. A particularly heavy burden for the Ukrainian budget is *military expenditure*, to maintain an army that still numbers 650 000 men. An independent researcher claimed that military spending absorbed over 16 per cent of GNP, and this without the (disputed) Black Sea fleet!

Now – *the currency situation*. The Soviet (Russian) rouble circulated in the Ukraine through 1991, though various measures were already being taken (when I was in Kiev in June 1991) to provide special coupons for residents, so that visiting Russians could not buy everything up. Part of wages were paid in coupons, part in roubles. Some items could be bought only for coupons. At the beginning of 1992, when Ukraine followed Russia in allowing prices to rise ten-fold and more, demand for rouble banknotes naturally rose very rapidly, and Moscow failed to provide enough of them. (This was not an anti-Ukrainian move: the undersupply of banknotes in Russia itself led to the accumulation of large-scale arrears in wage payments.) To cope with the problem of (literally) the supply of money, *and* to make it more difficult for visiting Russians to buy things up, the Ukrainian central bank issued much larger quantities of coupons, and it was decided that all retail trade (and so all wages) would be in these coupons, denominated in karbovantsi (which was in fact the Ukrainian name for roubles). It was intended to limit the issue to the level required to cover retail purchases, while wholesale trade and inter-enterprise payments continued to be denominated in roubles.

When introduced, the 'coupon' currency was supposed to exchange at a par with the Russian rouble. Within a few months the exchange rate became around 1.3–1.4 karbovantsi to the rouble. One reason was that too many were printed; another that many travel to Russia, where they need roubles. Meanwhile, wholesalers and manufacturers found that (until recently) they could exchange karbovantsi into roubles at 1:1 in the state banking system, while acquiring them at a cheaper rate, and one colleague described this as a sort of subsidy, which further helped to unbalance the budget. The rules have now been changed. In the street, deals are undertaken in 'coupons', in roubles, and finally also in dollars. The exchange rate in the official banks was 260 karbovantsi for the dollar, 510 to the pound. However, the free rate was nearer 320. (A ride in a bus or metro costs 50 kopecks – they are still using the metallic USSR small change. This is a good deal less than a farthing.) Yet another problem: coupons have been easy to forge. So the economy is supposed somehow to function with depreciating roubles (supplied in unpredictable quantities from Russia) for wholesale trade and some other transactions, and simultaneously with even more rapidly depreciating 'coupon' karbovantsi. All agree that this cannot go on.

Answer: real Ukrainian money to replace the coupon? Some have already been printed, under the name *hrivna*. However, in the view of all of my Ukrainian economic colleagues, and also of some ministers, to introduce the *hrivna* now could be a recipe for disaster – though Kravchuk spoke of introducing it already in October. Given the budgetary and banking mess, and lack of political control, the *hrivna* would speedily suffer the fate of the coupons. True, it may be possible for the Ukrainian government to get some 'stabilisation-fund' dollars from the IMF, but they now ask for as much as $6 billion, which will surely not be forthcoming. One hopes that wiser counsels will prevail. One expert recommended a limited introduction of the *hrivna*, to circulate in parallel with the coupons and the Russian rouble for a temporary period, recalling the gradual introduction of the *chervonets* in 1922–24. *That* was 'bipaperism', this would be 'tripaperism'. Meanwhile nationalist oppositionists are criticising premier Fokin for delaying the introduction of *hrivna* and for delaying leaving the rouble zone.

TRADE AND PAYMENTS

The Ukraine is heavily dependent on Russia for energy (oil and gas), timber, paper, textile raw materials (cotton mainly from Uzbekistan). Of the Ukraine's total trade, 70 per cent was with Russia, 9 per cent with other ex-Soviet republics. The collapse of Comecon, the shift to trade in hard currency with Hungary, Czechoslovakia, Poland, led to a steep fall in trade with these countries in both directions. As mentioned above, there is no reliable measure of what has happened with trade with Russia, but it has certainly declined, as is attested by anecdotal evidence about the breaking of long-established ties: for example, the non-arrival of pit-props for Ukrainian coal mines and sheet metal for the Zaporozhe car plant, while the Ukraine has been unable to supply Russia with grain and sugar-beet (sugar is one consumer item officially rationed in the Ukraine). But there are a multitude of barter deals and some sales for roubles in both directions. I met an energetic Ukrainian businessman, based in Kharkov, who manages a 'Konizern' with the name of EPOS (N. Ivashchenko), whose business includes production and sales of chemicals, textiles, building materials, and also construction and commercial banking, operating in Russia as well as the Ukraine, and, he insisted, legally. Yes, he admitted, there are complex problems, but there are successes, with the help of German associates. All this and more could be disrupted if the Ukraine's new currency goes its own way and leaves the rouble zone. The government knows this, and last week premier Fokin was in Moscow negotiating clearing arrangements with Gaidar. But he has nationalists to cope with.

If the Russians are too tough on oil and gas prices, the Ukrainians can counter by demanding high transit charges: Siberian oil and gas passes across Ukrainian territory. Right now the Ukraine is heavily in debt to Russia, because of the adverse movement in terms of trade (though Russia is not charging full world prices for its oil and gas). (But it is true also that some Russian firms owe money to the Ukrainians, as well as to each other). Several colleagues saw the trade-balance situation as critical. What can the Ukraine export, given the sad state of the Russian market and production bottlenecks in the Ukraine? Far from having grain to sell, Ukrainian officials have to beg for credits to pay for imports of grain, partly because the harvest is expected to be mediocre (drought in the south), partly because of the reluctance of farms to sell for depreciating 'coupon-money'.

As for gold and currency reserves, the head of the Ukrainian bank answered a question as follows: 'This is no problem: there are none.' The Ukraine has sought to get a share of the former Union's gold and precious stone reserve, but has not succeeded. It has accepted in principle to bear its share of the Union's foreign debt, this share being estimated at around $13 billion. It is supposed to be paying $1 billion a year in interest, but has at regular intervals sought a postponement, and plainly cannot pay. It has entered into credit negotiations with a number of countries, and by joining the IMF will have access to more. But it is hard to see, with the best will in the world, how it can manage its balance of payments crisis. The more so because capital flight is also in progress. Not only do traders and exporters try to keep their proceeds abroad, but there is also a capital flight to Russia, because the rouble looks like a better bet than the Ukrainian coupon, and because interest rates are much higher in Russia (see below). Foreign investors are still few. Ukraine's main source of energy, coal in the Donets basin, is in old and deep mines and high cost, and even with low labour costs its competitiveness is problematical. Tourism has good possibilities in the Crimea, but the status of the Crimea is itself in doubt; there is now a 'Crimea republic', probably strong enough to keep its own hard-currency receipts. (The Crimea, plus the Black Sea fleet, could be serious bones of contention with Russia).

PRIVATISATION – AND AGRICULTURE

Privatisation is proceeding slowly, but there has been a notable development in leasing industrial and service enterprises: as at 1 July there were 1200 leased enterprises, and another 1360 had become leased collective property, and together they produced 14 per cent of industrial output. Some leases are for as long as 90 years, and it was decided not to disturb them in the process of privatisation. As also in Russia, there are uncertainties as to how to privatise. There is a state property fund, which can dispose of state enterprises, but at what price, on what conditions, to whom? It has been proposed to follow Russia and to issue investment vouchers, but in the Ukraine these are supposed not to be saleable. Then what are they? Surely this is not real investment. A colleague called this 'Monopoly money' (the 'Monopoly' game is known!). The authorities do not seek privatisation for its own sake: the essential point is to have a responsible and efficient management, subject to market discipline. Small-scale privatisation and leasing will doubtless go ahead, but, to cite a speaker at their meeting, 'who will buy the steelworks and coalmines?'

Agriculture presents special problems. Universal privatisation is not an option: there would be far too few takers, given all the uncertainties, the absence of the small-scale machinery and equipment, lack of building materials, unfavourable prices. The generally-agreed proposal is to break up and divide up only those state and collective farms that are hopelessly loss-making and inefficient. The more effective farms will be encouraged to continue. There are many farms in between these two categories: there the idea is to encourage a variety of solutions, depending on peasant preferences: family farm, genuine cooperatives, partnerships, with or without long leases. All are conscious of the fact that 'depeasantisation' has gone far and deep, and so the numbers willing to leave the relative security of state and collective farms and to go it alone will be moderate. There may be a good opportunity for foreign specialists to start up some experimental modern farms. After all, the famous black-earth is still there (despite some losses through erosion, and more recently through the Chernobyl nuclear disaster), and both grain and sugar-beet have good longer-term prospects, *and* an assured market at least in Russia (even if the EEC's agricultural policy keeps them out of Western Europe).

INTEREST RATES AND INVESTMENT POLICY

Here there is a big difference with the policy adopted in Russia and other 'reforming' countries. Despite an inflation rate which in August reached 25 per cent a *month*, interest rates have been raised only to 15 per cent a *year*, which is a negative real interest rate with a vengeance! This reflects a more 'regulatory' approach. Of course with such an interest rate credits must be rationed, that is, they can be made to reflect government-determined priorities. Thus large credits have been made available to help finance 'conversion' of the military–industrial complex, and also to agriculture. My own view is that this is sensible, given the primitive (or non-existent) state of the capital market. If, as in Russia, interest rates rise to 80–100 per cent, no one can afford to borrow for productive investment. However, lack of resources is a major limiting factor, and the fact remains that investment activity has all but collapsed, as it also has in Russia. Yet how can one modernise industry and infrastructure without large-scale investments? There is hope for help from abroad, and something is being done by the Ukrainian diaspora. But there is a very big gap to be filled.

THE POLITICAL ECONOMY OF MARKETISATION: CAN THEY DO IT?

Last June the 'Gaidar' of the Ukraine, Lanovoi, was demoted by president Kravchuk, and in his place he appointed Simonenko, formerly a party official in Odessa. This reflects the government's reluctance to use shock therapy, a reaction also noticeable in Russia, with the modification of Gaidar's policies by the counterweight of industrialist Arkadi Volsky and banker Gerashchenko. There is pressure from the nationalists to go further in 'decoupling' Ukraine from Russia and Russian policies, which would damage the Ukrainian economy which is closely linked with the Russian. Evidence from many countries shows that macroeconomic policies can have perverse and undesired effects in countries where state ownership is predominant and markets still in a rudimentary condition. The Ukrainian government committee proposes some tougher controls over wages, an investment priority policy affecting both domestic and foreign capital, and is in no hurry for large-scale privatisation (while going ahead faster with the small-scale). One idea is to start with a pilot scheme in one region. There are, on paper, sensible proposals about new taxes, on personal incomes and on corporate profits, and tax holidays to attract foreigners. There is hope of covering more of the budget deficit through bond sales (but because past attempts were unsuccessful they prefer not to call them bonds, but rather 'state economic-development certificates', with guaranteed protection against inflation). It remains to be seen if firms and individuals will have enough trust in the government. Doubts on this score are legitimate.

A report for the Vienna *Institut für internationale Wirtschaftsvergleiche* states that Lanovoi's sacking has reduced the credibility of Kravchuk's commitment to marketisation, and that 'the international agencies are aghast at the government's refusal to deal seriously with hyperinflation. In mid-August the IMF threatened to break off talks on economic assistance unless measures are taken to reduce the budget deficit and to postpone the introduction of the *hrivna*.' Foreign businessmen 'wait for signs that the government has regained control over the burgeoning state budget deficit and can manage the currency'. An important unknown is the attitude of the population. Kravchuk is sometimes accused of 'populism', and it is surely the case that continued price controls (especially on necessities) plus spending on the 'welfare' safety-net have not been consistent with the harsh logic of marketisation. Thus bread still costs less than half what it costs in Russia, and no doubt requires a subsidy. But, although there has been a wave of strikes, public order has been maintained. So maybe these so-called populist concessions to public pressures were a necessary price to pay. The trouble is that decline in output is continuing, essential imports may have to be cut for balance of payments reasons, and there are opposition forces ready to take advantage of disorder and breakdown.

The Ukrainian government, led by ex-communist functionaries, must tread warily, coping with public resentment at falling living standards and seeking to prove their commitment to Ukrainian national interests. Their ideas stress the importance of Ukrainian *citizenship* rather than ethnicity, a distinction of vital political importance in a country with a large (11 million-plus) Russian minority (and both prime minister Fokin and army commander Morozov are ethnic Russians). The more extreme nationalists, a minority at present, urge the government to decouple the economy and the reform process from that of Russia, but this could be costly, given the degree of interdependence and cause ethnic conflicts too. There are, of course, also Russian nationalists who criticise Yeltsin, and are ready to make trouble over the Crimea (where most of the people are Russian and Tartar), over the Black Sea fleet and over the supply of scarce energy and materials at below world levels. Meanwhile, as also in Russia, the demise of the old communist party machine, which imposed discipline and in effect ruled the country, has led to a grave weakening of the political structure. Other parties are numerous but feeble, and many are the complaints about the non-implementation of policies, unclear demarcation of power and function, the inadequacies of the legal system, vagueness as to property rights and weak financial discipline ('soft budget constraint'). The government's committee recommendations include many sensible institutional measures, such as the setting up of a state insurance scheme to cover foreign investors ('of the type of Hermes in Germany, Cofas in France . . .'), and there are good proposals on reforming tax collection. It is (in my view rightly) proposed to retain the present controls over prices of key items, and also to set up an 'anti-monopoly committee' with powers. There are pages of business-like proposals. What is lacking is, first, sufficient emphasis on measures to stop the decline in production (many of the proposed reforms need time to have any effect). And, second, the government may lack the authority and the determination to impose monetary and fiscal order, in what is undoubtedly an extremely difficult situation.

They do urgently need help. But if I were a Western investor, I would regard the risk of a purely commercial venture to be too great, unless it is itself a hard-currency earner.

The Ukrainian economic crisis in perspective: April 1993

No one doubts that there is a crisis in Ukraine. Indeed prime minister Kuchma, shortly after taking office, declared that it is not a crisis, it is a catastrophe. He has also, according to *Vechirny Kiiv*, said: 'We are not a banana republic, but we are bankrupt.' In what respects does the Ukraine differ from other ex-communist countries, all of whom have in varying degrees suffered substantial falls in output and in living standards? Let us begin by analysing the causes of the decline. The actual figures can be questioned, because some private activity is unrecorded, and also because there is now a greater choice of goods at free prices (for those who have the money) than used to be the case under the old system. None the less, when all allowances are made for statistical gaps and distortions, output of most industries has certainly fallen, and most citizens are worse off than they were (say) three years ago. Why?

First on the list of causes: *the economic consequences of political disruption.* All the former members of Comecon (CMEA) have suddenly and drastically reduced the level of trade with each other, depriving some industries of markets and others of supplies. This has been the consequence of demanding payment in dollars at world prices. At the same time, the break-up of the Soviet Union has led to the erection of obstacles to inter-republican and even inter-regional trade, a switch to barter (due also to the rapid depreciation of the rouble), with disruptive effects on production and on supplies of consumers' goods. A few examples: Ukrainian coal production was adversely affected by the non-arrival of pit props from Russia, and the Zaporozhe car factory was similarly handicapped by non-delivery of sheet metal. (Russian factories have similar complaints about non-fulfilment of contracts.) Particular difficulty for the Ukraine arises from its dependence on imports from Russia of oil and gas. Russian oil production has been falling, supplies to the Ukraine have been reduced, and prices for both oil and gas hugely increased. Ukraine has tried to 'counter-attack' by threatening to charge high transit fees for Russian oil and gas which crosses its territory in pipelines on the way west. Ukraine has been seeking alternative sources of supply of both oil and gas, but costs are high, convertible currency very scarce.

Second, *the short-term effects of institutional transformation*. The collapse of the old 'command' system has disorientated managers and bureaucrats who were accustomed to work within it. Market institutions, market culture, commercial law, a modern banking system, a capital market, infrastructure, are either lacking or still in the process of formation. While most of industry remains state-owned, management is no longer subject to control by the 'owners', and operates in a highly imperfect market (with much monopoly power), and under conditions of complete uncertainty as to the future: will it be privatised, if so when, on what terms, with or without management or employee buy-outs? Under such conditions, how can there be a long-term view, or incentive for efficiency?

Third, *the effect of inherited structural distortions*. All the ex-communist countries had an overexpanded heavy-industry sector, and many (including Ukraine) had a large military–industrial complex. Furthermore a large part of civilian industry was in urgent need of modernisation. Some industries were responsible for intolerable degrees of pollution. All this called for restructuring, the abandonment of wasteful production and the conversion of arms factories, but this takes time, and also investment resources.

Fourth, *the effect of falling purchasing power*. In all of Eastern Europe, and in Russia too, prices, when released from control, increased much faster than money wages. The Ukraine was no exception. So while the fall in consumption is sometimes explicable by supply bottlenecks, in many instances citizens cannot afford to buy goods that are available. For example, clothing, and the dearer foodstuffs, remain unsold.

Fifth, *the effect of the collapse of investment*. In all these countries, there was a very rapid decline in investments. These were formerly planned and largely financed by the state. For reasons both financial (budget deficit) and ideological (state planning seen as wrong in principle), the state's role has everywhere been cut back. But neither private nor foreign investment has filled the gap. The result has been a decline in demand for, and output of, the construction industry and also machinery and equipment, in the Ukraine too.

Sixth, *the adjustment problems of agriculture*. These include the conversion of state and collective farms into – what? Genuine cooperatives? Or should the land be divided among the peasants? Should the children of former owners have a claim for land or compensation? How many peasants want to set up family farms? How to avoid disruption in the transition period due to all the uncertainties? Should land be freely bought and sold? Can family farms, if set up, be provided with the needed credits, machinery, building materials? And then in all these countries prices of industrial products have risen much faster than agricultural prices. This, and inflationary expectations, have adversely affected marketings of farm produce (also in Ukraine), and also the willingness of peasants to undertake private farming without price support (which exists in most Western countries, but the cutting of subsidies is a precondition of reducing the budget deficit).

Seventh, *import competition.* This is not, or not yet, a major problem in Ukraine, but in many countries (for example, Poland, the Czech Republic, Hungary) production is affected by a preference for Western goods, which can now be freely imported.

Eighth, and last, *the decline in services* (in Russia the decline in 1992 was 50 per cent) due to the marketisation and the phasing out of subsidies. Many cannot now pay for kindergartens, vacations, sanatoria, and so on. To these one could add *the effects of inflation.* This affects different countries in very different ways. The Czech Republic, Hungary, and, after a period of hyperinflation, now also Poland, have been able to keep inflation within tolerable limits, but today both Russia and Ukraine feel the painful and distorting effects of an upsurge in inflation. In both countries it is exceeding 30 per cent a month and accelerating. This is one cause of a very rapid decline in the exchange rate, which makes nonsense of international comparisons and of any attempt to align internal to world prices. (Thus if the Kiev metro charged 'world prices' for a ride, using the (subsidised!) New York subway fare as a guide, the fare, at the exchange rate ruling in March of this year, would be 1600 karbovantsi.) Of course it is true that if one does not align internal prices to world prices, there are undesirable consequences, including opportunities for corrupt deals and speculative excesses of many kinds. But if, for example, average wages at this exchange rate are less than 15 dollars a month, world prices for consumer necessities are out of the question.

WHY THE INFLATION IN UKRAINE AND RUSSIA?

At the end of 1991 there was a big gap between demand (that is, the level of personal incomes plus savings) and supply available at the official prices. This was also the case in Poland in 1989, and in Romania and Bulgaria too in 1990–91. Consequently the freeing of prices was bound to lead to a big rise in prices. It was hoped that this would be followed by a period of relative stability, assured by strict monetary and credit policies and a reduction in the budget deficit. Poland in 1991 (almost) conformed to the pattern – though the decline in output exceeded the reformers' expectations. But in Russia and Ukraine things worked out differently – and the fate of the two was linked since for most of 1992 Ukraine was part of the rouble zone. What went wrong? There are number of interlocking explanations.

First of all, it proved impossible to cut the budget deficit sufficiently. Revenues were affected by the decline in output, and also by difficult collection (thus the unfamiliar Value Added Tax presented big problems) and lack of tax discipline (avoidance, especially by the expanding private sector, and also retention of revenues by local authorities). Though Russia tried to cut back military expenditures, it proved unavoidable to increase pay and also meet the cost of moving occupation troops back to Russia. And Ukraine had to pay for its own army, while military costs used to be covered by the all-union budget. The parliaments of both countries, responding to public pressures, passed laws increasing pensions and benefits. There would have been large sums to pay in unemployment benefit if unemployment had greatly risen. It did not in fact greatly rise, but this was due to the fact that bankrupt firms were given financial support, by subsidy or low-interest credits, and this helped to speed up inflation. In the first half of 1992, the Gaidar government attempted to impose a strict monetary policy, but one result was that enterprises, short of working capital, ceased to pay each other for supplies: by June 1992 unpaid debts exceeded 3 trillion roubles. (Similar tendencies were to be found in other countries too.) State enterprises and the state itself owed large sums to their own employees, due to lack of cash. It proved impossible to hold back the flood, and since then the deficit and credit cash emission have both grown. In Ukraine the budget deficit was proportionally higher than in Russia (Kuchma spoke of the incredibly high figure of 40 per cent of the Gross National Product), and the karbovantsi-kupony depreciated faster than the rouble.

Political and economic pressures have, until now, made impossible the imposition of strict financial and budget discipline. It is hard to see how this can be achieved in either country without strong governments of national unity commanding national confidence. Of course there are large budget deficits also in the United States and Great Britain, yet inflation rates are low. But this is due to the fact that they are not covered by money creation, but by the sales of bonds in financial markets. Needless to say, both the Ukrainian and Russian governments know this, and both have proposed to do the same. However, they are victims of a vicious circle: who would buy bonds so long as inflation is both high and unpredictable, and it is bound to remain high unless the government stops financing the large budget deficit by printing money. As for bank credits, if the inflation rate exceeds 1000 per cent per annum, a positive interest rate would have to exceed this figure. But who would borrow at, say, 1100 per cent, other than to finance the most short term of short-term deals.

This leads me to a key problem, common in varying degrees to all these countries: *the collapse of investment*. The modernisation of restructuring of industry and agriculture, and of infrastructure, the conversion of military to civilian production, the need to deal with ecological disasters inherited from the old system; all call urgently for more investment. Instead of that, in all these countries, including the Ukraine, investment has fallen so far that it is in all probability below the replacement rate, that is, net investment is negative. This would in itself ensure a fall in output in the future. How is the necessary investment to be financed? There are few legitimate private fortunes. The new commercial banks see little profit and much risk in lending other than for short-term profit, which in the main comes from dealing, not producing or investing. In the present inflationary uncertainty, this is not surprising. State enterprises have no incentive to reinvest their profits (if any), given the uncertainty they face about privatisation. Foreign investors are welcome, but few. So – should the state, in Ukraine, Russia, Poland, anywhere, have an investment strategy, channeling credits or grants on favourable terms to priority sectors? This question becomes an important source of politico–ideological dispute. Those who have become converted to 'Chicago' free-market concepts reject (in Britain too!) the very notion of an industrial or investment strategy, believing that the market should decide. They also point to the lack of competent officials, the power of lobbyists, the opportunities for corruption. However, in much of Eastern Europe, in Ukraine too, the capital market is not so much imperfect as non-existent. As also in Russia, one cannot rely on what does not exist. Furthermore, there are a number of other relevant experiences: in Japan, South Korea, Taiwan, in Western Europe in the years of recovery after World War II, the state played an active role in encouraging investment in what were judged priority areas.

What of *privatisation*? In all these countries it is the subject of much controversy. All agree about small-scale privatisation (of shops, cafes, various other services and small workshops), as well as legalising new private businesses in these and other areas. But progress has been slow, as also in Ukraine. Shortage of private capital and credit, lack of entrepreneurial experience, legal unclarities over property rights, bureaucratic obstruction, cause delays and frustrations. Some countries have issued privatisation vouchers to all citizens, but these can cover only a fraction of the capital value of most firms, and many of the poorer citizens will be tempted to sell them. The larger firms will remain state property for years yet, and it is important that they and their managers and employees have reasonable incentives to be efficient. Some of the privatisation ideology looks naive: it seems to have in mind an owner–manager–entrepreneur, whose appearance is indeed desirable, but is encountered (west as well as east) in small firms. The larger ones, whether its shares are sold to the public or purchased with vouchers, will (like most western corporations) have managers nominally responsible to numerous and anonymous 'owners'. Unless, that is, there is a managerial buy-out. Or there could be cooperative ownership by the entire workforce. Or state enterprises could be leased to management for a number of years, until in more normal and less inflationary times it is possible to value the capital of the enterprise. There can also be disputes about the full desirable extent of privatisation, with some arguing for a mixed economy in which energy and large-scale heavy industry remains in the public sector. Some are attracted by the Chinese model, where private and cooperative (and also foreign-financed) property has greatly expanded alongside the state sector, and where great strides towards the market have been accompanied by growth, not decline. But, of course, it is no easier to imagine Chinese methods being applied in Eastern Europe than Japanese ones introduced in Great Britain! (Though some Japanese managers are trying.)

FOREIGN TRADE AND PAYMENTS, CONVERTIBILITY

In such countries as Hungary and Poland, management has had for many years direct access to foreign markets, so that the necessary experience in the conduct of foreign trade is fairly widely dispersed. This was not the case in Russia, for the reason that, until recent years, the 'state monopoly of foreign trade' meant a monopoly for the trade corporation under the Ministry of Foreign Trade. The position of Ukraine was, of course, even worse, in that nearly everything was centralised in Moscow. There are, inevitably, gaps in organisation and experience. Experience with balance of payments deficits also varies between countries. Thus some (Poland, Hungary) have inherited large hard-currency debts, while Romania under Ceauşescu paid them all off (the people suffering hardship in consequence). The depreciation of the currency in all these countries has made labour extremely cheap by international standards at the free exchange rate. The cheapest of all would appear to be Russia and Ukraine. In the year that followed the drastic depreciation of the zloty, Poland achieved a sizeable trade surplus, but as the real exchange rate improved (that is, wages and costs rose faster than the zloty–dollar rate), there is again a trade deficit. The opportunity for Russia and Ukraine to sell competitively in the West seems very good, on paper. In fact as we know many thousands cross borders to engage in what could be called bazaar trade. It is probable that some very real large-scale trading opportunities are missed through lack of marketing skills and contacts. However, one must recall that (as Hungary and Poland have already found) that success could lead to Western import restrictions.

As already mentioned earlier, the disruption of trade within the former Soviet Union, and between ex-members of Comecon, has harmed everybody. Russia's difficulties are exacerbated by the continuous and continued fall in oil output, this being by far her largest hard-currency earner, and on top of this the breakdown of authority and financial discipline has been such that most proceeds from exports in terms of trade with Russia owing to the enormous increases in prices of oil, gas, other materials. The many cross-border barter deals can be obstructed at any time by the newly-erected customs barriers, whose appearance was deplored by Kuchma in a recent interview in the Moscow *Argumenty i fakty*. He also complained that Russian firms have not paid their Ukrainian suppliers – though in Moscow one hears the opposite complaint. The essential point is that trade with the ex-USSR is impeded by confusion over money and payment. (Thus a few months ago Russian post offices were refusing to accept parcels of any size addressed to Ukraine; maybe this is still the case.) I would have expected Moscow to be using its considerable economic bargaining power to bring ex-Soviet republics closer together. Yet instead one finds a tendency to be quite ruthless in ignoring their interests. But in order to trade one must have exportable products.

Ukraine is, one gathers, in no position to export grain or sugar-beet to Russia, which has need of them, and indeed Ukraine has been buying grain in the West. In any case, western Europe severely restricts imports of farm produce. Many products of Ukrainian (and of Russian) industry should be competitive in the West in due course, but in the short run there is advantage in deals with Russia – if that country can avoid a slide into chaos. Ukraine may be able to avoid paying its share of Russia's (the Soviet Union's) debt, since it has not been able to acquire a share in the gold and currency reserves (Russia's have greatly diminished in recent years, so there is little to share out in any event). So Ukraine finds itself in an extremely difficult situation, analogous to that of a country like Bulgaria, with no gold and valuta reserves at all. Foreign credits have been few and far between. This raises the question of convertibility and the linked question of trade liberalisation. Is it right in a critical situation, when many suffer hardship, to allow firms and individuals freely to acquire highly scarce valuta for imports of luxuries? Countries not in acute crisis can do so, for example, Hungary and the Czech Republic. Can or should Ukraine? In the first ten years after the war convertibility was strictly limited in western Europe. Referring to Russia, the German banker Axel Lebahn wrote: 'It is for me incomprehensible, when individuals and firms are mainly interested in remitting a quick profit abroad, that anyone should propose to introduce convertibility within two months.' (*Stand*

und Perspektive neur deutsch-russischer Wirtschaftskooperation, Berlin,
1992.) Of course there are arguments the other way, including the desirability of import competition. But even the IMF, despite its 'liberal'
ideology, must surely appreciate that if its loans are wasted on luxury
imports for the new rich, instead of being used for modernisation of
potential exporters, the money will disappear down a black hole?

Last but not least, what of *wages, social services, living standards*?
Again, experiences of different countries greatly vary. It is surprising to
find that the most severe policy towards wages was applied in Poland,
despite the role of *Solidarnosc* in bringing down the communist regime.
In 1990 all prices (almost) were freed *except* the price of labour, which
was severely restricted, which led to criticism even from Milton
Friedman. To this day, through the so-called Popiwek, state enterprises
are financially penalised if they raise wages. In the Czech Republic, by
contrast, despite the dominance of 'Chicago' ideology in the person of
Vaclav Klaus, there is an effective minimum wage, and there is much
greater freedom also in Hungary, and in Russia too. The problem arises
wherever rapid inflation has to be combated. How does one break the
wage–price spiral? Is it politically acceptable or socially fair to hold wage
rises down below the rise in prices? Should one impose a temporary
freeze on both? In all these countries there has been a truly huge increase
in the degree of income inequality. Is this to be welcomed, heralding the
rise of a capitalist class? Or deplored because so little of the new riches
have been acquired by producing anything? In Russia there is much talk
of corruption, 'the mafia' and former *nomenklatura* feathering their own
nests. All these issues either have arisen or are bound to arise in the
Ukraine too. Linked with them is the problem of taxation: too high a
level discourages genuine enterprise, too low a level ensures a continued
budget deficit. This is at present a source of dispute in both Poland and
Russia. The former Soviet regime was in some respects paternalistic.
Pensions, education, medical services, housing, kindergartens, and so on,
were all too often of mediocre quality but were free or subsidised. What
should happen to them now? Should they all be marketised? In many
countries, Russia especially, birth rates have fallen very sharply, deaths
much exceed births, because people can no longer afford to bring children
into the world. Should this not worry us? Is not life preferable to death?
The decline in the availability of social services has been accompanied by
a big fall in financing of science, research, culture. This could be due to
budgetary constraints, but also to the triumph of free-market ideology.
This is yet another dilemma for the Ukrainian authorities.

Ukrainian report: July 1993

It is important to realise that Ukraine is one of Europe's largest and most populous countries, larger in both respects than France, with a high economic potential: excellent soil, skilled labour, a sizeable part of the industry of the former Soviet Union. However, right now Ukraine faces a most serious crisis, and, though the long-term prospects can be viewed with optimism, the immediate future is both bleak and economically, socially and politically dangerous.

POLITICAL POWER, OR LACK OF IT

Until the collapse of the Soviet Union, Ukraine was one subordinate republic among many. Decisions of importance were taken in Moscow. They were passed down through communist party channels to Kiev, where the party officials were fully subordinate to the central committee in Moscow. As in the USSR itself, the state administration carried little weight, the 'elected' parliament was of little significance, the country was run by a bureaucracy of party functionaries. And since power and influence resided in Moscow, ambitious Ukrainians tended to move there seeking promotion (rather like many Scots move to London!). Less than two years ago the Union collapsed, the ruling party disintegrated, and Ukraine became an independent state which had to create its institutions almost from scratch. So, in the view of all our Ukrainian colleagues, a very important obstacle to change and to efficiency is the lack of administrative cadres, of experienced and responsible politicians, of an efficient civil service, of persons acquainted with commercial law, public finance, tax collecting. There is lack of experience in marketing, lack of market culture and infrastructure. Laws and decrees are adopted which contradict one another, the rules of the game are frequently altered.

Matters are further complicated by splits in the political leadership: president Kravchuk and premier Kuchma both believe that the emergency requires emergency powers, but dispute as to who should exercise them. There is the parliament, elected when the Soviet Union still existed, with fragmented and small political parties, which have no very clear economic agenda – their differences are in many cases centred on nationalist issues, including the sore question of relations with Russia. President Kravchuk himself is the former ideological secretary of the Ukrainian communist party, and many of the chiefs in the provinces are former communist officials. None the less, there is a strong feeling in the Ukraine among the radical reformers that the political establishment is dragging its feet, and that this is why reform in Ukraine is way behind Russia's. A further difficulty is due to the very poor pay of Ukrainian officials. Kuchma himself, in an interview last month, gave his own salary as 60 000 karbovantsi (Ukrainian roubles, hereafter karb.) a month. At present free exchange rates, this is $15. I am told it has just risen to $25! Other pubic servants get much less. In the same interview, he asked rhetorically how they could fail to be corrupt. They have to feed their families! Energetic and ambitious intellectuals go into business, rather than into government.

There is supposed to be a referendum in September, which would enable the citizens to declare their lack of confidence in the president and in parliament. New elections to the parliament would surely produce less conservative deputies, which would facilitate the reform process. However, some doubt was expressed (for example, by the well-informed Bohdan Kravchenko) as to whether the September referendum will occur at all. Meanwhile, to cite a report by the Centre for Market Reforms (Kiev):

> The essence of the problem is that neither the president, nor the premier, nor parliament, nor the parties, nor influential elite groups . . . , have yet proposed to society an ideological doctrine and programme which could unite the healthy elements of society for the creation of a civil order, a market economy and democratic Ukrainian statehood.

And Kuchma himself 'had to admit the low effectiveness of the administrative hierarchy, the failure to control regional administrative and economic authorities'.

RELATIONS WITH RUSSIA

This is the key issue for several reasons. One, which happened to 'blow up' while we were in Kiev, is the question of the Crimea, Sebastopol, the Black Sea fleet. The second is concern that the large Russian population in the Donets coal basin and other parts of the eastern Ukraine may demand autonomy and that this demand is being encouraged by Moscow as a means of exerting influence. Some regard the recent miners' strike as political in this sense. Meanwhile there are anti-Moscow protest demonstrations (for example, in Kiev, 16 July). Tension with Russia affects military expenditures. The Ukrainian army is much larger than the state can afford, and it wants half of the Black Sea fleet as well. Then there is the retention of nuclear weapons. None of this helps reduce the budget deficit. Vital for Ukraine are its *economic* relations with Russia. Typical were the comments of the director-general Ponomarev (of a corporation which was part of the military–industrial complex): apart from the drying up of military orders, his problems included trying to secure material inputs which previously came from Russia, and to find customers, most of which (military or no) were in Russia and other ex-Soviet republics.

Most of industry, whether or not military, faces a similar situation. Obstacles to trade included difficulties in payment (partly due to currency convertibility problems, now the Ukraine is out of the rouble zone), partly to insolvency of many enterprises. It should be recalled that inter-enterprise debt reached astronomic dimensions, in both Russia and Ukraine. The old planning system established many monopolies, that is, single enterprises producing all the output of (for example) a particular machine or vehicle for the whole Union. This causes severe losses (of inputs, and of markets) when political disintegration is accompanied by economic blockages. Customs barriers, export and import quotas, limited and confused clearing arrangements, obstruct trade. Ukraine imports from Russia most of its oil and gas. Russia's oil output has been falling, its price demands have been rising. While formerly (that is, before 1992) supplying Ukraine at the low internal price, Russia by stages is moving towards world prices, which were many times higher. At his press conference, Kuchma confirmed earlier reports, that it had been agreed that the price charged for crude by Russia to Ukraine would rise to $80 per ton in the third quarter, to $90 in the fourth quarter, $100 in the first quarter of 1994 (world price is, I believe, $120). Ukraine suffers both from reduction in deliveries, and from a very substantial worsening of her terms of trade with Russia. A fall in export proceeds, due in large part to disruption of established ties, has contributed to a balance of payments crisis, which is reaching a critical stage now.

It is in this context that one must see the (surprising) agreement, reported in detail in the press here on 14 July, signed by the premiers of Belarus, Russia and Ukraine. The agreement (or, strictly speaking, an agreement to set up a joint group to draft an agreement) envisages closer integration of production, investment, foreign trade, fiscal and monetary policies, market-reform measures, so as to stop the disruption of economic ties and to create a single economic area or common market. All tariff and non-tariff barriers should be removed, there should be free movement of capital and labour between the three republics.

Coordinating organs would be created to ensure that consistent policies are followed. The detailed draft is to be ready by 1 September, and three vice premiers (Zalomai, Shokhin and Landyk, one from each republic) are to draft it. Economically all this is evidently desirable. At his press conference Kuchma defended his own signature to the agreement, pointing out (as did many others we spoke to) that Ukraine suffers greatly from the breaking of traditional ties, that it is absurd to make unnecessary investments, to fill gaps in supply created by the new state boundaries, that the whole area has been integrated for centuries, and so on. But the political problem looms large. On the very day this decision was published, the Ukrainian press featured prominently the declaration of the Russian Supreme Soviet on the Crimea and Sebastopol. Suspicion of Russian 'empire-restorationism' is strong, and may well stand in the way of progress. We should believe in the tripartite free trade area when and if we see it. Yet if this fails, the cost will be vast. Example: *Pravda Ukrainy* (17 July) reports Kuchma's visit to a large factory in Kirovograd, which used to make *all* the sewers for the whole USSR. Now, cut off from orders, it has stopped production for two months. Its workforce is in effect on paid leave. It is economically silly to close it altogether. Its future, as Kuchma duly pointed out, depends on the tripartite agreement working.

RECESSION, INFLATION, THE BUDGET, INCOMES OF THE POPULATION

We received somewhat contradictory information on these vitally important subjects. The country memorandum of the World Bank, dated 2 June 1993, shows net material product to have fallen by 11 per cent in 1991 and another 16 per cent in 1992, but the rate of decline notably slowed in the first months of 1993, according to 'Ukraine in Figures', a bulletin issued by Pynzenyk's office in the Economic Reform Ministry. The same source claims a fall in the rate of inflation in March. There was even a small budget surplus in the first five months of 1993, according to the Minister of Finance. So was Kuchma exaggerating when he spoke repeatedly of crisis, imminent catastrophe, the need for a state of emergency?

Unfortunately, the balance of evidence points to Kuchma being right. Hyperinflation is here, unless vigorous steps are taken to halt the slide. It is important to note that there are statistical deficiencies, both in the measurement of output and particularly in price indices. This is due partly to the existence of multiple prices, with partial price control also being exercised by local authorities, while there are also free prices for the same items. The *retail* price index (official) looks like this (source: Pynzenyk's office, per cent rise over previous month): Sept. 92 (14.4), Oct. (19.2), Nov. (19.6), Dec. (29.7), Jan. 93 (79.8), Feb. (32.3), March (19.2). The same source gave *wholesale* price increase in January as 141. The leap in January was due to a very steep rise in prices that had been controlled and subsidised. This was followed by a moderation in price rises, until June, when there was another leap, estimated by Kaufmann (World Bank representative in Kiev) at between 40 per cent and 70 per cent in that single month. According to several sources, the June price rises, affecting many necessities in both state shops and in the market, were and are resented, and touched off damaging strikes in the coal mines. The high rate of inflation, paralleled (and partly fuelled by, as well as reflecting) the rapid depreciation of the karbovanets, is attributable to a combination of factors.

First of all, the budget deficit – or surplus – has little meaning, unless combined with credit emission by the central bank. If one goes down the other goes up. Most credits are at a (very) negative rate of interest, may or may not ever be repaid, and are scarcely distinguishable from direct budgetary subsidies. According to Lanovoi's Centre for Economic Reform, in 1992 the budget deficit was 15 per cent of GNP, but if one adds bank credits one reached 34 per cent. There were particularly large increases in bank credits during the period of so-called budget surplus in the first half of 1993. Just how large is in dispute. Thus according to Kaufmann the cost of the settlement with the miners and of the financing of agriculture, plus extra financing of social services, came to 13 *trillion* karb., which guarantees a speed-up in inflation. (This combines credit emission with extra budgetary grants.) Lanovoi agreed. He expected 60–70 per cent a month inflation for the rest of this year, a 90-fold rise in prices in 1993 as a whole. He said that president Kravchuk, addressing a congress of collective farms, promised not only to leave the farms unreformed for years, but also 'limitless' (*bezlimitnyi*) credits at 30 per cent interest (bank rate is 230 per cent, inflation ten times above *that*), to be repaid by the harvest. (Kuchma, at his interview, also referred to these credits being issued *pod urozhii*, secured by the harvest, that is, that this was a sort of advance payment.) However, there will be no check on how the money is used, so Lanovoi expects much lower subsidy figures were cited by the minister of finance (an old-style official with 55 volumes of Lenin on his office shelves!).

If the budget plan announced for 1993 is carried out, planned revenue would absorb 55.3 per cent of GNP (in 1992, 30.2 per cent), and expenditures 71 per cent (47.4 per cent in 1992), the difference being covered by emission, according to Lanovoi's institute, but hyperinflation would create havoc with the figures. The point being made was the rising *share* of the budget in a declining total. '80 per cent of value-added is absorbed by the budget' (but tax avoidance is also a fact). Of course there is no point in introducing the long-promised new currency, the *hrivna*, as this too would be swept away. The *price system*, if it can be so called, was described in detail by Lanovoi. Sixty per cent (by value) of wholesale prices are controlled. The control takes two forms. For basic items like fuel and metal the prices are fixed. For many others (including machinery and metal-working) there is a limit in profit margin, expressed as a percentage of cost (thus making it profitable to inflate costs).

The agricultural procurement organs (still monopolist and state-owned) and retail trade in basic foodstuffs also have limits on profit and retailers' margins. In this way prices of many items in state shops do get controlled (with local variations), but there are also many private and leased shops (or counters inside state shops) where prices are free. And then there is the free market, for example, the large one, 'Bessarabka', which we visited. But prices there may or may not be much higher than state prices, depending on circumstances and on costs. State price controls are adjusted at intervals, which causes disproportionate leaps in prices (and so also in costs of production and of living) when a rise is decided. Hence the big upswings in prices in January and June of this year. Thus the cheapest sausage in state shops leapt from 800 karb. to 5000 karb. overnight. Yet even after the June price rises, 30 per cent of milk and 40 per cent of meat costs are covered by subsidy, according to Lanovoi. Prices are so high in relation to incomes that one wonders how people survive. *Average* wages are of the order of 25 000 to 30 000 karb. a month. ($9 a month, or 8 cents an hour), and here are some food prices, observed in state shops and the market (karb. per kilo unless stated otherwise): Loaf of bread (164), Chicken (3270), Sugar (1500), Rice (1900), Potatoes (300–500), Mushrooms (12 000), Pork (7500–8000), Beef (5000–6000), Lard (6000), Milk, 1.5 (408), Butter (1633), Ham (7884), Best sausage (11 664), Poor sausage (6200), Eggs, 10 (900–1000), Bananas (4000), Lemon, each! (5000). How do people live, if one lemon or one kilogram of meat equals one week's wages? Even the economist Chernyak, who told me that *he* makes 90 000 karb. a month, says he cannot afford to buy clothes, or restaurant meals. Yet people look well fed, and many women are smartly dressed. The statistics seem falsified by what one sees. Are they just wrong? The answer given was: Yes, most people make an extra income, by some second job, by dealing, by having a relative in the country to send them food, by drawing on past reserves (for example, of clothes, shoes, and so on.). But life *is* tough for many. And surely productivity on the main job suffers. *Wages* were out of control last year. Efforts to limit wage rises were made, but they can have only limited chance of success when prices are rising so fast. The Supreme Rada (parliament) passed a law recently granting the low-paid a cost-of-living bonus of over 6000 karb. a month. Miners get double the national average at least. As usually happens when hyperinflation takes hold, price rises seem often to exceed the growth of money supply, and one hears complaints of shortage of money.

Kuchma, in his press conference and in his speech at the Kirovograd factory, hinted at emergency measures that would include bread and meat rationing, tighter controls over what state enterprises do. He also stressed the need for elementary order. Thus export goods are left on the dockside if 'commercial structures' pay bigger bribes. The *exchange rate* reached 4200 karb. to the dollar while we were there. Why is it so unfavourable? Among the explanations, along with the obvious consequence of inflationary expectations, are the following sources of demand for dollars. One can borrow from a bank at a very negative rate of interest, buy dollars and wait. Patience will be amply rewarded. Or would-be exporters of raw materials under-invoice on a big scale, and the extra dollars are placed in a foreign bank account by the Western partner (a favourite route for capital flight, it seems). And many Ukrainians journey to neighbouring countries to bring back goods for resale, which again stimulate demand for dollars. At the same time, exports have plummeted, so the dollar supply is down. The central bank has virtually no reserves with which it could interfere. We asked: is the fact that the central bank is responsible to parliament a significant cause of its inability to control the flow of soft credits? The reply of the deputy-governor of the bank was, I believe, not deliberately evasive. 'Until quite recently we had no central bank, no president, no real parliament.' In other words, no one is in effective control of the deteriorating situation – though he himself said there was no need to panic. But maybe there is.

PRIVATISATION

Progress in this direction has been painfully slow, even in respect of small-scale enterprises. Reasons? One is to do with legal complications, which few are competent to handle. Thus most small enterprises are not state but municipal, and some were leased to the workforce. Indeed, 1500 industrial enterprises were so leased during 1992, accounting for 20 per cent of industrial production. Some see leasing as an obstacle to outright privatisation, others as a useful stage in an ongoing process. The privatisation plan for 1993 was rejected by the parliament. It is intended, according to minister Pryadko, to privatise 20 000 enterprises during the year, but so far only 155 have been. Delay, we were told, is in the interests of local officials, since many have a (corrupt) hand in 'spontaneous' privatisation which is in fact taking place in unofficial ways. An original scheme of spreading ownership was decided on last year (I heard about it on my previous visit). Privatisation certificates or vouchers are to be issued to all adult citizens, and their value is to be 70 per cent of all capital assets. In mid-1992 each was worth 30 000 karb., by the end of the year it was 55 000. Now of course it would be much higher. The certificates will be indexed in line with capital asset revaluation. One reason for delay is that they have not yet been printed (shortage of good paper and printing capacity!) (Americans will print them!). These vouchers, unlike the Russian ones, will be for investment only, bear the owner's name, cannot be sold. There are also to be certificates (vouchers) valid for the purchase of land and for the purchase of housing. They can be switched: that is, if the individual already has an apartment and/or does not want to acquire land, he can exchange for other categories of vouchers. Each employee could use a certificate for purchase of shares in his/her own enterprise, plus the right to *buy* more, up to half the value of the certificate if he/she so wishes. In small enterprises this could mean majority employee ownership, but not so in the larger ones. Investment (mutual) funds are at a process of creation. There is to be a functioning stock exchange, and shares will be bought and sold. Larger enterprises are to be 'corporatised', though still state-owned.

My impression is that, despite the slow start, the intention of the president and the government is to get privatisation moving, on the populist principle of wide share ownership with the exception that, after the initial egalitarian gesture via the vouchers, there will be concentration of capital and that a class of entrepreneur proprietors will start emerging. However, some influential political groups may block the way. The minister in charge, Pryadko, spoke of a 'socialist' block in parliament which is opposed to all but small-scale privatisation, and the economist Chernyak (who has close links with the opposition leader and with *Rukh*) doubts the commitment of part of the government. Several times I heard the view that the old party *nomenklatura* is split: some are actively engaged in turning themselves into capitalists and so favour privatisation (on their terms), while others, left in the cold, bitterly oppose it. The World Bank country memorandum (dated 2 June 1993) warns:

> The NBU (National Bank of Ukraine) has only just started to develop a basic understanding of the difficulties of preparing a voucher scheme and the logistic problems of implementing it. The Savings Bank, responsible for non-cash accounts, is also in the early stages of understanding the complexity of this process. Neither agency is close to developing an implementation program.

And, of course, the whole process is also thrown out of gear by hyper-inflation. Catch 22: radical market reform requires stabilisation. Stabilisation requires radical market reform. And continued inaction equals disaster.

INDUSTRY AND INVESTMENT

All agree that a radical restructuring of the real economy is indispensable. One needs what Schumpeter called 'creative destruction', as hopeless loss-makers are phased out and the economy adjusts to a new demand pattern. However, this requires substantial investments, otherwise there would be what one colleague called 'uncreative destruction'. The printing of investment vouchers is not real investment, of course. This has fallen dramatically since 1990. Ukraine inherited a large and relatively modern military–industrial sector, but outside of it most industrial plant is obsolete, worn out, energy-intensive, with heavy industry having long had priority over consumers' goods. How can the needed restructuring take place when net investment is negative, below replacement rates? To make things worse, one has what Lanovoi's institute calls 'structural perestroika in reverse'. Subsidies go to heavy industry, and its output has fallen by less than that of light industry and agriculture. The institute's reports point to inconsistencies in government policies: support is given to market institutions, while other measures protect state monopolies and grant lavish credits to large state enterprises, preserving the old structures.

I witnessed an exchange of views between a World Bank official and Chernyak. They finally agreed (as did I) that continuing to subsidise all lossmakers was a recipe for hyperinflationary disaster, while allowing them all to close would destroy the economy. The only solution is selectivity, to rescue, and encourage investment in, essential and/or promising sectors, with foreign aid and credits as part of the package. The World Bank official pointed to the evident difficulty, amid present-day chaos, of identifying such sectors. Chernyak replied that such a special government commission was currently engaged in this task. Lanovoi is less inclined to interventionism, yet he and his institute, in their 'programme for 1993', are surely correct when they argued as follows:

> Given conditions of hyperinflation, the absence of private and enterprise savings and the presence of a budget deficit, the sources of internal capital accumulation are meagre. It is essential to create the conditions for the redistribution of the national income in favour of sectors with favourable perspectives, while reducing its use in declining sectors, while encouraging the flow of foreign investment.

This calls for selectivity. Whether a weak and divided government, under pressure from lobbyists, will be able to select correctly, and then implement the chosen policy, is quite another question.

Much depends on the future of Russia as a market. Thus minister Pyatachenko noted that Ukraine has surplus oil refining capacity which could refine Russian oil for re-export, also that while Ukrainian machinery may not be of a quality to sell in Western markets, it is saleable in Russia. Uncertainty as to the Russian market is a major problem. It has been estimated that between 60–70 per cent of the machinery and engineering industry supplied the military, and that 40 per cent of industrial fixed capital was in energy and metallurgy. Structural change is called for, but financed how? Meanwhile credit emission is keeping these sectors afloat, fuelling inflation.

AGRICULTURE

Ukraine has some of the most fertile soil in the world (though there is a drought risk). In the course of my journey through the Poltava province one could see confirmed the reports that this year's harvest would be a good one, despite some rain damage. As a result it is hoped this year to do without imports of grain. However, total production shows a steep downward trend. Meat, butter, milk, sugar, declined by upwards of 20 per cent in 1992, and the decline is continuing. Agriculture receives massive subsidies, direct and indirect. In part this is a consequence of the effect of inflation on devaluing working capital: thus farms were paid for the 1992 harvest at mid-1992 prices, and since then the prices of all inputs (fuel, fertiliser, herbicides, farm machinery, and so on, and goods consumed by peasants) have risen tenfold, putting even the more efficient farms into bankruptcy. However, there is plenty of evidence of inefficiency in the state and collective-farm system, and even more in the still-monopolist state-run procurement and wholesaling organs. Losses in the fields, in storage, in transport, are notoriously high. The fall in output has been due in part to two contradictory trends, which in fact have cumulative effects. One is the substantial worsening of terms of trade (price relativities) between agriculture and industry. The other is the steep decline in urban purchasing-power: when meat costs the equivalent of one week's wages per kilo, few can afford to buy it, and in the recent miners' strike it was pointed out that the minimum monthly wage could not buy a kilo of good sausage (of course the miners earned much more, but even for them it was tough). Despite all this there is still a subsidy for livestock products! Farms accuse the wholesalers of underpaying them, and there have been government decrees limiting the profit margins of state trading organs.

So radical reform is called for – and little actually happens. This is for several reasons. One, cited by just about everybody, is the power to obstruct exercised by local officials and (especially) farm management, plus the state wholesalers. They try to hold on to power and easy pickings. But at least equally important is the attitude of the bulk of the peasantry. How many, even if one abstracted from present uncertainties, would wish to set up as private farmers? The consensus is: not many. Add to this the lack of small-scale machinery, doubts as to availability and prices of other inputs, legal obscurities concerning land ownership, the fact that the peasants' simple needs are more or less met in state and collective farms without hard work and responsibility (and they may have a private plot as it is), and privatisation as a short-term solution looks plainly unrealistic. Some Ukrainian colleagues are attracted by encouraging the creation by the peasants of genuine cooperatives. (The collectives were phoney, pseudo-cooperatives.) It is plainly important to break the monopoly of the state wholesalers, surely by the opening up of these activities to private traders. Other issues, too, spring to mind. What is the optimal size of a farm in the Ukraine? On similar land in Canada farms are big, but the rural population in the Ukraine is many, many times higher. A switch to efficient mechanised farming would deprive many of a living, and this at a time when urban unemployment is set to rise. What kind of price support or subsidy schemes should there be? We in Western Europe cannot preach the virtues of free market prices in agriculture without blushing! And finally, suppose Ukraine increases output and achieves a sizeable export surplus, where are these exports to go? Again, as minister Pyatachenko noted, the most promising market is Russia.

FOREIGN TRADE AND FOREIGN INVESTMENT

Here again there has been steep decline, particularly in trade with Russia and other ex-Soviet republics, but also with foreign countries (exports to them fell by 38 per cent in 1992). In this area even more than elsewhere statistics are incomplete and inaccurate. Thus goods move to and from Russia over a long and unpoliceable border at values unknown, since many are barter deals. As already noted, exports for hard currency are frequently underinvoiced, the difference remaining in Western bank accounts. Ukraine has been getting deliveries from Russia (especially of oil and gas) on credit, and debt to Russia lays Ukraine open to demands for prepayment, and at very much higher prices. There is also inter-firm debt, with payment delays in both directions. But, especially given the soaring price of oil and gas imports, Ukraine faces an immediate balance of payments crisis. On my previous visit to Kiev, last year, I heard the bank director answer very briefly a question about gold and currency reserves. He replied 'u nas ikh net', 'we have none'. The foreign investment story is likewise a gloomy one. Lanovoi's institute has calculated that these amounted to less than $1 billion in 1992, and only $114 million in the first quarter of 1993. On both counts, along with problems connected with hyperinflation and supply and other bottlenecks, much responsibility rests with the contradictions of government policy. Export quotas, export licenses, export taxes, all involving bureaucratic paperwork (and opportunities for corruption), plus some irrational import duties, introduce much confusion and frustration. Private exports are taxed when state trading organs are exempt. With its very low labour costs, the Ukraine could surely make some impact in foreign markets, given much-needed help in marketing *and* the sweeping away of administrative and financial obstacles. A new journal, *Ukrainski Kommersant*, featured a critical article about changes in regulations and failure to keep promises, instancing president Kravchuk's solemn promise on his visit to America not to alter the regulations concerning currency conversion and profit remittances, and then altering them. How, asks the paper, can anyone trust such a government?

Ukraine badly needs foreign capital and foreign aid. In my view it could and should be targeted to fit into the government's restructuring priorities if these are judged to be sound. Thus, to cite just one example, if private farming is being encouraged, aid in the form of small-scale equipment, now lacking, would have a positive effect. So would investment by GM, or Rover, or Volkswagen, in the context of modernising the car industry (the Zaporozhets car was little better than the late unlamented Trabant, if better it was. Its output has been handicapped by non-arrival of components from outside the Ukraine).

FINALLY, SOME CONCLUSIONS

The crisis is acute. Many fear that, if present trends continue, the long-suffering population will stop work. Strikes are threatened soon on the railways, where worn-out equipment is not being replaced. Urgent measures are needed, possibly calling for a real state of emergency, with full powers for the executive. The key to everything is money. By that I mean that no reform measures, no privatisation schemes, no sort of market, can work so long as the 'coupon' karbovanets currency is worthless and depreciates at 50 and more per cent a month. How can one talk of a banking and credit system, or the financing of investment activity, if a positive interest rate equals 3000 per cent per annum? The absence of real money undermines even the most sensible government actions, explains some of the ad hoc and inconsistent measures, too. Thus export licensing and export taxes are intended to deal with the consequences of the wide gap between internal and world prices at a very peculiar exchange rate. The same gap facilitates corruption. Yet how can one align internal to world prices if, at this exchange rate, the average citizen earns $9 a month? And a balance of payments crisis is looming. There *must* be drastic action on the monetary-fiscal front, since without this other measures cannot succeed. But other measures too must be taken. A whole programme has been elaborated by the Centre of Market Reform, at the request of premier Kuchma, and I have a copy of this. The 'basics' are all there: support for private enterprise, commercialisation of those state enterprises not privatised, trade and payments arrangements with ex-Soviet countries, agricultural reform (carried out gradually and cautiously, as it must be), changes in banking and foreign trade procedures, selective rescue of lossmaking enterprises, strict energy-saving measures, plus steps to attract foreign investment – with pride of place for measures to bring inflation down. Can these, can other proposals, begin the process of convalescence? After all, Ukraine has, in the long term, great potential. Can breakdown and disintegration be avoided? Asked this question, Chernyak thought that, if wiser policies were adopted now, recovery would still take 5–10 years. Cooperation with Russia would be economically beneficial, but he too was worried about Russia's 'imperial ambitions'. He feared 'not Latinamericanisation but Africanisation'.

Ukraine needs help, and needs it more than Russia. Like Russia, its weak and divided post-Soviet government is having to grapple with immense problems of transition and adjustment. One is struck by how little our own theories can help them in their unprecedented task. The September referendum, if it takes place, may or may not clarify matters. An autumn crisis, political and economic, is on the cards.

What went wrong with André Gunder Frank?[1]

A very challenging argument! Like most of his other work, this one raises fundamental points in a vivid and controversial spirit, and this is a good thing. Let me say right away that I agree with several of his key points, and, as will be seen below, am myself a critic of the ideology which has become dominant in Eastern Europe, and which is responsible for an unnecessary degree of economic decline and hardship for the majority of the population.

The main disagreement is in the weight to be ascribed to what could be called 'world-economic reasons' in explaining the collapse of the 'east'. Interestingly, a broadly similar point was made, from a very different theoretical position, by Robin Matthews.[2] He too wondered whether the coincidental economic troubles of the West and East were merely coincidental. Might they not have some causes in common?

In my view it is important in this context to see the Soviet Union as a special case. Clearly, the smaller countries of Eastern Europe were and are bound to be heavily dependent on external markets. Similarly (say) Peru, Chile, or for that matter New Zealand, cannot exist other than in close connection with larger economic partners. Whereas the former Soviet Union could, if it wished, insulate itself from world economic crises to a much greater extent. A spectacular example was the very different economic history of the early 1930s. Though the world slump did adversely affect terms of trade, and so added to the cost of the first two five-year plans, none the less the steep decline in the West was coincident with a crash programme of industrialisation in the USSR. And in the late-Stalin period, due partly to deliberate intent and partly to Western embargoes, the USSR depended little on foreign trade. This isolation had its cost, of course, especially as it was associated also with self-imposed cultural–scientific isolation, which contributed to technological backwardness.

But let us begin at the beginning. Yes, the eastern half of Europe *was* for centuries less developed than the western half. There were deeply ingrained reasons for this, which resisted attempts to overcome them under every regime or ideology. Here Frank is right. To take some other well-known examples, the *mezzogiorno* in Italy continues to contrast with Lombardy, and Macedonia and Kosovo remained far below the level of Slovenia, despite decades of effort by the respective governments, Christian-democrat and communist. In the then-communist east, anyone would easily guess the 'productivity ranking-list'. East Germany would be followed by the Czech lands, which would be followed by Poland and Hungary, with Romania and Bulgaria coming last. The USSR, like the Russian empire before it, would be very unevenly developed, with segments of high tech and excellent science and culture coexisting with backward areas and especially backward villages, which seemed centuries behind even those of Poland, let alone Bohemia. Within the USSR itself, the Baltic republics were top, the Central Asians bottom, in the income and productivity 'league'. 'Relative positions changed but little', writes Frank. Agreed. But why is this a major reason for collapse, for 'what went wrong', if it reproduced a centuries' old situation?

As I intend to concentrate on the case of the former Soviet Union, let me agree with Frank that some of the basic troubles of the smaller countries did arise out of their attempt to integrate more closely with the world economy, at a time when this economy was itself in trouble. This applies, for instance, to Poland, when Gierek tried his *fuite en avant*, to borrow his way out of trouble in the hope of repaying the debt with Polish exports of manufactures. Hungary also incurred a substantial debt, but this for different reasons: to mitigate the effects of a sharp worsening of terms of trade. The Czechs had much lower debts, the Romanians (as Frank noted) actually repaid theirs. A key point in common for all these countries was that they could no longer depend on the Soviet Union, they *had* to look west. And this because the Soviet Union's own economic dynamism, and political–ideological self-confidence, were on the wane. Frank would argue that this, that is, the wane, was decisively due to the Soviets' participation in the world economy. This is where my disagreement comes. Other reasons were surely of greater importance. Indeed for a few years the Soviets derived benefit from the (for them quite unexpected) improvement of terms of trade, the very thing that did so much harm to (for example) Hungary. This, and also so-called détente, also enabled them to borrow. But the debt (before the process of disintegration began) was proportionately far lower than those of Poland and Hungary, and even in absolute terms well below that of Mexico.

If *participation* in the world economy was not a decisive factor, the effect of low growth on *comparisons* with the West did have an effect on what I have called political–ideological self-confidence. If one emblazons on one's banners the slogan 'catch up and overtake', and evidence accumulates that no such thing is happening, this begins to matter. There was also the burden of the arms race, but the size of the military–industrial complex was an obstacle to, not the cause or consequence of, closer integration in the international division of labour.

A small detour is called for at this point. We have agreed that Eastern Europe for centuries was behind the West and that the causes were deeplying. One of the causes, we would surely agree, relates to the human factor, explicable by history and sociology at least as much as by economics. German (or Japanese) tend to be more efficient, as workers and managers, than Russians or Serbs. But we have two examples of the *same* people developing under two different systems for over 40 years: Germany, East and West, and Korea, North and South. The contrast was to some extent concealed by statistical gerrymandering, but it has proved to be vast. Frank cannot account for the gap in terms of association with the (single!) world market, unless he is willing to grant that the much closer association with it on the part of West Germany and South Korea greatly benefited both the economy and living standards of the mass of their peoples. If such a contrast exists, and the poorer half of the same people know it, then the preservation of the 'soviet' half is necessarily dependent on Berlin walls, thirty-eighth parallels, military force and strict control over politics and the media, and collapse is bound to follow once the barriers are removed. I do not think, *pace* Frank, that 'little East Germany advanced to become the world's ninth greatest industrial power', unless you consider a Trabant equal to a Mercedes. East German growth statistics were, it seems, exceptionally exaggerated. And Frank himself agrees that the Czech lands and Poland, and probably the Baltic states too, like Finland, are culturally more in the West than in the East, and that they would never have had Soviet-type regimes were it not for their occupation by the Red Army. From which, again, it follows that Gorbachev's signal to the effect that he would not prop up these regimes, and not their problems with world markets (though they *had* problems with them!), was the decisive and immediate cause of the collapse of their basically imported and imposed regimes. The Soviet Union was different. *It* had done the imposing, and the system there had developed for its own internal reasons. What *were* these reasons?

One, which it shared with the Tsarist Empire, was the task of mobilising the people of a relatively poor country to create and maintain the material basis of a great power. (This could not, for obvious reasons, be the raison d'être of a regime in, say, Bulgaria or Poland.) 'Peter the Great was the first Bolshevik,' wrote the poet Voloshin. 'Peter's methods were purely Bolshevik,' wrote the philosopher Berdyaev. Here Frank and I seem to agree: Stalin's industrialisation can be explained by the same sort of 'catch-up-the-West' syndrome that motivated Peter the Great and such tsarist ministers as Witte. Marxist ideology and the class struggle were mobilised for this task, and played their own mobilising and legitimising role, but 'the universal service state' was a common feature of Peter's and Stalin's Russia. Theodore van Laue has long argued that a key, maybe *the* key, to Russian and Soviet history lies in the gap between great power aspirations and the relative poverty of the human and material resource base, which help to explain the authoritarian features of successive tsars and of the successors of the tsars. Ideologists as different as Pobedonostsev in the 1890s and Suslov in the 1970s doubtless shared the conviction that strict control from above was essential for the preservation of the state and the enhancement of its power, particularly in a multinational state.

In my view, the centralised planning system which was imposed under Stalin was correctly described by Oskar Lange as a *sui generis* war economy. In many respects it resembled the economies of capitalist warring countries: central control over resource allocation, the supercession of the market by politically imposed priorities, price control, rationing, all justified by the overriding needs of the struggle. Stalin not only used military language ('fronts', 'bridgeheads', 'shock brigade', 'campaigns'), he deliberately adopted policies which emphasised (or even created) crises and emergencies. It has long been argued, and with good reason, that this system was inherently incapable of administering the complexities of a modern industrial economy, that (to cite Tatyana Zaslavskaya's 1983 memorandum) the forces of production had come into contradiction with relations of production. So long as there *was* a sense of emergency and struggle, so long as there was a supreme despot to impose priorities, the system could continue to function, though generating much waste and many inefficiencies. But under Brezhnev one had a loss of 'dynamism from above', in a system which (as Gregory Grossman noted a great many years ago) required 'pressure' to combat built-in 'routine and inertia'. When Molotov, in retirement, was asked what he thought of the peaceful life under Brezhnev, he replied: 'When life is peaceful (*kogda spokoino zhivetsa*) Bolsheviks are not needed. Absolutely not needed.'

By the early 1980s, *before* the collapse of the oil price, stagnation had set in. The system was petrified, it was degenerating, losing its raison d'être, its sense of legitimacy, and surely 'blame' for this cannot be assigned to the fact that trade with the West grew in volume. It is the sense that something was indeed rotten that led the reluctant top bureaucrats to elect Gorbachev, though at the time neither he nor they knew how far the reform process would go. Then followed a catalogue of errors and inconsistencies, ranging from the anti-vodka campaign and an even sillier campaign against 'unearned incomes' (in 1986–87), to inflationary printing of money combined with price control and soaring subsidies, loss of control over incomes, and so on, which led to growing shortages. *Glasnost'* and *demokratizatsiya* meant freedom for increasingly assertive nationalisms, and the exposure not just of Stalin's crimes but also their roots in Leninism, the delegitimation of the October revolution itself. The one effective administrative authority had been the party, acting through its full-time functionaries. In downgrading the party, Gorbachev was gravely weakening the entire power apparatus. Frankly, the world market does not and should not figure prominently on the list of causes. Yes, Gorbachev declared that the Soviet Union should participate more fully in the international division of labour. But as oil prices *and* Soviet oil output fell, actual participation fell with them.

My interpretation looks very different from that of Frank. But then our paths converge. My views about the path being followed by Russia and most other East Europeans today are close to his. I am appalled by their sudden conversion to Chicago economics, and agree with him that this puts them well on the way to the Third World. On a recent visit to the Ukraine, one of their brightest economists remarked that what threatens is not even Latinamericanisation but Africanisation. There was, in my view, no alternative to seeking to rely much more on the market mechanism, despite the formidable practical difficulties in replacing the centralised allocation system by a functioning market. To me this suggested caution, a mixed economy, a sort of new NEP. I agree with Frank that obsession with privatisation has gone beyond all reason (as it has also in Great Britain). In Russia there is neither a capital market nor adequate accumulation of legitimate private capital, so that investment has collapsed. The advice of the IMF is counterproductive even from the IMF's own point of view, in that its loans will never be repaid so long as its dollars are freely bid for by seekers after short-term profit. Rather than being devoted to the needed reconstruction of the economy, to the conversion of the over-expanded military–industrial complex, the provision of a modern infrastructure, they are being spent on luxury imports for the new rich or simply deposited in numbered accounts in Western banks. Meanwhile science, medicine, the arts, high-tech industry are in a state of collapse, while the small group of nouveaux-riches make money out of dealing, with the help of underpaid and corrupt officialdom. The stage is being set for a most unpleasant outcome.

There is an alternative: China. Far be it from me to idealise the Chinese model, which carries with it its own dangers and distortions, but the contrast with Eastern Europe leaps to the eye. Instead of decline and impoverishment, China has seen large increases in both consumption and investment. This has been the result not of privatisation of state

enterprises, but of the freedom given both to provincial and local authorities and to private firms, with or without foreign (often expatriate
Chinese) capital, to set up all kinds of enterprises. Many of these are
cooperative and municipal, as well as privately owned, some competing
with state enterprises. Chinese experience confirms the validity of Frank's
view that ownership is not of itself decisive: markets and competition
provide an adequate discipline whoever is the ultimate owner of means of
production. It is too soon to say whether the mixed economy of today's
China is a stage on a gradual road to capitalism or a durable species of
mixed economy, which could be called 'socialist'. (It does almost corre-
spond to what I had envisaged in my *Economics of Feasible Socialism*,
which, oddly enough, was translated into Chinese.) But in either case it is
a path far less painful for the mass of the people, far less harmful to the
forces of production, than that chosen by Russia and the East Europeans.

Naturally, there are features of the Chinese situation (including the
specifics of agriculture, as well as the nature of the people) which cannot
be replicated in Russia, Ukraine, Poland. But that is no reason to ignore
that experience, or the very different experience of Japan and South
Korea, successful in raising themselves high on the international ranking
lists while very actively participating in the international division of
labour, but not through laissez-faire.

Frank surprisingly states that the East Europeans and the Soviet Union
'had no other choice' but to participate in the world economic system and
then he *criticises* 'really existing socialism' for offering no alternative, for
regarding 'delink as illusory and dangerous'. Do we find ourselves in the
world of Samir Amin, in which poverty and underdevelopment are due to
the links with the world market? But does this make sense? It is one thing
to see the deficiencies of the IMF's prescription – trade liberalisation and
full convertibility, plus the abandonment of any investment strategy: here I
am fully on Frank's side. It is quite another to imagine that participation
in world trade at world prices impoverishes the poor. That would imply
that Brazil would be better off if she did not export coffee and rejected the
foreign investment and know-how that came from and with Mercedes, or
that Malaysia is impoverished by exporting rubber and tin to countries
richer than itself, or that Cuba would not better its position by exporting
sugar to the United States as and when the embargo is lifted, and so on.
Such countries as South Korea, and indeed *Western* Europe in the first
postwar decades, gave priority to reconstruction, did have a strategy
(including export-led growth), did not leap directly into import liberalisation, postponed full convertibility of their currencies. *These* are lessons
with which to counter the IMF's laissez-faire ideologists. Frank's alternative is less than clear. Or have I misunderstood him?

NOTES

1.   André Gunder Frank, 'The Thirdworldization of Russia and Eastern Europe' in Jacques Hersh and Johannes Dragsbaek Schmidt (eds), *The Aftermanth of 'Real Existing Socialism' in Eastern Europe*. Volume 1. *Between Western Europe and Asia* (Macmillan, 1996), pp. 39–61.
2.   R.C.O. Matthews, 'Political and Economic Causes of the Economic Slowdown', *Scottish Journal of Political Economy*, **40**(2), May 1993, pp. 129–42.

Russia in March 1994: a brief report

Sergei Glaziev, chairman of the economic committee of the Duma, refers to 'a desperate situation'. Boris Yeltsin speaks of 'accelerated economic collapse'. 'We are on the edge of an economic crisis which can paralyse the whole country', to cite L. Paidiev, senior official of the Ministry of Economics. But first about the political crisis.

1. *Politics.* 'Yeltsin's days are numbered', assert a number of well-informed persons. They point to his health and to his mental state. 'He will not last till 1996.' There would have to be a presidential election, maybe even this year. Maybe this is so. Who then will run, and with what chances? A major article is devoted to this issue in the journal *Zavtra*, and though the journal is very much of the slavophil opposition, the article is regarded as serious. So – who? *Gaidar*? No, no chance of electoral success ('Strobe Talbott has already written him off'). *Shumeyko*? First deputy-premier: 'Centrist'. Ambitious. But no – no backing. *Shakhrai*? (Leader of the 'party of united consensus'). Did not do well in elections last time. Lacks popularity and financial support. *Luzhkov*? Mayor of Moscow. Supported (so it is alleged) by some big banks. Often accused of tolerating corruption. *Chernomyrdin*? The most probable successor. Has solid financial and media support. Possible alliance with Skokov and Luzhkov. But he lacks decisiveness, and others too call him a ditherer. May be a stop-gap president. *Zhirinovsky*? Could pick up a lot of votes if elections are held very soon, but his reputation as a 'cheap demagogue' is growing, lessening his chances. So – very unlikely (thank goodness! A.N.). *Rutskoi*? Could unite the opposition. Serious candidate. But 'while offering patriotic slogans, he lacks political, economic and organisational experience'. (Others speak of him as an honest muddler, a lightweight, war-hero.) *Zyuganov*? Communist party leader. 'Even in the west he is seen as an acceptable leader of a civilised party and not an extremist.' Lacks finance and media support, and business is hostile. But Zyuganov could be a valuable ally for the 'patriots'. *Skokov*? Former secretary of

the president's security committee, now chairman of the 'commodity producers of Russia', described as 'a clever and calculating technocrat'. Gaidar once called him his most dangerous rival. But not widely popular. He used to oversee the KGB and so has compromising materials on many of *his* rivals. Also mentioned as possible are *Baburin* (more likely to be in alliance with communists and agrarians), and *Yavlinsky* (good business connections, but described by an American journalist as 'another Gaidar, a little thinner and a bit more sensible, but another theoretician prone to macro-experiment'. He lacks popularity, especially in the provinces). Finally, the author reminds us not to write off *Zorkin*, the ex-chairman of the Constitutional Court, who has 'coalition potential'. But he lacks political support and has no known economic policy. So – who? My St. Petersburg colleagues would put their roubles on Chernomyrdin, though without much enthusiasm. And of course Yeltsin may bounce back.

All agree that the present situation is one of power-vacuum. As Shatalin put it, 'not a single state structure is capable of exercising authority . . . In this situation it is quite pointless to devise any reform programmes, which can only be doomed to failure.' With Yeltsin ineffective, the government is not trying, in discussions with the Duma, to come up with a 'save the nation programme'. Yeltsin's message to the parliament was lacking in substance. The proposals of the 'three academicians' (Abalkin, Petrakov, Shatalin) seem inoperable: price and income control, plus fixed exchange rates, are not practicable. However, as reported in previous weeks, the idea of a 'selective' strategy, financed via a new investment bank or newly-organised industrial–financial corporations (like Japanese *keiretsu*?), seem likely to be pursued. I saw a copy of a letter from Yeltsin to Fedorov and Gerashchenko seeking measures to ensure that credits be so targeted that they cannot be misused. There is now a major scandal concerning a large credit issued to GAZ (the 'Gorky' car plant): the directors used the money, supposedly granted for retooling, to buy millions of vouchers and then to buy the firm for themselves! Accusations of corruption, links with organised crime, rackets connected with privatisation, are frequently encountered. No one has yet noticed any change for the better in behaviour in the management of newly privatised enterprises. Stories abound of would-be entrepreneurs having to pay off officials, and pay protection money, and very heavy taxes, which helps to explain why there are still so few cafes, to cite an example of an obviously felt need still not filled.

2.   *Taxes* on legitimate business are a major source of complaint. This, plus rapid inflation, exhausts working capital speedily. Of particular nuisance value is the Russian version of the Polish *popiwek*, that is, tax on

excessive wages. In Russia until recently 'excess' meant any sum over four times the minimum wage. But the *average* wage is well *over* four times the minimum wage! So this further impoverishes the enterprise. (A large increase in minimum wages has been decided.)

3. *Strikes in the coalfields* are spreading. The government faces a dilemma. The Vorkuta coalfield (like the Donbas in the Ukraine) is a major loss-maker. It should be a leading candidate closure. But the political and social consequences are seen as disastrous. The Vorkuta miners are not only demanding payment of wage arrears, but also making a political challenge.

4. *Policies towards the 'near abroad'.* An intelligent appraisal by a leading Kazakh commentator ('The Monroe doctrine à la russe') appeared in *Nezavisimaya gazeta*, 13 March. Citing Kozyrev's claim that the CIS plus the Baltic republics are in Russia's sphere of vital interests, the author (U. Kasenov) points to the consequences: Russian troops will not be withdrawn, Russians will be 'protected'. The political journalist Migranyan (a member of Yeltsin's council) argued that Ukraine is artificial and weak and is due to disintegrate, and north Kazakhstan may drift towards Russia too. There is some similarity between Kozyrev's claims and the so-called Brezhnev doctrine. The restoration of the empire, it appears, 'is most effectively pursued by the economic, political and ethnic destabilisation of the former Soviet republics'. One line is to offer Russian inhabitants of other republics dual nationality. All this worries the author. N.B. The same Migranyan, in *Literaturnaya gazeta* (9 March, front page) expresses scepticism about the possibility of political consensus in Russia. Policy differences and rivalries run deep. If the situation continues to worsen, 'then it is possible that the army will have the last word, if, that is, some popular generals are prepared to take the responsibility. Then, with the participation of some civilians, a military–civilian administration could govern in an emergency. Of course, this would be an extreme solution.' Things could drift that way. *But* as against the neo-imperial view, several of my economist colleagues asserted that the last thing they need is for Russia to take over Ukraine with its economic crisis. Even Belorussia is seen as a burden. The Russian economist–politician E. Saburov has become vice premier of the Crimean Republic, without becoming a Ukrainian citizen. The Crimean parliament has proposed the right to dual nationality and making Russian an official language. Kiev can hardly accept this, so trouble is brewing.

5. *Gas: Ukraine has been siphoning gas* off the pipeline leading to Western Europe, as an alternative to paying for the gas with money it does not have. Agreements have been signed with Russia and Turkmenistan

about payment of the debt. Payment is partly to be in shares in Ukrainian enterprises. Radio has reported a similar deal with Estonia: gas debt has been 'paid' by granting Russia's Gazprom half of the shares of Estonian processing plant.

6.   *Science and R&D.* Financing of research and academic institutions was miserable in 1993, it is to be worse in 1994. Academicians are about to picket the ministry of finance.

7.   *The fall in production is no myth*, argue Baranov and others in *Izvestiya*'s business supplement (10–16 March). They answered the allegation by A. Illarionov that the decline is only moderate. He also claimed that real incomes rose by 10 per cent in 1993, an assertion completely at variance with output statistics (though these may be an appreciable amount of unrecorded imports). Industrial output in December 1993 was either 55 per cent or 50 per cent of the level of January 1990, and the year 1993 saw a fall either of 16.1 per cent or 18.6 per cent, depending on methodology. That is really shocking, assert Baranov et al. Furthermore, another article in the same issue is headed: 'Demand for Russian industrial products fell in February at record speed' (this from S. Tsukhlo of the 'Gaidar' institute). Also yet another article speaks of imminent danger of collapse of the motor vehicle industry, due to the big decline in purchases of lorries, especially by agriculture. They hope that large credits to agriculture would revive demand, but these same credits are a major burden on the budget. *Official figures*: in February 1994 industrial output was 24 per cent down on the previous year, machinery 48 per cent down!

8.   *'Valuta credits', large profits opportunities* are pointed to in the same *Izvestiya* supplement. Given the very high bank-rate in Russia (21 per cent), and the comparative stability of the rouble–dollar rate, Western bankers are said to be realising that converting dollar credits into roubles can 'more than compensate the risk of investing in Russia'. But . . .

9.   *Inflation prospects*, according to Makarevich, of the Russian Bankers' Association, look grim. Currency futures have risen to 3071 roubles per dollar (July), or to 3331 (for August). (I changed at 1707 on 10 March. A week later the rate was 1720. A.N.) Central bank reserves may prove insufficient, and new and tough-looking controls over currency deals may well not be effective, the more so as some regions and republics are demanding freedom to deal in foreign currency. (The present law banning the use of dollars in cash payment is widely ignored or circumvented.)

10.   *The 'reform' proposals of the 'academicians'* (that is, the report of the Academy of Sciences and the 'International Reform' foundation). My colleagues believe that, while the government would accept most of

the diagnosis, it will water down the practical proposals. But tighter control over foreign trade and payments is indeed likely, as is an attempt to target priority sectors and to target credits, probably via specialised investment banks. (But there is still no bankruptcy, no determination to close what must be closed, so the inflationary consequences of current policies remain, despite many brave words about holding down the budget deficit.)
11. *The 1995 financial picture*, plus recommendations for 1994, emerged in a long paper presented by the Ministry of Finance, prepared while Fedorov was still minister. A brief summary of its contents:

(a)   Fedorov denies that there was 'shock therapy', and blames 75 per cent of inflation on monetary causes, 25 per cent on cost-push. Elementary financial discipline was lacking in government and parliament, populist promises on expenditure were made. He again attacks the central bank for its credits to the 'red directors'.
(b)   Monetary aggregates in 1993 given, including estimates of accelerated velocity of circulation. Herewith a table, (in billion roubles):

| | | 1993 | | | |
	1992	1st qr	2nd qr	3rd qr	4th qr (est.)
Credits to government	2789	3927	5291	7942	11206
Credits to banks	2624	3888	5791	8655	11272
Credits to CIS (ex. cash)	907	1703	2022	2105	2533
Total Central Bank credits	*6320*	*9518*	*13104*	*18702*	*25011*
Money base	4284	6344	9304	14817	21426
Money aggregate MZ	7187	10932	16219	38138	35775
Velocity	5.0	7.4	6.9	8.2	–
Monthly inflation (retail)	25	24	21	23	17

(c)   *Incomes* (real) rose by 10 per cent, the dollar equivalent of wages trebled to $100 a month. Fedorov deplores big increases in income differentiation, claims to have proposed higher taxes on the rich. (Doubt that 10 per cent is real. A.N.)
(d)   *Savings* remained far too low, but many have 'invested' savings in commercial banks, some of dubious soundness.
(e)   GNP fell by 12 per cent, industrial production by 18 per cent.
(f)   The *budget* data for 1993 includes details of revenue and expenditures. Revenue reached 29.5 per cent of GNP (29.4 per cent in 1992). Towards the end of the year it is admitted that, by failing to

pay *its* debts, 'the state itself to some extent initiated the growth of unpaid debts', 13.8 trillion roubles of commitments were 'not financed'. Details are given of state-financed investments, which were below original intentions.

(g) *The financing of the budget deficit* (billion roubles). 'Expanded' government deficit 14816 (9.2 per cent of GNP), of which: Credit to federal budget (9860); Assets of local budgets (–1300); Assets of extra-budgeting funds (–700); Treasury bonds and so on held by banks (185); External source, loans from abroad (4384); Unpaid obligations on foreign debt (1566).

(h) *Internal debt* as at 1.1.94 equalled 35 349 bill. roubles, or 21.8 per cent of GNP.

(i) *Monetary and credit policies* described. Important decision: to end subsidised credits, taken on 23 September 1993. *Bank rate* (that is, interest charged on centralised credits issued by the central bank) rose as follows: 29 Dec. 1991 (20 per cent); 10 Apr. 1992 (50 per cent); 1 July (80 per cent); 30 Mar. 1993 (100 per cent); 2 June (110 per cent); 22 June (120 per cent); 29 June (140 per cent); 15 July (170 per cent); 23 Sept. (180 per cent); 15 Oct. (210 per cent).

(j) *Non-payment of debt*: causes analysed, with figures by sector, for example, in August 1993 77.9 per cent of debt was owed to the fuel sector, 18.7 per cent to ferrous metallurgy. Leading in the list of non-payers were the food industry (27.8 per cent), non-ferrous metals (24.1 per cent), light industry (16.1 per cent).

(k) *Credits issued to CIS republics*, figures given (bill. roubles): Ukraine (247.5), Belarus (65.7), Tadzhikistan (81.9), Uzbekistan (55.9).

(l) *Foreign currency dealings* (total turnover, $million): 14 711, of which sales by commercial banks accounted for 10 689, the central bank for 4022.

(m) *Reserves of the federation*, 1.1.94 (estimate): Central Bank foreign currency holdings ($4556.1 million); Gold held by Central Bank (128 tons); Ministry of Finance currency holdings ($197 million); Gold held by Ministry of Finance (177.8 tons); Debt of Ministry of Finance ($2306.6 million); *Net* international reserves ($4876.6 million, 6050 billion R.).

(n) *Capital flight*. Fantastic figures have been alleged, real ones are much lower. Estimates: $5–10 billion of export proceeds kept abroad, about $20 billion are held officially by Russian firms in dollar form. Estimated 'flight' in cash was $3.7 billion in 1993. Illegal flight hard to measure.

(o) *Foreign credits* during 1993 (including IMF, EBRD) and also other credits utilised, totalled $4.2 billion. *Total debt* (including of former

USSR) was $80 billion at the end of 1993. The budget for 1994 includes debt service of payments of $6.4 billion.

Fedorov forecast for 1994. Warning on 'Ukrainisation'. Even a moderate emission support for production, which could result in 11–12 per cent inflation at mid-year, plus a 9.5 per cent of GNP budget deficit, would lead to a $-rouble rate by the end of the year of 4500–5000 R. But he fears much worse, especially because of carryover of budgetary debt from 1993. Danger of hyperinflation could lead to imposition of controls on prices and incomes, and the reform process would (in the view of the authors) be reversed. Various scenarios are given numbers. (But these forecasts are 'ideological', because it is assumed that a softer credit policy must lead to a *greater* contraction of production, which is unlikely in the short term. A.N.)

12.   *Import tariffs* have been raised sharply on many consumers' goods (16 March). Effect will be sharp rise in prices in Moscow and St. Petersburg, where imported goods just about dominate, in food, drink and manufactures.

13.   *Defence expenditure*: Defence Minister Grachev announces publicly that the draft 1994 budget provides less than half (47 per cent, he said) of the defence financing. The army must number almost 2 million men. Many colleagues agree that the military do now have more say in policies.

14.   *Belorussian currency* crashes against the dollar by 50 per cent in a week following decision to spend much more to subsidise agriculture.

15.   *Finally*: moderate pessimism seems appropriate. Yeltsin's future, possible election of a successor, government divisions, a power vacuum, very strong pressures to support existing structures, coexist with some determination to cut subsidies and keep the budget deficit within bounds. A new strategy, and agreement with parliament is possible. The government itself may (should) decide to choose a strategy, based on some sort of consensus and an emergency coalition 'to save Russia'. But few of my Russian colleagues can see such a coalition emerging, though on 17 March parliament (led by Shumeyko) is considering declaring a 'state of economic emergency', whatever that would mean. Yeltsin meanwhile is taking two weeks holiday. (The rumour is that he can only work for half a month, but rumours could be being spread by his rivals). Very worrying is the continued fall in output, with no sign of a tunnel, let alone a light at the end of it.

There *must* emerge soon an emergency package. Muddling through is not enough. But *nothing* can be done unless the authorities are strong enough to exercise authority. A market needs a legal order, entrepreneurship cannot function amid corruption and protection rackets, and 'interventionism' requires honest and determined 'interventors'. My colleagues described the present government as largely composed of sectoral lobbyists, incapable of acting together. Perhaps the sight of catastrophe can concentrate their minds. I certainly hope so.

Letters to Morgan Stanley,
August 1991–April 1994

1991

The Coup, 19 August 1991, Glasgow

A few thoughts about the chief actors.

(1)   YANAEV. Party apparatchik without any visible qualities. His appointment by Gorbachev as his vice-president puzzled observers. Not the expected hard-line leader (I thought Lukyanov or even Gidaspov as more probable). Probably only the nominal head just because his post as the (legal) vice-president gives some semblance of legitimacy to what is plainly illegitimate.

(2)   PAVLOV. Premier. Apparently committed to a radical-sounding reform programme. Clearly suspicious of Western influences. The promise now to freeze prices and raise wages does not augur well for a sensible economic policy. But we must await a policy statement.

(3)   KRYUCHKOV. Head of KGB. Also clearly suspicious of Western influences. As KGB heads go, he was not known to be particularly harsh, but he may now have to go.

(4)   PUGO. Minister of the Interior, and so in charge of internal security troops. Known hard-liner. Why did Gorbachev appoint him?

(5)   YAZOV. Minister of Defence. Doubtless deeply concerned at the effect of loss of centre's powers (including revenue-raising powers) on the survival of the military–industrial complex.

I think there is a sixth member, a senior economic minister, but this needs confirmation [Baklanov].

The coup caught us all by surprise, at least in respect of its timing, but, since it also caught Gorbachev by surprise, we cannot blame ourselves too much. Note that this was *not* a procedural replay of the ouster of Khrushchev in 1964. That was by a vote of the central committee of the party. Only a few weeks ago Gorbachev had got support from the central committee. *The* key issue now is: will they get away with it? Will they be able to impose their rule? On Yeltsin and the Russian republic (will they now detain and/or muzzle Yeltsin), on the crowds in the streets? On strikers? In the dissident republics? And will the soldiers shoot if ordered? I would guess that the attitude to foreign countries of the new leadership will be one of wary isolationism, rather than outright cold-war-type hostility. But much may depend on whether they use force, with blood flowing, in (for example) the Baltic states and perhaps in the Ukraine too. We can only wait and see.

The Coup II, 20 August 1991, 8 a.m., Glasgow

The following are key passages from the Emergency Committee's first decree. The paragraph numbering is the decree's. The first few paragraphs relate to the exercise of power over all of the USSR, suspension of other authorities, bans on demonstrations and strikes, control over the mass media, and so on. Then:

9.　... 'Ensure the normal functioning of enterprises in all sectors of the national economy, strict fulfilment of measures to preserve and restore, for the stabilisation period, vertical and horizontal ties between subjects of economic management throughout the territory of the USSR, and the unfailing achievement of planned targets regarding production and supplies of materials and components. (The translation is theirs, A.N.) Establish and maintain austerity arrangements concerning the use of materials, equipment and foreign currency, and work out and implement specific measures to combat mismanagement and squandering . . . Wage a decisive struggle against the shadow economy . . . Create favourable conditions for all sorts of enterprise that obey the laws of the USSR.'

11.　'The cabinet of ministers is hereby instructed to take stock of all available sources of food and other essentials, and report to the people what the country has at its disposal, and to take under strict control their preservation and distribution. Any restrictions established to prevent transportation across the USSR territory of foodstuffs and consumer goods, as well as materials for their production, should be proclaimed null and void . . . Proposals should be submitted within a week for streamlining, freezing or reducing prices for certain categories of consumer goods and foodstuffs, first of all for children, everyday services and public catering, as well as raising wages, pensions and compensation sums to different categories of citizens. Measures should be worked out to streamline (? A.N.) the pay of leaders at all levels of state, public, cooperative (!, A.N.) and other establishments . . .'

12.　'Taking into account the critical situation in harvesting and the threat of famine, extraordinary measures should be taken to organise the procurement, storage and processing of farm produce . . . , providing machinery, spare parts, fuel . . .'

13.   'Plots of land of up to 0.15 hectare for fruit and vegetable-growing be provided for any city dweller if he so wishes.'

14.   'The cabinet of ministers should complete within two weeks the drawing up of plans for emergency measures to pull the country's fuel and power complex out of the crisis and prepare for winter.'

Plainly these are intended to be emergency measures. It does not prove that Pavlov has abandoned his moderate marketisation and limited privatisation plans. The sixth member of the emergency committee is BAKLANOV, a party official closely connected with the military–industrial complex. One report also mentions STARODUBTSEV, leader of the farm management lobby, known to be cool towards private farming. Will they get away with it? Will the army shoot if ordered? How many soldiers will back Yeltsin? What will the republics do? A key player is Kravchuk, Ukrainian leader in Kiev, a party man now nationalist. Civil war cannot be ruled out. And *unless* they shoot, the emergency committee may not be obeyed. We can only watch events. It is all to play for.

The Coup III, 21 August 1991, 9 a.m., Glasgow

It looks as if the conspirators have failed. The crowds in the streets, Yeltsin, the negative response of many republican and provincial officials, divisions of opinion and loyalty in the army and the KGB, lacklustre and mediocre leadership (who would follow Yanayev and his like to the barricades?), would all be part explanations for the failure. Also there was lack of ruthlessness: surely the junta could only hope to establish their authority throughout the Union by being prepared to kill a lot of people. The contrast with the overthrow of Khrushchev is not only because the experience of five years *glasnost'* has emboldened the people and given them voice. The coup was technically illegitimate even within the party. Khrushchev was ousted by a large majority of its central committee, at a time when the party dominated society. Gorbachev was not being removed by or through the party. He was being replaced by the vice-premier, not by the deputy general secretary. So to call the conspirators hard-line *communists* is a trifle misleading. Their appeals used no communist slogans anyhow. Hard-liners they certainly are. If they have failed, I do not think that the Western response played a major or decisive role. The putchists (including Pavlov) made no secret of their dislike of dependence on Western aid or IMF-imposed policies. They were the kind of people who would say that Russia can and should solve its own problems and proceed by some peculiarly Russian road without Western interference. But, as noted previously, some of the political and military hard-liners were not opposed to marketisation – so long as the military–industrial complex was safeguarded. The coup was to some extent provoked by the impact of the proposed new Union treaty on the existence and financing of the military–industrial sector. In my report on my trip to the Ukraine last June, I cited the economist and deputy Chernyak, saying (apropos Gorbachev's journey to London) that, contrary to the view of many of his nationalist colleagues, it is desirable to support Gorbachev, because, for the time being, he is an obstacle to a takeover by military and hard-liners. The same point was made, in correspondence, by Sergo Mikoyan, who criticised the radicals who have been attacking Gorbachev for not understanding this. We now hear that the radicals are being self-critical about this.

What now? If the coup will indeed have failed (and I may be wrong about this, of course), the whole political balance will have changed, and for the better. Out will go the hard-liners who planned and supported the coup. Republican independence movements will be strengthened. Gorbachev, if he survives as president, will have to collaborate closely with Yeltsin, and conservative resistance to the marketisation process will be much weakened. But what will be left of the Soviet Union? In Kiev, Kravchuk has kept a low profile, but further swift moves towards Ukrainian real sovereignty are very likely. Balts too. Meanwhile all the economic problems which have been accumulating – unbalanced budgets, conflicts of laws, a feeble rouble, hyperinflation, falling output, shortages, internal trade barriers, and so on – remain to be tackled. It may need a state of emergency to tackle them, but under more enlightened auspices.

The Coup Fails – What next?, 23 August 1991, Glasgow

A few first impressions.
1. In my first note, I had expressed surprise that the coup had been led by the colourless Yanaev, and not the more likely Lukyanov. It is now being said by Yeltsin and his supporters that it was indeed Lukyanov (chairman of the Supreme Soviet of the USSR) who 'masterminded' it.
2. Yeltsin is evidently in an extremely strong position to impose what-ever conditions he wants. If the draft Union treaty, that left very little authority to the centre, is further revised, this would leave Gorbachev with just vague coordinatory and ceremonial duties. Then Russia and all the other republics that would remain 'in' become genuinely sovereign. And of course the six that want out are on the point of leaving and will be allowed to do so.

3. Most important is what has happened to the communist party. Although, as I had noted, it was not in any formal manner involved in the coup (the politburo and the central committee did not meet, the plotters did not act in the name of the party, indeed never mentioned it), the public-in-the-street saw it – not without some reason – as a hard-line *communist* plot. The party has therefore been further discredited, and its functionaries at all levels faced with very awkward problems, to say the least. Yet in many parts of the country the party's appratchiki were still a force to be reckoned with, as obstacles to implementing reform measures, or (as in Leningrad, for instance) as rivals to progressive elected officials.

4. But, but, but, who is the highest party functionary of all? The general secretary, none other than Mikhail Gorbachev himself. On Channel 4 TV, Peter Frank rightly pointed out that, having in his nationally televised press conference aligned himself with the party, albeit a purged and reformed party, Gorbachev puts himself on a collision course with Yeltsin and millions of those who blame the party both for the coup and for the deplorable state into which the country has fallen. The pulling down of Dzerzhinsky's statue in Lubyanka square is bound to be followed by similar actions in respect of Lenin and other symbols of the Bolshevik revolution. Some provincial party secretaries may be pulled down too, literally so. One can see how difficult it was for Gorbachev to announce there and then that he is following Yeltsin in resigning from the party of which he is the nominal leader. But then he is associated with a discredited organisation, which even now lost control of its own political organ, *Pravda*. Under these conditions, how long can he last? Just imagine that he wants to hold an annual parade on Red Square on 7 November (anniversary of the 'October' revolution), and Yeltsin forbids it, saying that Red Square is in 'Russia'!

The entire political structure will now quickly evolve. Much will depend on whether the key republics – Russia, Ukraine, Belorussia, Kazakhstan – will agree on a joint course of action. The centre is in no position to enforce anything.

Addendum

The text of the Union treaty as it stood was in many respects ambiguous. Thus it proclaimed the Union to be a 'democratic federal sovereign state', but also that 'each republic is a sovereign state', with 'the right to decide independently all questions of its development', having 'the fullest political power to determine their own national and administrative structures'. The power of the Union is limited to such functions as are 'voluntarily granted it by the republics'. They (the republics) are granted 'the right to establish diplomatic, consular and other links with foreign states, to exchange diplomatic representatives, to enter into international agreements'. As one Soviet commentator put it, 'the draft in practice ignores the sovereignty of the Union . . . What we would have is something between a confederation and a treaty between states.' The centre would have vaguely defined functions in respect of foreign policy, customs and trade policy, making general rules about contracts and social policy, in the hope presumably that the republics which will sign the treaty will make up a free trade area. There was to be a joint defence policy and a joint military–industrial complex. But financed how? In the first draft of the treaty, the Union would have only such funds as the republics would choose to grant it. The republics would in practice have full powers over natural resources, their use, and presumably also their prices. They would presumably have control over foreign currency earnings, and would somehow divide among themselves the contributions to servicing past debts. The chairman of the State Bank, Gerashchenko, pointed out that there would be insufficient authority for the centre to carry through the needed fiscal and monetary policy, or limit credits from the now very numerous banks. If this draft is to be revised to give even more powers to the republics, then indeed it is the end of the Union as an effective authority – unless exercised in the form of joint interrepublican committees, like committees of EEC. And western business must now pay much more attention to the republican authorities.

The End of the Soviet Union?, 26 August 1991, 7.30 a.m., Glasgow

Gorbachev is about to address the all-union Supreme Soviet. But how many will show up to hear him? What are the functions and powers of this 'Supreme' Soviet, indeed of the all-union government? Is Gorbachev losing out to Yeltsin in a personal power struggle, or is he becoming irrelevant because he is president of a now non-existent state, the Soviet Union? Is Yeltsin acting to transfer power to Russia, or is he aiming to replace Gorbachev on what is left of an all-union stage? What *is* left of the all-union stage when the Ukraine and even Belorussia declare their independence? If all this is transitional, then transitional to what?

Let us look at the possible scenarios. Suppose Russia under Yeltsin calls together a crisis meeting of representatives of the sovereign republics, to discuss a joint programme to avert economic catastrophe, how many would actively participate, and on what terms? Or would the independent republics negotiate bilateral trade agreements with each other? Would some sort of loose alliance or confederation emerge with the Ukraine and Belorussia plus the Central Asians? There would be no centre capable of imposing financial discipline, there would be no common currency, no central bank. And where does the military–industrial complex fit into all this? Would there be a multitude of internal customs barriers? What happens to any trade or other agreements negoti-ated with what was the Soviet Union? And what of its 60 billion dollar debt? The mind boggles. Yeltsin still needs to impose order in Russia itself. The old structures of power depended greatly on communist party functionaries. While in some republics there are viable nationalist party organisations, in Russia the alternative parties are weak and fragmented. There is no Solidarnosc or Forum ready to provide an alternative, as in Poland and Czecho-Slovakia. In the Ukraine too there are twelve small parties, though the national *Rukh* could act as a temporary non-communist rallying centre. In Russia a new structure of authority has yet to be created. Yeltsin did speak of appointing a species of plenipotentiary (neo-commissars?) to represent the centre in Russia's many national-minority autonomous republics, provinces, proud cities like what now must be called St. Petersburg. But how many will obey him, once the euphoria is over and the troubles of daily life and economic breakdown accumulate? He may need authoritarian methods. But where is the mech-anism of implementation, the needed constitutional legal structure? He has formidable problems in his own republic, to secure the political basis for implementing the much-needed programme of marketisation. It is good to see Yavlinsky as vice-premier, but of what? If of the USSR, then he is vice-president with no power to do anything (except possibly to draft a proposal which could be discussed with the Ukraine, Belorussia and Kazakhstan). If of the Russian republic, he will doubtless remember that he held the post before, and when he resigned nearly a year ago he publicly blamed his colleagues (Yeltsin too) for being irresponsible pop-ulists with no sense of financial discipline. But Yeltsin does have good advisers (Yavlinsky included), and he is capable of learning.

Where in this confused and changing situation can one fit Western aid and Western investment? Aid to whom? Will there be a centre through which it could be channelled? Should we press for closer inter-republican cooperation (for example, by channelling aid through a coordinating centre in Moscow), or will we find ourselves dealing with what amount to separate states? We are clearly about to recognise the three Baltic republics. Are we then also to recognise the Ukraine, Belorussia, Georgia, etc.? Whatever now happens, Western business must surely establish links with the potentially viable republics. A journey to Kiev becomes particularly urgent. And between the wars Britain was a major trading partner of the Baltic republics (though this was before the Common Agricultural Policy!).

Much still depends on how Yeltsin will play his very strong hand. I fear more drama and not a few disorders before any sort of clear pattern emerges. And is it certain that the provincial party structures will all meekly fade away? The economic mess will provide ample ground for exploiting grievances while republics' independence may lead in the short run to accelerated decline through supply disruptions – unless they can get their act together.

The End of the Soviet Union II, 26 August 1991, 8 p.m., Glasgow

I saw a large part of the Supreme Soviet session on satellite TV. Gorbachev spoke quietly, like a man not long for political life. He said all the right things: marketisation to be pressed ahead with, land should be made available to the cultivators, a market infrastructure must be brought into being, private enterprise encouraged, there should be sound money, the rouble should become convertible, the republics should have full rights within a new Union treaty (less those that want out), the aim being 'a united economic area'. The full Congress of Soviets is to meet in early September, with elections to follow. But it all seemed to matter little, since he (and the all-union level) lacks power to implement. When he sat down there was silence, no applause. He was followed by Khazbulatov, one of Yeltsin's deputies. He spoke with eloquence and *was* applauded. He emphasised the vital importance of private property. The scheme for Russia is not to transfer authority from all-union ministries to Russian-republic ministries, but to turn enterprises and kombinats speedily into independent *firms*, which can and should attract foreign investment. Priority must be given to agricultural reform, 'previously blocked by Starodubtsev and the so-called peasant union, which represented no peasants' (true, it was the collective and state farm managers' lobby, A.N.). Peasants must be free to leave state and collective farms with land, if they so wish, and be provided with credits, equipment, etc. He urged immediate and substantial defence cuts, by as many as 50 billion roubles, achieved by abandoning on-going programmes, such as building aircraft carriers. The KGB must be drastically cut too, its functions totally redefined. The budget must be balanced. He spoke of the need to be quite tough with those autonomous republics and others within the Russian federal republic that refuse to carry out the radical new policies. He also spoke of signing a redrafted Union treaty. But who else will? While neither he nor the other speakers I heard referred to the Ukraine and Belorussia, several supported the Baltic republics' claim to independence. Another speaker did praise Gorbachev for pushing ahead, against obstacles, to achieve democratisation, his tone implying that we should be grateful for past services (as indeed we should, A.N.) and not that he is man of the moment. It was also proposed from the floor that Yakovlev be made vice-president and Shevarnadze foreign minister, but this was not acted on.

There was a certain air of unreality about the whole proceeding. What power had this assembly to decide anything? Would they ever meet again in the present not-very-democratically-elected composition? Is there ever going to be a new constitution of the Union, where there could well be no Union anyhow . . . The division of responsibilities between the Russian republic and all-Union officials (even when the latter have in effect been nominated by Yeltsin) remains unclear. And the new minister of defence, Shaposhnikov, will command over what area? Is the Ukraine really to have its own army? Who is to control all these thousands of nuclear warheads? I will be in Stockholm from 1 September to 25 September. There is a meeting due there with Shatalin and Petrakov. They may well clarify the many obscure elements in a mighty complex situation.

Can Economic Chaos be Avoided?, 31 August 1991, Glasgow

Clearly, the USSR as a political structure is ceasing to exist. But economic–technical interdependence of the republics is a fact. Few factories and farms can continue to produce unless they can draw materials, fuel, components, and so on, from producers located in other republics. And in many cases the users of these products are also in other republics. So declarations of *economic* independence can bring about a precipitous decline in output of most goods, as well as a food crisis in some areas. Gorbachev spoke of a 'single economic area' again a day or two ago. No doubt, such men as Yavlinsky and other sensible economists agree. But he, and they, can achieve nothing if they act within a Union structure that no longer has political meaning. Nor can the all-union 'Supreme' Soviet. Yesterday two of their number bitterly complained that their apartments had been searched by (Russian-republic) detectives, despite their immunity as deputies, and no one could do a thing about it. Yeltsin is stepping into the central power vacuum, initiating bilateral negotiations with the Ukraine, Kazakhstan, the Balts, with the apparent aim of easing transition and achieving a minimum of economic collaboration. Without

it, we would see the continuation of beggar-my-neighbour policies, with a
sharp increase in the number of beggars in all the republics, each asking
the West for alms. The decline of production would be unnecessarily
large, as would be the aid required. It is plainly in the interests of the
'seven' to channel help in such a way as to encourage inter-republican
collaboration, through some newly-devised joint emergency mechanism,
until a real market with real money can be brought into existence.

But the auguries are not good. Nationalism and mutual suspicions are
strong. When Rutskoi and Sobchak, representing Yeltsin's Russian government, arrived in Kiev, a large crowd booed them and chanted:
UKRAINA BEZ MOSKVY! (Ukraine without Moscow!). They may
recall that in 1920 the Ukraine was supposed to be a separate (if by then
soviet) republic, but in next to no time it was fully subjected to Moscow.
So when Ukrainian leader Kravchuk signed the agreement with
Moscow's representatives, he had to watch his back, especially as his own
political past was, from the Ukrainian-nationalist viewpoint, somewhat
dubious. I recall that when I was in Kiev in June, several of my Ukrainian
colleagues thought that many Russian liberal democrats would be unwilling to accept a fully independent Ukraine. Nor is this paranoia, since
millions of Russians regarded Kiev as 'the mother of Russian cities', the
border cuts the Donets coal basin into two, with most miners on the
Ukrainian side ethnic Russians. Yeltsin doubtless shares such sentiments;
hence his tactless remark about revising borders. These mutual suspicions
are obstacles to a desperately needed economic collaboration, especially
given the dire situation that faces them all, when the slogan 'chacun pour
soi' has evident short-term attractions. But I shudder at the consequences.

3 September 1991, Stockholm

. . . ten republics have reported to having signed up for coordinating the
way out of the crisis. But it is far too soon to judge if they have devised a
structure that can function, with power to implement unpleasant decisions. Indeed, I for one doubt if Yeltsin has yet devised such a mechanism
for his own republic. My pessimism is shared by Grigori Khanin, who is
here in Stockholm. But he and I hope that we will be proved wrong.
Meanwhile it does seem important that Western aid be significant AND
that it should be channelled in such a way as to encourage closer inter-
republican collaboration. Separate beggar-my-neighbour policies will
have the effect of hastening the slide to perdition and increase the numbers of beggars.

Forecast: Storm and Gloom, 6 September 1991, Stockholm

1. Energy Crisis. Output of oil, coal, generation of electricity, are all declining. Few power stations being built, the nuclear generation programme largely abandoned. Older pipelines, including for district heating, urgently need repair (due to corrosion, and so on). Power cuts already beginning. All republics vulnerable. Strikes can make things even worse. Fear of winter cold.
2. Food Crisis. Harvest well below last year. Livestock being slaughtered for lack of fodder. Some areas very short of skilled and sober labour. Some republics and regions blocking movement of food. Privatisation cannot help in the short run. Local food shortages highly probable. Again: fear of winter and of disorders.
3. Monetary and Fiscal Crisis. Hyperinflation imminent. Money incomes rising 2.5 times. Shortfall in revenues and excessive union and republican expenditures threaten a combined budget deficit of 300 to 330 billion roubles, or upwards of 20 per cent of GNP. The currency and banking systems are collapsing.
4. Trade and Payment Crisis. The debt burden is rapidly increasing, while hard-currency receipts are steeply falling, with rapid decline in oil and timber exports in 1991. Debts are being incurred to finance current purchases, very little for investment. Despite drastic cuts in imports (by some 45 per cent this year), reserves are being rapidly exhausted. Control over payments and credit by the centre is also disintegrating. The free rate for the dollar has more than doubled since December 1990.
5. Investment Crisis. Investment has been heavily cut, below replacement level in some key sectors. Conversion of the military sector is slow, impeded by the general breakdown. Neither market forces nor the plan function in this or other areas.

As G. Khanin put it in the journal *Kommunist* (No. 12, 1991), any one of the above crises would give great cause for concern. But all five together equal catastrophe. All this calls for drastic remedial action. The new political agreement signed by representatives of ten republics, with still another structure for decision making and implementation, may seem a hopeful sign. But there are many suspicions (thus Yeltsin's Russia has, for some republics, 'changed from being an ally in the struggle with the centre into the potential successor to the Empire', to cite *Komsomolskaya pravda* of 3 September). In any case this is only a new structure, not an agreed programme of action. There is nothing that can compel any republic to take necessarily unpopular remedial action. Disaster scenarios beckon. 'Our country is like a grenade with its pin extracted', concluded the above-cited article in *Komsomolskaya pravda* (a liberal daily, despite its title). Killings are likely in Georgia, between Azerbaijan and Armenia, in Moldova, many of the 15 million Russians in Central Asia could have to flee . . . Maybe the situation is slipping out of anyone's control. I certainly hope all this gloom and doom will prove to be alarmist pessimism. Some republics (for example the Balts) may do better.

A Russian Shock Therapy?, 12 September 1991, Stockholm

The situation is evolving fast. The dissolution of the Union proceeds apace. This affects the position not only of the president Gorbachev, but also of those economists and technocrats who have been trying to preserve any sort of coordinating power even for inter-republican institutions. Shatalin and Volsky look like being sidelined. As recently as 4 September *Izvestiya* published a 'draft convention on an economic community'. On the same day in a speech in the Supreme Soviet of the USSR Boris Yeltsin urged 'the preservation of a united economic area', the union as a 'free commonwealth of sovereign states'. Just a week later one has the impression of a complete break-up into separate republics with separate and uncoordinated reform strategies, separate currencies, and even separate armies (there is now being formed a Ukrainian army, though its commander, General K. Morozov, is an ethnic Russian). The Russian republic looks like trying to go it alone, adopting its own version of Polish shock therapy, while making trade agreements with other republics and also foreign countries (Balcerowicz was recently in Moscow to sign a Polish–Russian trade agreement). The radicals around Yeltsin follow the advice of Jeffrey Sachs and Anders Aslund, who favour instant immersion in the cold water of freed prices and drastic expenditure cuts to balance the budget, plus strict control over wages and a speed-up in privatisation. The Yavlinsky programme is regarded as too slow and cautious. New with influence include Burbulis, Shakhrai, Skokov and Saburov, names new to me, plus an older man I know well, Viktor Volkonsky. But all this may change. There are many unanswered questions about shock therapy even in Poland, let alone Russia.

I tried to find answers in discussions with Shatalin and Petrakov who were visiting Stockholm. They agreed that the situation is dire, tax collection has broken down, including in most of the republics (notably in Russia and Ukraine). There is little immediate hope for close inter-republican coordination. Some have civilised governments and coherent policies (for example the Balts), but attempts by Uzbeks, Turkmens, and so on, to go it alone can mean instant catastrophe, while the 'fascist' (sic) leadership in Georgia is on a collision course. Armenia is in urgent need of help, but the centre is in no position to help anyone, as it is ceasing to exist. 'Moscow' now is the Russian republic. It too has an immense budget deficit. It also has a radical programme of stabilisation, marketisation and privatisation. Shatalin and Petrakov agree that difficulties are immense. Yeltsin and his government have no clear constitutional authority. Its orders may not be implemented. While drastic cuts in expenditure are discussed, with some extra revenue from sales of state assets, the cost of the social safety net, and the declared intention of having low taxes on enterprises, leaves many doubts around the budget, and so concerning restoring health to the rouble. Shatalin, however, is of the opinion that Russia, going it alone, may be able in a short while to create an authoritarian political structure and could then make a reality of a stabilisation programme. All is not necessarily lost, he insists, though the situation is critical. What will happen in Ukraine is a political–economic question mark too, which fully justifies a visit to Kiev. Petrakov urges Western aid for Russia concentrating on: currency stabilisation, credits to private enterprise (including via multinationals), conversion of defence plants, the energy sector and ecology. Aid, he says, should be for specific purposes. Shatalin and Petrakov seemed to have as little notion as to what will happen next as the rest of us, judging from the way they answered questions. Summarising my general impressions:

1. Although economic officials in all the republics are well aware of the need for coordinated efforts, this is in fact unlikely to happen. While no doubt they will make some trade agreements with each other, one can envisage endless arguments about prices, barter terms of trade (literally barter), past debts, who exploited whom, and so on. Beggar-my-neighbour policies might prevail. Each will try to sell for hard currency if they can. The damage all this will do will vary in different republics and regions. The centre is vanishing, or turning into Yeltsin's Russia.

2. The huge budget deficit is destroying the rouble, and I see no hope of joint action to save it. Separate currencies will appear. This may well soon include a new *Russian* monetary unit (the *chervonets*?), at some unknown conversion rate with respect of the paper roubles. But the new currency too would depreciate unless the budget deficit is greatly reduced. I have yet to hear of a convincing plan to do this. Or of a way to control the wage explosion (unless unemployment becomes massive, as it might).

3. Privatisation (still proceeding quite slowly) will be accompanied by controversy about alleged management and 'nomenklatura' buy-outs

at very low prices – but what is the right valuation amid all the uncertainties? With multiple exchange rates, many currencies, shortages, bottlenecks, half-formed internal customs barriers, shady dealers will make fortunes.
4. All the republics will be trying to attract foreign capital and foreign loans, competing with each other to offer favourable terms.
5. Russia is likely to make a deal with Japan, which will include the southern Kurile islands.
6. Western advice and training will be of particularly great value in such areas as commercial banking, marketing, market research accountancy, corporate and personal taxation, information flows, and also on the needed legal structure and how to prevent large scale fraud.

I am not yet convinced that Yeltsin will be in effective control of Russia, or Kravchuk of the Ukraine. Each would have to impose unpopular stabilisation policies, and may shift away from trying. *Note*: the latest news from Georgia are most disturbing. The local boss seems to have lost his head, and full scale riots are probable.

Is an Economic Union After All Possible?, 20 September 1991, Stockholm

Today there arrived a copy of *Izvestiya* (the best daily newspaper these days) of 17 September, carrying the headline, 'An Economic Union is Needed and Possible'. And indeed a meeting of the State Council, with Gorbachev in the chair, with the heads of most republics there (including Yeltsin and Kravchuk) adopted 'in principle' Yavlinsky's scheme. This would provide for free movement of goods and services, the encouragement of private enterprise, a joint monetary, fiscal and banking policy, balanced budgets, a joint price policy leading to free prices, and coordination of foreign trade and payments policies. However, as *Izvestiya* itself pointed out, there have been other plans adopted 'in principle' which remained on paper, and Yavlinsky himself expressed serious doubts in an interview with the *Herald Tribune*. Good resolutions may or may not emerge from the State Council (the last remaining institutional shred of the former Union) but, alas, real life will go on as before, only more so.

Two examples from this week's Soviet press. Vologda province announces a bilateral deal with Krasnodar province, swapping metal for grain. This, they claim, will assure bread supplies for citizens of Vologda. But note that both these provinces are in the Russian republic, and this conflicts with the notion of freedom of trade even within that republic.

(It is not a market-type deal, it is inter-local-bureaucrat barter!) The second example relates to the Ukraine. State grain purchases are way below plan and urban needs, and pressure is being exercised on farms and peasants to sell more. Despite which they expect to be at least 3 million tons short of the amount required to cover basic needs, and are contemplating importing this amount. But the Ukrainian government has hardly any hard currency, whereas enterprises in the Ukraine have considerable holdings. President Kravchuk is trying to 'borrow' from them the equivalent of $500 million, 'to avoid the disgrace of the former food-supplier of the Union having to ration bread'. Meanwhile there is a ban on exports to other republics of food and scarce goods of other kinds. Wages in the Ukraine will be paid in conjunction with new coupons 'now being printed in Paris, pending the introduction of a national currency'. *Izvestiya* comments: 'It is easy to see that all these measures render much more difficult direct links between Ukrainian firms and those of other republics of the former Soviet Union.' And the grain so far procured will last only until Christmas, and what then? And this in the Ukraine, potential grain exporter . . . No wonder Yavlinsky has pessimistic thoughts about the fate of his own plan. I (and he) would be happy to be wrong.

23 September 1991, Stockholm

The attached arrived by fax here. It relates to one of several arbitrary actions by Moscow's mayor Gavril Popov. (He has also tried to control retail prices, and seized two other public buildings). If he can get away with such actions in Moscow, under the eyes of Yeltsin's republican authorities, imagine what could happen in the remoter areas! Is anyone in charge? Yavlinsky is still putting forward plans for an economic union of sovereign states. But Khazbulatov, one of Yeltsin's deputies, in an interview in Tokyo, 'offered' him to the Japanese: 'he keeps sticking his nose in other people's business, reproducing Japanese and American ideas as his own. Enough of him!' (Khazbulatov may have been drunk?) Aslund has just returned from Moscow feeling very pessimistic. No one is getting their act together.

An Economic Union of Sovereign States?, 2 October 1991, Glasgow

Once again we hear hopeful sounds: at their meeting, this time in Alma Ata, representatives of 12 republics sign a declaration about economic collaboration. This seems to be a version of the plan drafted by Yavlinsky. I have a copy of the version he submitted on 5 September, but according to *Izvestiya* (30 September) he was compelled to water it down. It is necessary to await details of the agreed text before venturing any comment, except to repeat earlier expressed scepticism. Vague declarations of good intent which no one has the power or the will to implement cannot prevent catastrophe. The three Baltic republics have jointly decreed a customs union (and have refrained from signing the above declaration). But . . .

Most newspapers in the Ukraine have ceased publication, because there is no paper. Paper will not be supplied by Russia unless and until it can be bartered for Ukrainian food (*Izvestiya*, 28 September). Kuzbas (Siberian) coal is being bartered for Urals consumer goods. Armenian industry is being halted by power shortage. 'Tatarneft' (the Tartar oil enterprise) has signed a 600 million dollar deal with PANOCO, which might commit much of the oil to foreign markets, while 'the Russian government is left out' (yet the Tartars are supposed to be in the Russian federation; so is the Kuzbas and the Urals). No doubt because it wishes to assert control, the Russian government has issued a decree imposing export and import licensing of a huge list of goods (the decree and the list is published in *Ekonomika i zhizn'*, No. 40). But, firstly, this conflicts with the objective of free movement of goods to and from other republics, and, secondly, will such decrees be obeyed? Meanwhile the budget deficit already exceeds 200 billion roubles, as was reported to the (all-union) committee for operational control of the economy (headed by an unhappy Silayev, with Volsky as his deputy). They agree that the situation is dire, but have no power to remedy it, as there is in effect no Union. There is little hope that the Alma Ata agreement will bring the much-needed financial stabilisation nearer. Meanwhile *Izvestiya* (30 September) reports Yavlinsky as saying that the gold reserve is now only 240 tons. 500 tons were sold in Ryzhkov's time, batches of 70 to 80 tons under Pavlov's premiership. 'The country is bankrupt.'

As already stressed on previous occasions, it is not only that Gorbachev and the remnants of the former Union have no authority, but the situation is anything but clear in Russia itself. *Kommersant* (16 September) accuses Yeltsin of arbitrariness, riding roughshod over his Supreme Soviet (as Popov, mayor of Moscow, does with the Moscow Soviet). The formal power structures of the Russian republic are confused and probably unconstitutional as well. Effective control is lacking. I still see no grounds for optimism.

Possible Scenarios, 11 October 1991, Glasgow

Let us begin with the *Russian Federation*. (1) Disorder, strikes, steep decline in output. Yeltsin declares state of emergency and presidential rule, dissolves elected soviets. He might under martial law try to impose Polish-style shock therapy en route to the market. Evident dangers of mass unemployment and yet more disorders. (2) Yeltsin is replaced by, or enters into alliance with, Russian nationalists and neo-slavophils. Solzhenitsyn returns. Even a constitutional monarchy is not totally out of the question (with the capital in St. Petersburg?). The radical 'marketeer' reformers would then be sidelined. The slavophils tend to be suspicious of Western mercantile ideology. There may be territorial conflicts with other republics. (3) Russia too disintegrates. A period of anarchy is followed by a strongman dictator, presumably right-wing nationalist. (4) (Unlikely but not impossible.) Muddling through, keeping decline in GNP to 20 per cent, with slow and painful recovery in 1992–93, with a new currency. In all four scenarios foreign creditors will see little of their money.

Now to the *Ukraine*. If (repeat *if*) Kravchuk and the nationalist *Rukh* can keep extreme nationalism quiet and not antagonise the large Russian minority (for example, in Kharkov, Odessa and the Donets coal basin), there could be greater political order than is likely in Russia. But there is heavy dependence on Russia for energy and timber, and economic reform has been moving very slowly, especially in agriculture. There are virtually no reserves to back the proposed new national currency. There are bound to be severe difficulties because of the close ties with the Russian economy, but it should be possible to avoid chaos and breakdown.

It is hard to conceive of an independent Belorussia. Not impossible is an economic alliance with the Ukraine, the Balts, even Poland and Hungary, if the latter are coldshouldered by the EEC. Anything could happen in Central Asia, including strife between Uzbeks, Kirgiz and Tadzhiks, plus Islamic fundamentalism. It may be hard for Kazakhs to run a country where they are a minority. Georgia is close to civil war now. Armenia, cut off by a hostile Azerbaijan, faces instant economic disaster. But each such republic needs separate assessment.

Is there light at the end of the tunnel? Right now I see no tunnel (23 October). The Ukraine's refusal to sign or collaborate bears out the pessimistic mood.

The Yeltsin Programme, 30 October 1991, Glasgow

I now have the text of Yeltsin's speech. Eloquent, very radical indeed. I hear that he has been taking advice from E. Gaidar, which is good news:

Gaidar is a particularly talented political economist. The key features of the plan are: (1) Russia goes it alone, unless other republics wish to join in a joint programme. Those that do can expect to be charged at world prices. (2) Prices (or nearly all prices) to be fully decontrolled, already in 1991. (3) Wages too will be decontrolled, except that tough financial discipline will be imposed on enterprises (they will have to find the money). (4) The budget must be balanced, or close to balanced, in 1992. There will be new taxes, and (unspecified) cuts in expenditure. (5) 'Tough mechanisms against uncontrolled issue of money and credits', 'a real reserve banking system with hard money'. Unless the other republics renounce intention to have their own currencies, the Russian state bank will issue Russian currency. (6) There is to be a Russian republic customs service. (7) Privatisation of small and medium-scale enterprises is to proceed speedily. About 10 000 such enterprises could be sold in the next three months, 'raising about 100 billion roubles in revenue'. (8) Successful state and collective farms should continue, the unsuccessful broken up and sold off. Help for farmers includes import of small-scale machinery, credits, etc. (9) De-monopolisation measures. (10) Social guarantees, in the main targeted to particularly vulnerable groups (measures include soup kitchens, special supply arrangements, and so on). Freeing prices will be accompanied by large pay increases to teachers and doctors, also pensions, etc. (11) 'Competitive sale of import and export licences for roubles.' Measures to encourage foreign investment (to be spelled out). (12) Remaining all-union institutions are to shrink, as Russia will no longer finance most of them. At first all this will lead to lower living standards, but there is no other way and Yeltsin hopes that by the second half of 1992 some positive results will become visible. Meanwhile he will become his own prime minister and will acquire power to rule by decree.

Some preliminary comments: (1) Bold and resolute emergency programme, not really different from my scenario 1 for the Russian Federation as outlined in my fax dated 11 October. (2) Has Yeltsin and his government power (real power) to implement it? (3) Are the measures outlined in his speech sufficient to balance the extremely unbalanced budget? Yes, subsidies will be cut, military expenditure too, and there will be revenue from privatisation. But the gap is said to be around 120 billion roubles at least. Will they devise an effective tax collection mechanism? Can the rouble be turned into real money? (4) Will it be politically possible to impose financial discipline, and close down bankrupt enterprises, without disastrous social consequences? (5) Can a hyperinflationary wage–price spiral be avoided? (6) Will people stand it? Will there be a wave of strikes and riots?

This is the last chance. Yeltsin deserves praise for taking the bull by the horns, and taking good advice. But where will the bull take him?

11 November 1991, Glasgow

A few remarks and comments. (1) *Yeltsin's powers and the Russian Federation*. The gloomy forecast on disintegration is, alas, well founded. Not only has the Chechen-Ingush autonomous republic revolted, but the Russian parliament now refuses to back Yeltsin's emergency measures to stop the revolt. Yet the example is bound to be infectious. Bashkir, Tartar, Yakut, Cherkess, Ossetians (the last two close neighbours of the Chechens) could kick up hell at any time. Meanwhile I do not see Yeltsin in control of Russian cities either. Popov unilaterally introduces all-round food rationing in Moscow, Sobchak entertains the Grand Duke Vladimir in St. Petersburg. Yeltsin's representatives in the provinces have little power *vis-à-vis* local functionaries and soviets, unless and until he declares a real all-round emergency, and even that may not work. (2) *The Ukraine* remains in a state of flux. Kravchuk and Fokin, former party functionaries turned nationalists, know very well that it would greatly hurt the economy to refuse to sign an agreement with Russia or with what remains of the Union. But can they, politically? And are they in effective control over the largely non-Ukrainian Donbas coalfield and Crimea? And indeed, as *Analytica* put it, 'there is lack of a coherent programme'. A former graduate student of mine, Bohdan Kravchenko, is said to be advising. I cannot see a coherent programme emerging from him. But if I get there I might talk to him, and this judgement *may* prove unfair . . . *Finally*, *Ekonomika i zhizn'* has again reprinted details of the purchase price of a broker's seat on various stock and commodity exchanges: hundreds of thousands of roubles, here and there even a million . . . There must be a lot of money to be made! But with hyperinflation due at any moment, ultra-short-termism must rule . . .

1992

More Trouble in Store . . . , 14–15 January 1992, Glasgow

It is important that Khazbulatov, chairman (speaker) of the Russian republic's Supreme Soviet, has denounced the government's economic policy. So has Rutskoi, the vice president. There may be a vote of no confidence in the Supreme Soviet, with many deputies facing their constituents' outrage. It is not clear what Yeltsin can and should now do. Right now he is backing Gaidar. There was an excellent piece in today's *Financial Times* about the perils of doing business in an environment with no real 'market culture': fraud, false promises, corruption, are all too common. This is not even 'capitalism red in tooth and claw.' Some Russians distinguish between 'market' (*rynok*) and 'bazaar'. But even a bazaar seems preferable to what is now going on. There is as yet no defined system of commercial law, contractual obligations are too often ignored. One cannot have a market without free prices and real money. One cannot have free prices and real money unless there is a market.

Catch 22. The energy crisis is compelling the Russian republic to cut back drastically on oil supplies to other republics. This can cause havoc there. The Ukraine is very much affected. It also sits astride pipelines to the west. Will it use this fact in bargaining with Moscow? With what consequences? Are they are still arguing about the Black Sea fleet. (What idiot gave the Crimea, plus the naval base of Sebastopol to the Ukraine?) Layard in *The Independent* makes a powerful case for large-scale Western aid. He is right: without it, if we simply provide charitable relief supplies, there is virtually no chance of avoiding hyperinflation, chaos and a new authoritarianism. The sum required has been repeatedly estimated (also by him) as about 16 billion dollars, to buy imports (which can be resold for roubles and so help balance the budget) and to help stabilise the currency at a less absurd exchange rate. (At today's free rate Gaidar's salary is indeed about 6 dollars a week!) A rate of about 20 roubles to the dollar, he thinks, might be sustainable with strong Western support. I do sympathise with Layard's arguments and objectives, but I feel he gravely underestimates the government's powerlessness and the all-pervasive corruption. As things now are, both imports and Western hard-currency would be diverted, while large sums would continue to 'leak' into holdings in Western banks . . . A key point too frequently forgotten is the desperately urgent need to direct funds and resources to deal with emergencies, for example, the energy crisis. Yet what little private capital there is goes either into speculation or into the purchase of privatised assets, while the state includes itself out. The same problem is arising in Poland, also in the energy sector. Given inflationary expectations the rate of interest is bound to be sky-high, so it is only logical to chase a *fast* buck. So who is to invest?

Trouble in Store, 29 January 1992, Berkeley, California

The latest news remains grim. Interesting conversation here with Russian Supreme Soviet deputy Viktor Sheinis. He is himself a member of the commission now drafting a constitution for the Russian republic. But even if the present draft is accepted by the needed majority, what he called the 'nihilistic' attitude to law, ingrained in the society, may lead to the continued paralysis of state structures. Obedience under the old system was based on the party and its *nomenklatura*. No adequate substitute for this has yet emerged. Popular discontent is reaching critical levels, with prices soaring and output falling. Discontent among the military is also widespread, for evident reasons. Rutskoi is a brave and honest man, but he could effectively challenge the economic programme and press for authoritarian solutions. Sheinis is also concerned by worsening relations between Russia and Ukraine: he would lay much of the blame on the Ukrainian leadership, which, being old communist apparatchiki have to go all out to prove their nationalist credentials. Sheinis himself was sent last year to persuade the Azerbaijanis and the Armenians to settle peacefully the dispute over Nogorno-Karabakh; unfortunately, much blood will now flow, in fact is already overflowing. As for Georgia, he strongly supports the view that Gamsakhurdia is an irresponsible thug, who got elected simply because he had suffered under the Moscow-dominated communist regime. His policies were provocative and disastrous.

A detailed study of the *Ekonomika i zhizn'* article, in a special issue, on the oil crisis makes very disturbing reading. In 1991 total exports were to have been limited to at most 65 million tons, yet licences were issued to sell twice that amount, and the author speculates about the size of the bribes. It is this that compelled Yeltsin to impose an export ban in November. But this meant that contractual obligations had to be broken. Many oil importers are in dire trouble. Someone just back from Latvia confirms stories to the effect that few buses are operating, for lack of fuel. For the same reason problems are accumulating in Ukraine. Lack of fuel and of other supplies has led to a state of emergency and rationing (and a political crisis) in Estonia. Meanwhile Russian oil output is expected to decline, due to wasteful exploitation practices in the past, inadequate exploration and drilling, lack now of essential improvements. It is suggested that the time is fast approaching when oil exports from Russia will fall to zero, that some oil may even have to be imported by the end of 1992. The consequences for the balance of payments hardly bear thinking about.

Political in-fighting in the Yeltsin team is a continuing complication. Rutskoi's criticisms of the Gaidar programme have been repeated by Khazbulatov, the 'speaker' of the Russian parliament, but apparently Khazbulatov is regarded as a demagogue and may not carry enough weight to upset the government. A more serious conflict involves Matyukhin, head of the Russian State Bank. He is being blamed by the Gaidar team for printing too much money, but he points out that he has no alternative: wages and pensions must be paid, and he has no effective control over the credits granted by the innumerable new commercial banks. Meanwhile the budget deficit is still being covered by money creation since the tax collection mechanism is not (or not yet) adequate to its task. The new constitution, if and when adopted, envisages dividing the Russian federation into geographic and national *regions* (the word *zemli* is used, the equivalent of the German Länder), with separate representation in an Upper House. Some fear that they may become mini-states which could adopt autarkic policies and undertake their own foreign trade deals. At issue is the power, or lack of it, of the Russian governmental structure. Local authorities are now under pressure from the public to limit price rises. The point is made that, with yet hardly any privatisation and with wholesale and retail trade still largely monopolised, prices could be set quite arbitrarily by local trade officials. It is one thing if (say) a town has 50 food shops owned and operated on some sort of competitive basis, and quite another if all of them are under one official local trade trust. Privatisation of thousands of Moscow shops is due very soon, but critics have argued that this should have preceded freeing of prices.

It has been reported that Russia will try to import 20 million tons of grain in 1992 (as against 16 million in 1991). It will surely be impossible to pay for this without large Western aid. Yeltsin has issued a decree on agricultural land which could have far-reaching consequences if implemented. Land reform commissions are being set up to help overcome the expected opposition from local vested interests. Any peasant will be entitled to withdraw from state or collective farms with land, which can be bought and sold (though only for agricultural purposes). Collective farms are to become genuine cooperatives. But this last measure already figured in the 1988 decree on cooperatives, and little changed. True, political conditions are now different, and there is much more determination to proceed with privatisation in agriculture. The unknown factor is: how many peasants will willingly undertake the responsibility of private farming in the face of a multitude of uncertainties: they need assured supplies of material inputs, credits, etc. And many have been effectively 'depeasantised'. Also, if I understand the decree correctly, townsmen (as distinct from peasants) will not have the right to buy land. Yet, with the expected rise in unemployment, some move back to the land should surely be encouraged. But I have yet to see the detailed text. In any case, the measure is unlikely to have much short-term effect.

The energy and food crisis affects different parts of the former USSR very unequally, but everything is being made worse by disintegration and by beggar-my-neighbour policies. Looming catastrophe could compel the republics to breath some life into the Commonwealth structures and adopt joint remedial policies. But more likely is that each will try to go their own way, blaming disasters on the others. I hope to be wrong about this, but . . .

More Evidence of Gloom, 5 February 1992, Berkeley, California

A batch of newspapers has arrived. The following are some key points.

1. (*Moskovskie novosti*, 26 January): 'The whole idea of reform is being discredited. People see a definite connection between democracy and chaos and between the market and universal beggary. We will soon know how it will end, in a social explosion or a new putsch.' The author of these remarks, V. Lipitski, spoke for the 'People's Party of Free Russia'. Its leader is vice-president Rutskoi.
2. In the same issue the mayor of St. Petersburg, Sobchak, demanded the abolition of VAT on food, predicted tenfold price increases, warned that privatisation auctions will mean that the mafia will buy. The *Financial Times* reported on 4 February that VAT on many foods has been cut to 15 per cent, that is, a sort of compromise with Sobchak's demand. The same report stated that Khazbulatov convened a meeting of 'prominent economists' and that the well-known Pavel Bunich demanded lower taxes and more subsidies.
3. *Nezavisimaya gazeta* of 16 January prints an article by V. Desyatov which states: 'Taxes in the form in which they have been promulgated are not only unreal, but are in principle uncollectable. Not even the tax inspectorate know how to compel payment.' He and others say that the reform plan resembles that of the ill-fated Pavlov, that nearly all regions of the republic control or ban the movement of goods, that the high taxes inhibit enterprise.
4. The same paper on 14 January printed an interview with Yavlinsky. He too says that 'taxes will not be collected'. 'There is total lack of political clarity and responsibility, a basic inability to carry through any serious policy . . . Hyperinflation, mass beggary and unemployment, fall in output (an 18% drop in the first quarter over the last quarter is forecast in the issue of 23 January) will lead to further disintegration, regionalisation, a rise in criminality . . . ' There must be an effective state. He attacks those liberals who weakened the state and expected the market to do the necessary. '*It is a crisis of the democratic movement*' (emphasis his). Today's entrepreneurs are engaged mainly in dealing, not in production, with links to organised crime and corruption.
5. *Moskovskie novosti* of 19 January contains sharp criticisms by N. Petrakov. The Gaidar plan he sees as 'a mechanical copy of the Polish reform'. He too sees similarity with Pavlov's (pre-coup) reform plan. Experience showed that there would be hardly any investment. An investment strategy is desperately needed, for example, for energy and for

sectors capable of exporting. (Yes, indeed this is a major weakness of
Jeffrey Sachs, to whom, unfortunately, Gaidar listens too much, A.N.).
6.   It has been reported that on 7 February there is to be a 'conference of
patriotic oppositionists' which may be addressed by vice-president
Rutskoi. 'Gaidar is unpopular with the people because of prices, with
entrepreneurs because of taxes.' (*Nezavisimaya gazeta*, 18 Jan.). Fear is
expressed by many about the break-up of Russia. There is a movement
for an independent Siberia (hoping to attract Japanese capital), and a
Cossack republic is spoken of.
7.   Finally, *Nezavisimaya gazeta* of 23 January published what is supposed to be the draft budget of the Russian Federation, but the figures
appear to relate to the entire public sector (i.e., including the expenditures financed by state enterprises) and the figures seem devoid of
meaning. Thus on the revenue side there is an item foreign trade revenues (228 billion roubles), while expenditures also have an item for
foreign trade (220 billion roubles). A Russian colleague here is as much
in the dark as I am as to what this might mean. Anyhow, here we are in
February and there is yet no budget for 1992. None of this gives any
grounds for optimism!

Russia After the Congress, 15 April 1992, Berkeley

Not surprisingly, for lack of any alternative, the Congress deputies, after
making critical noises, have gone along reluctantly with Yeltsin's reform
plans. The danger now is from an indignant public. Also the Congress
may get bogged down debating several alternative drafts of the constitution and in the end adopt none. Yet there is plenty of evidence that the
Russian governmental structures are confused and ineffective. How can a
market exist without a legal order?
   Forecast for 1992, prepared by the Ministry of Economics, has been
published by *Ekonomika i zhizn'* (No. 13). Compared with 1991, industrial output is expected to fall between 25 and 30 per cent, the volume of
retail sales by 20 per cent, oil output by 14 per cent (or by
64 million tons), food industry by 18 per cent (meat by 22 per cent, butter
by 13 per cent, vegetable oil by as much as 28 per cent). By the end of the
year wholesale prices will have risen (on rather optimistic assumptions)
more than 8-fold over the last quarter of 1991, or 10 to 11 times if one
includes VAT. Total investments of all kinds will be 30–40 per cent below
1991 levels. The value of Russian exports in 1992 is estimated at $36.3
billion. Another article in the same issue forecasts a larger fall (20 per

cent) in oil output, but the collapse of industrial production should reduce demand, ensuring an adequate export availability. Source quotes an expert of the TOTAL oil firm to the effect that to restore oil output to the levels in 1988 Russia would require $30 billion of investments. Some detailed statistics have appeared in the same journal of *foreign trade in 1991* with a country breakdown and quantitative data on the former USSR, and also (for commodities) for Russia separately. Compared with 1990 exports of virtually everything are greatly down. There is one exception: aircraft (a rise from 102 planes to 116). *Export taxes.* A new decree lists literally a thousand or so items subject to export duty (the evident cause is the still substantial disparity between internal and world prices, if the free exchange rate is used). The export duty is payable in ECU. Examples: vodka 160–230 ECU per ton, manganese 8–11.5, crude oil 20.8–29.9, uranium 400–5750. The lower rate of duty is applicable if the firm is liable to transfer a large percentage of its export earnings to the centre (at a rate far below the free one). This may replace or supplement export licences, which have notoriously involved corruption. *An anti-corruption drive* is being given much publicity, amid allegations that it is reaching record levels. A 'special commission' to fight corruption bears a not unfamiliar acronym: Cheka.

Industrialist critique of reform. The president of the Russian Union of Industrialists and Entrepreneurs, Arkady Volsky, answering a correspondent's question about what he sees as the 'weak spots of the reform', replied: 'Above all, the measures taken do not stimulate the growth of output. The way out of our country's crisis lies in the providing of stimuli for growth, and the quality and quantity of goods for the people. Instead the main effort is directed towards macroeconomics, while output is on catastrophic free fall . . . The government does not seem to understand the scale of the catastrophe. It seems mesmerised by macroeconomic problems, and the need to balance the budget, yet the fate of the reform will be determined by dozens and hundreds of specific (micro) events: closedown of production, unemployment, the aggressive anger of hungry people.' He denounces the imposition of customs barriers, licences, quotas, ill-considered intervention by national and local incompetent officialdom. Volsky used to have high party connections, but seems genuinely concerned to make the new reform work. His Russian Union includes both managers of state enterprises and new entrepreneurs. And his criticism of Gaidar (and Jeffrey Sachs) for over concentrating on macro stabilisation (necessary, of course) while micro is left to market forces is soundly based. The market has yet to be created. And in the present climate of high uncertainty it is most unlikely that private capital will be used for productive investment.

More on the budget. Writing in *Izvestiya* (20 March) Otto Latsis stated that in 1991 the combined deficits of the USSR and the republics exceeded 20 per cent of GNP. It is hoped to reduce this already in the first quarter (for Russia) to 5.3 per cent. There are great difficulties in collecting revenues, especially the unfamiliar VAT at the high rate of 28 per cent. Some are failing to pay, but many others fail to understand about value-added and pay the whole 28 per cent, which is then levied several times en route to the final customer. According to Latsis, the Ministry of Finance is so short of revenue that it is failing to inform the overpayers that they are overpaying! In Stanford last week I met Bernshtam, an émigré who often advises the Russian government. He showed me a memo he and some US colleagues had written, about the overoptimistic revenue projections for 1992. Undercollection has been the rule, both for VAT (despite some overpayments) and, especially, the projected revenue from foreign trade. *Izvestiya* of 28 March reports the rejection by the Supreme Soviet of yet another draft of the budget for 1992. But, as it points out, how can any credible budget be drafted amid all the inflationary uncertainties? (Thus only a couple of weeks ago I reported on the huge increases in energy prices definitely due in April. Now they are to be increased not in April but later in the year to avoid further increasing costs in agriculture. But this means still more trouble for the budget, as some fuels, especially coal, require large subsidies, and corruption will continue to flourish when there are such large differences between official and free prices for energy, oil especially.) *Finally, universal bankruptcy*. The same issue of *Izvestiya* reports an enormous rise in inter-enterprise debt. As costs rise steeply, most enterprises are unable to pay their suppliers, which leads to a chain-reaction of payments defaults, and also to pressure for emergency credits from a banking system that has been instructed to restrict credit. The following figures tell their own dramatic tale: Value of bills unpaid (payments delayed): On 1 January 1992 (39.2 billion roubles); 1 February (140.5); 1 March (390); 20 March (676) !!!

Have the Gaidar Reforms Failed? The Yavlinsky Critique, 16 June 1992, Glasgow

Here a summary of an eight-page analysis which appeared in *Moskovskie novosti* of 24 May, by a team of the 'Epicentre' research institute, headed by Yavlinsky.

1.   *Economic Liberalisation.* Privatisation is exceedingly slow: still less than 1 per cent of trade, catering and other services. Quotas, licences and

export taxes inhibit foreign trade. A cut in import duties has contributed to turning last year's trade surplus into a large deficit. Most export receipts in valuta do not reach the centre. Budget revenues from foreign trade had been planned to be 228 billion roubles in the first quarter; actual receipts were 30 (another source gave even lower figures, A.N.). Russian firms and individuals have accounts in Western banks estimated at between 5 and 20 billion dollars. Multiple exchange rates provide ample opportunities for corrupt gain: thus 'centralised imports' pay 5.4 roubles per dollar, there is a commercial rate of 55, others go as high as 160. While many state enterprises have been 'commercialised', management has neither incentives nor the means to invest or restructure. Though the number of private farms have rapidly increased recently, they account for only 2 per cent of farmland. Agriculture is badly hit by prices: inputs have risen 10–15 times, farm produce 5–7 times.

2. *Financial Stabilisation.* The budget deficit has been 'lowered' by creative accountancy. In fact it is 15 per cent of GNP. Payments from regions and firms are delayed. The lack of financing of health and education have put both in a critical state. Foreign credits are improperly included with budget revenues. Despite big rise in emission, there is a grave shortage of bank notes. The free exchange rate has been kept from collapsing by bank intervention, using dollars owed as interest payments to foreign creditors. Hyperinflation will be stoked up by the (necessary) rise in energy prices and by the abolition of the 'centralised-import' subsidised exchange rate, and by irresistible pressure to raise money wages. A stricter credit policy and high interest rates have led to the bulk of enterprises becoming insolvent: a bankruptcy law, not yet adopted, is in practice inapplicable. Credit is having to be expanded. A growth in the numbers of bills of exchange will add to inflationary pressure. '*Financial stabilisation will be impossible without restructuring the economy, without a consciously directed industrial strategy*' (emphasis mine – and his!).

3. *Fall in output* continues due to supply disruption and falling demand. Higher prices do not stimulate higher production. The biggest declines are in the food and consumer-goods industries, which deepens impoverishment. Worn-out equipment is not being replaced, as investment has fallen steeply to below capital replacement levels. Foreign investors are few, 'the capital flight from Russia is massive'. Liberal monetarism is plainly inadequate as a cure, since it assumes a functioning market mechanism.

4. *Disintegration.* Yavlinsky is critical of lack of effort to reach agreements with ex-Soviet republics, and also the loss of Moscow's control over resources within the Russian federation, with control passing to regions and such national republics as Tatarstan.

5.   *Foreign Aid*. The $24 billion can make little difference, especially as some of it is tied, or not new money. (It is in any case only a small fraction of what West Germany is spending on East Germany, which has a population of 16 million.)

6.   *Popular Attitudes and Living Standards*. Compared with a year ago, wages have risen 6.9 fold, prices 11.2 fold. Yet supply and demand are not in balance, local authorities fix some prices and interfere with deliveries and contracts. Food consumption in calories has fallen from 2600 to 2100 a day, 'not enough to feed an 11 year old'. State medical services and other social services are collapsing. The public is demoralised. *Yavlisnksy's Conclusion*. 'It must be recognised that the effort at economic stabilisation has failed, that the economy faces hyperinflation and the collapse of production.' Deaths exceed births. Discontent grows.

My Comment. While some Russian critics have spoken of 'sour grapes', I fear that Yavlinsky's critique is well founded, though *his* critics accuse him of not putting forward a viable alternative. The same journal in its issue of 31 May cites a senior manager, G. Faktor: 'The most dreadful thing today is the investment climate. If output has fallen by 30%, investment has fallen by 60%.' And in the issue of 7 June, L. Grigoriev writes on 'the crisis of accumulation'. Investment in 1992 will be barely a quarter of 1990 levels. It is essential that existing investment resources, also from abroad, be channelled to the most effective sectors. Foreigners will only invest 'if there are clear property laws, contract discipline, financial responsibility, commercial ethics . . . Yet foreign potential investors observe with surprise that the investment climate in the Russian federation is no better, or is even worse, than in the former USSR. 1992 saw the collapse of Vneshtorbank, an increase in profits tax from 25 per cent to 32 per cent, the abolition of two-year tax holidays, very high export taxes on oil, repeated changes in the regulation of foreign trade', the possibly imminent imposition of a 60 per cent income tax on foreign personnel, and 'confusion of functions and responsibilities between central, provincial and local organs'. *Izvestiya* (25 May) reported that the bank rate, raised two months ago from 20 to 50 per cent, has gone up to 80 per cent. Well, yes Gaidar is now prime minister. But can he stick to laissez-faire in the face of catastrophe?

Notes from the Hebrides, 22 July 1992, Isle of Coll

Excellent short-wave reception here. So have kept partially in touch by ear. *Ukrainian–Russian relations*. Both countries are aware of the harm to their economies through obstructing trade. A meeting between Yeltsin and Kravchuk has given hope of positive steps. This was followed or accompanied by a joint meeting of the industrialists' organisations of the two countries, the Russian group being led by A. Volsky. They are pressing for a relaxation of tension and for a trade and payments agreement. But this does not yet exist. *Privatisation in Russia.* Still slow, but gathering pace. The man in charge is 36 year-old Anatoli Chubais (who was my host in Leningrad in 1989, where he lived in one room with his family in a communal apartment!). He has just been promoted vice-premier, which gives him more power to speed-up the process. Large state firms are to be turned into limited companies, and citizens will get vouchers to buy shares. Proceeds from sales of retail stores and consumer service undertakings will be retained by local authorities and, said Chubais, used to relieve poverty via the local budget. *Agriculture.* Yeltsin has stated that the harvest in 1992 should be better than in 1991. In a radio interview, the peasant leader Chernichenko stated that progress in private farming is still slow. About 2000 state and collective farms which are hopelessly bankrupt are to be sold off, but the effects of inflation on farm costs have been such as to deter takers. He expressed the view that land should be made available for sale to foreign agricultural interests, who could introduce new technology, seed varieties, livestock breeds. 'Otherwise we will stay hungry for 15 years.' *Debt moratorium.* The 'seven' had no choice but to accept a moratorium on debt interest payments.

If the *Guardian* is correct, debt has risen by 10 billion dollars in the past year. Since this coincided with a steep decline in the economy, and may have been due in part to this decline, it does not augur well for the effectiveness of the 'new' Western aid package. The more so as its contents and its timing are quite unclear. If the release of even a part of it is conditional upon Russia putting its internal house in order, prospects would seem even bleaker. There are proposals to write off a part of the debt in exchange for the acquisition by the West (how? by whom?) of natural and capital assets in the former USSR. There are indeed ample natural resources, often in remote areas, but how can one fail to agree with the *Guardian* correspondent?: 'Doing business in a country with no established financial infrastructure and a legal system which leaves property rights uncertain is not so much daunting as utterly terrifying.' Even on what on paper could be favourable terms, Western investors are thin on the ground. And nationalists such as vice-president Rutskoi drum up political support against large-scale Western takeovers. With a sizeable part of export earnings kept abroad, lack of tax-collecting ability, and irresistible resistance to drastic cuts in expenditures, plus continued expectation of even higher inflation, I cannot see how promises made to

IMF or the 'seven' can be kept, even with the best will in the world, and this even assuming the absence of major strikes or disorders. *Politics*. Moscow radio reported a speech by vice-premier Rutskoi, in which he (again) attacked Gaidar's policies, which 'achieve not macroeconomic stabilisation but chaos.' His alternative he did not make clear. Meanwhile there are repeated broadcast denials that anyone in the Ministry of Defence or Security is/are planning a coup. *The Russian budget*. Moscow radio reported the adoption of the budget for 1992. If my ears did not deceive me, it provides for a deficit of 900 billion roubles, or some 25 per cent of total budgetary expenditures. *Food subsidies again?* Moscow radio reported Gaidar (now acting premier) as announcing a 36 billion rouble subsidy. In today's roubles the sum is small, but a principle is involved. Local authorities in some areas also subsidise basic foods, to avoid riots over prices. *Banking and Currency*. Katyukhin having resigned as head of the Bank of Russia, his designate successor, Gerashchenko, ex-head of the USSR State Bank, has criticised him for using $500 million in recent months for supporting the rouble free rate, instead of paying interest on debt. *Conflict over the Press*. The Russian Supreme Soviet passed a resolution demanding control over *Izvestiya*, an excellent independent newspaper, but nominally its organ. Yeltsin defends *Izvestiya*. It is another instance of friction, which also affects economic policy and legislation.

Another Russian Miscellany, 28 July 1992, Glasgow

Relations with Ukraine. Further complicated by escalating quarrel over the Black Sea fleet, with one small warship mutinying and sailing to Odessa so as to be Ukrainian, and the Russians still in charge of Sebastopol, which the Ukrainians claim to be their territory. Another Yeltsin–Kravchuk meeting is due to sort things out. But suppose someone opens fire? *Relations with Balts*. No so good either. Estonian irregulars have been sniping at Russian troops. Meanwhile the Russians are bitterly criticising the Estonian nationality laws, which deprive the Russian minority of most rights, including, according to one report, even access to the health service! Latvian laws are about as bad for the non-Latvian residents, that make up almost half the population. There need be no immediate trouble in store, but it does darken the future, and provide a more nationalist Russian government with a strong motive to intervene. *A Ukrainian note*. Reform is in trouble. The vice premier in charge, Lanovoi, described to me last year as a sort of Ukrainian Gaidar, has been sacked. His replacement, Simonenko, is reported as uncertain as to whether to end the still very large bread subsidy. *A Brighter Note. A*

Russian Belorussian Confederation? Both *Izvestiya* and *Nezavisimaya gazeta* report positively on this possibility. It would make good sense, particularly for Belorussia (now called Belarus). *The Russian Budget*. My ears did not deceive me. A budget deficit in excess of 900 billion roubles was voted by the Russian 'parliament'. However, it was not agreed by the government, which is opposed to some of the extra expenditures which parliament has voted. As far as I can see, this leaves us with no meaningful state budget for the rest of this year. But not only parliament takes financially 'baseless' measures. *Nezavisimaya gazeta* of 23 July reports that Yeltsin has allocated 90 billion roubles to army housing, 'but it is not clear from where this money is coming.'

First Half Year Statistics. *Izvestiya* (20 July) published some of the official figures. Compared with the first half year of 1991, GNP is down by 13.5 per cent, oil output by 13 per cent, food industry output by 23 per cent. In many cities in June there was hardly any meat, sugar or vegetable oil. In June the average wage reached 4400 roubles a month, a fourfold rise since January, but prices have risen much faster. Foreign trade has declined steeply, but imports have fallen so rapidly that there was a small trade surplus (exports $15.4 billion, imports $14.9). There is continued alarm about the huge rise in inter-enterprise debt: it had risen 1.7 fold between 1 May and 1 June, exceeding 1900 billion roubles. *Ekonomika i zhizn'* (No. 26) deplores the fall in total investments, on a scale unheard of in Russian history in peacetime. Machinery and equipment, and chemicals, have been particularly hard hit. 'Clearly there is no investment policy, the reductions have been chaotic.' By May capacity utilisation in industry had fallen to 64.7 per cent. A report in the same issue from their Institute of Forecasting speaks of 'creeping deindustrialisation', with the fall in output due now more to deflation than to supply bottlenecks.

More Forecasts. According to an official report by the influential E. Yasin and S. Vasiliev (*Ekonomika i zhizn'*, No. 26), in the whole year 1992 GNP will be down 15 per cent, industrial output 13 per cent, construction 30 per cent, agricultural production by 11 per cent. They hope the price index will be 'only' 1600 by the year's end, but fear it might be 2500 or even more if their output predictions prove to be overoptimistic. The budget deficit might fall to 5 per cent of GNP, but, they add, if tax collection lags then the deficit could reach 13–14 per cent of GNP. (That's more like it, alas! A.N.) *Another Critique*. In the same journal (No. 27), V. Shprygin goes on the attack: 'Not only has there been a catastrophic fall in output, but also worsening quality, greater financial instability, continued budget deficits. The basic policy error was to give top priority to cutting the budget deficit through price rises and high taxes, without tackling the basic disproportions in the real economy. Instead of tackling the causes of chaos, they try to deal with its consequences.' Instead of structural change we see the deepening of disproportions.

Oil: The Latest Forecast. It will fall from 451 million tons in 1991 to 393 million tons in 1992 (source, as above). (David: in your recent note you expressed the view that, since the bulk of the oil of the former USSR came from the Russian federation one should not worry about political disruption. Unfortunately, some of it comes from the Tatar and Bashkir ex-autonomous republics, and they are claiming the right to retain hard-currency earnings. This is apart from oil and earnings from oil sales leaking out into numbered accounts abroad.) *Finally, Nezavisimaya gazeta* of 17 July headed an article: 'A Coup is Likely, but also impossible'. That's a safe forecast!

26 September 1992, Glasgow

A few pointers to Russian developments. As I surmised, Gaidar has survived the latest attempt of oppositionists in the Supreme Soviet to unseat him. But policies have been modified. There is no doubt of the greater influence of Volsky and Gerashchenko. A strict monetarist restrictiveness would have throttled industry. In *Izvestiya* of 21 September Otto Latsis speaks of 'retreat': inflation had fallen in June and July, but rose sharply in August. Economic correspondent Berger, in the same issue, points to Gerashchenko (State Bank chief) giving conscious priority to saving production, loosening credit controls despite adverse effects on the rouble–dollar rate and on the budget. K. Kagalovsky, government linkman with the IMF, reported (*Izvestiya*, 17 September) that the bank issued 500 billion-worth of credits in the last two months. Large increases in prices of energy in September have also given a twist to the inflationary spiral, leading to a further sharp fall in the rouble–dollar exchange rate. Kagalovsky criticises the Bank for also granting credits to ex-union republics, including the Ukraine (to buy Russian goods) and 'to finance war in the Caucusus'. He estimated the total foreign debt at $84 billion, and of course Russia cannot pay. *Izvestiya* of 18 September prints an analysis by an economic research centre. The fall in industrial output has speeded up. Over the same period in 1991 it had fallen by 13 to 15 per cent in the first six months of 1992, by 21.5 per cent in July, by 27.2 per cent in August. In the first 8 months oil output fell by 14 per cent, gas by 3 per cent. Financial discipline is beginning to bite, one cannot now produce without selling. There are also supply bottlenecks (for example, textile materials fail to arrive from other republics). Wholesale prices rose 15 per cent in July and again in August. Bread and flour have sharply risen in price (particularly in areas where prices had been administratively held down), and (according to *Nezavisimaya gazeta* of 19 September) there is this month a 50 per cent increase in charges for domestic electricity, gas, heating, water (but, since wholesale prices have risen faster, this will require a subsidy still). In the first 8 months the value (in dollars) of foreign trade fell by 28 per cent: exports by 34 per cent (in August by 31 per cent), imports by 21 per cent (in August by 45 per cent) (!!). The research centre forecasts a decline in exports by over 40 per cent in the whole year 1992, compared with 1991. A thoughtful article by A. Lifshits (*Izvestiya*, 10 September) analyses dispassionately the pluses and minuses of 'Gaidarnomics'. There is some real progress towards a market economy, including in human behaviour. Though there is much poverty, goods have appeared in the shops. But he also strongly criticises (as I do) 'indifference towards the investment process, calm contemplation of its collapse, unwillingness to do anything for economic infrastructure', and also unrealistic promises to the IMF about reducing the budget deficit. Amid such widespread poverty it is shocking to see output of consumers goods falling so fast. But prospects are not all black.

30 September 1992, Glasgow

Ukrainian premier V. Fokin has resigned. No successor has yet been appointed. What does this mean? Possible interpretations are: (1) Someone must be held responsible for the economic crisis, and in Kravchuk's view, it is better that this be Fokin than Kravchuk himself. (2) Fokin, an ethnic Russian, has been under attack for allegedly not being tough enough in negotiations with Moscow, for not leaving the rouble zone, delaying the introduction of Ukrainian money (the *hrivna*), and so on. Then his departure would be bad news for negotiations with Russia. (3) Some may blame him for slowing the economic reform process. But I have heard nothing in Kiev to suggest that Fokin was blocking reform, or any more so than Kravchuk. There have been demonstrations demanding Fokin's removal. Kravchuk finds it politic to go along. If there are policy changes, this will show when we know who will be the appointed successor, and whether policy will in fact change, and, if so, in which direction. Watch this space . . .

6 October 1992, Glasgow

A few random and relevant notes. First, *Ukraine*. According to *Izvestiya* of 2 October, the resignation of premier Fokin was followed by the adoption by the Ukrainian parliament of a vote of no confidence in the government. President Kravchuk was given ten days in which to find a new premier. It must be surmised that the majority 'against' reflected the deteriorating economic situation, and included those who attacked the government for not marketising faster and those who believe in tighter state controls, plus disgruntled nationalists. A possible guess is that Simonenko, moderate reformer and ex-party hack, may succeed Fotkin. *Russia* has established 64 customs posts on its borders with other ex-Soviet republics. Gaidar has just visited Baku and was going to Yerevan, to establish trade and payments ties (in roubles) with Azerbaijan and Armenia. Meanwhile, according to *Pravda* (3 October), Lithuania has eliminated the rouble and has replaced it with temporary tokens of its own.

In Russia, fears of more inflationary spirals has sent the rouble tumbling yet again, with *Izvestiya* of 1 October reporting a rate of 309 roubles per dollar, 54 up on the previous week. The influential head of the managers' lobby, A. Volsky, was interviewed in *Izvestiya* (30 September). While supportive of the marketising strategy, he proposes some 'correctives'. Thus to avoid 'collapse', it is necessary to stop 'the massacre of production' which is now occurring. They should aim at a mixed economy with a regulatory role for government, 'as in China'. It is necessary to adopt policies to deal with the 'structural crisis', deciding 'what sectors to close down and which to support and at what cost'. The free fall of investment 'must be stopped' (yes! A.N.). He proposes a price freeze on essentials plus a wage freeze, as immediate emergency measures. He was lukewarm on the investment vouchers scheme. Unless carefully managed, it may seem like 'a trick played on working people.' 'Voucherisation' was violently attacked in the neo-communist *Pravda* on 1 October. The author of the scheme, Anatoli Chubais, is reported as saying that the poor will be able to sell them and so relieve their poverty. The *Pravda* critic argues that racketeers and the new rich will thus be able to buy up coupons and become owners of undervalued state enterprises, that this is highway robbery of what was the property of the whole people, etc. etc. Without going along with the spirit of this critic, I must admit to many doubts. 10 000 roubles (the face value of the voucher) is little more than £20 even in today's depreciated pounds. So unless the value of the capital stock has been drastically written down, it cannot provide a basis for ownership, and insofar as the poor will try to sell the vouchers, these will represent extra roubles in peoples' pockets (so more inflationary pressure), while contributing nothing to real investment. In real terms it is a kind of hand-out, politically useful. What else is it?

25 October 1992, Glasgow

My immediate purpose in writing these few words is to draw attention to the probability – I put it no higher, but also not lower – that Yeltsin and his programme are subject to speedy derailment. The refusal to accept his request to put off the meeting of the Congress of Soviets, which visibly angered him, means that this assembly, when it assembles on 1 December, may very well pass a vote of no confidence in the government, notably in Gaidar, while at the same time cutting off Yeltsin's emergency powers. There are clear signs that the hitherto disorganised opposition groupings are trying to get their act together. One can see vice-president Rutskoi as a key player, plus Volsky and his industrial managers. As also in the Ukraine, one of their demands will surely be that the still-dominant state-owned sector be controlled, subject to orders from somewhere, made responsible to someone. Priorities would be imposed. Some Western correspondents have noted the contrast between relative order in the gas industry, run by the republican Gasprom, with the fragmented chaos of the decentralised oil industry. There may be a programme of emergency powers run by a Comité du Salut Public, with military support, with much verbiage on the need to suppress (widespread) corruption and speculative excess. All this may not add up to an alternative policy. They may exert pressure on Yeltsin rather than try to remove him. Or of course Yeltsin may try pre-emptive action this month, dissolving the congress and calling for new elections. But no one knows what sort of parliament this would produce. Anyhow, the next weeks will be filled with uncertainty, and the rouble–dollar rate will probably fall further when the new rich try to off load roubles. However, one hears of a counter-tendency: if purchase of newly privatised housing and also privatisation shares will be in roubles, some of those hoarding dollars will find a reason to off load them. But for what it is worth, my guess is that we shall soon see over 400 roubles to the dollar.

A thought. In a previous note I referred to the effect of privatisation-anticipation on the behaviour of management in Russia and in the Czech lands. Judging from today's *Observer*, exactly this can be observed in British Railways today. The government's particular mode of privatisation strikes me as particularly crazy, destroying the system, but whether this is so or not, investment plans are abandoned as there is no sort of long-term perspective for management. This is having a knock-on effect on suppliers of rail equipment. (Il ne manquait que cela!)

22 December 1992, Glasgow

It is still quite unclear what is going on in Moscow. Yeltsin's sudden
return from China is another example of impulsiveness and mental confusion. This surely must further weaken his political clout, and
correspondingly increase that of Rutskoi, Volsky, Khasbulatov – and of
the new premier Chernomyrdin. If Gaidar becomes Yeltsin's chief economic adviser, and, as is being reported, my old friend Nikolai Petrakov
accepts the role of Chernomyrdin's economic adviser, then, bearing in
mind Petrakov's quite virulent criticisms of Gaidar's strategy, where are
we? And where are the Western advisers such as Sachs and Lloyd? There
is contradictory talk of currency reform, but I gather that this will be the
issuance of new Russian banknotes to replace the Soviet ones still in circulation (with Lenin's head on them). Apart from replacing Lenin's head,
and creating new payments problems in what remains of the rouble zone,
little will have changed. It would not be a new hard internal currency,
that is, a replay of the chervonets of 1923, though that may come after
hyperinflation has really taken hold. As I anticipated, Chernomyrdin
seems to be thinking in terms of selective investment-directed credits at
modest interest rates. One can hardly insist on interest rates above the
rate of inflation: who would borrow for investment purposes at 2000 per
cent!? But demand from industry for credits may prove irresistible. Or it
would be resistible only by a strong government. But we are now about to
witness a confused struggle between the president, the prime minister, the
legislature, a semi-independent state bank, the lobbies, the regions . . .
Who now has the power to act, to implement policy, if and when they
decide what to do?

28 December 1992, Glasgow

The appointment of Boris Fedorov is an important piece of good news.
He knows inside and out both the Russian financial system (he had been
Minister of Finance of the Russian federation when there was still a
USSR, and resigned in protest against the unsoundness of policies then
followed), *and* Western banking, and the views of potential western
investors and international bodies. I met him first when he was a highly
critical adviser to the party's Central Committee, in 1989. With him as
vice-premier, and most of the reforming ministers still in place, what could
emerge is a sort of coalition government, with Chernomyrdin (and,
behind him, Volsky) in a position to persuade the managerial–industrialist
group to go along with essential stabilisation policies. Fedorov and his

reforming colleagues would surely insist that in future credits can no longer be granted indiscriminately, that the need to sustain production requires the earmarking of credits for specific purposes. (Experience has shown that large issue of credits since July have been misused both by commercial banks and industrial enterprises). The research institute of the Ministry of Economics recently recommended the setting up of a new state-sponsored investment bank, pointing out that Western aid and investment is more likely if there exists a development plan or strategy, with future export earnings high on the list of priorities. Credits must be denied to loss-makers in non-priority areas. A government headed by Chernomyrdin may be able to resist pressure from these interest groups better than one headed by Gaidar, precisely because Chernomyrdin speaks their language ('set a thief to catch a thief', only de Gaulle could get the French out of Algeria, and so on). Of course this may not be possible. But, judging from his past behaviour, Fedorov would demand action and resign if thwarted, as he did in 1990. There may not yet be light at the end of the tunnel, but maybe there is a tunnel . . .

1993

27 January 1993, Glasgow

Further fall in the rouble. The spectacular fall in the rouble–dollar rate yesterday was partly due to inflationary expectations, and partly to an immediate panic over rumoured issue of new currency and so of a compulsory exchange of old bank notes. It is this apparently which led to the rush to sell roubles. *But what meaning has the exchange rate? Izvestiya* (13 January) pointed out that even at 450 to the dollar, GNP in 1992, 13.7 trillion roubles, amounts to a mere $30 billion, or less than Greece or even Pakistan, and a per capita GNP of $200. But exports amounted to $35 billion, that is, at this exchange rate, to 16 per cent more than GNP. The American Jan Vanous is quoted as saying that an exchange rate of 12 to the dollar would be closer to price and income relativities. (12 is too low! A.N.) *Hyperinflation* is already here. In the week ending 5 January food prices rose 9.5 per cent. The budget deficit suffers from what *Izvestiya* (5 January) calls 'the budget war'. Autonomous republics and some regions simply refuse to channel revenues raised on their territories to the federal budget. It reminds the author of what happened to the Union budget in 1991. *The stillborn price decrees of Chernomyrdin* had, according to *Izvestiya* (13 January) been drafted before he became premier, but the previous government had put them on ice. Chernomyrdin signed them without any prior discussion in the cabinet. Fedorov was in Washington (he commutes regularly between there and Moscow), and instantly protested. He has tough proposals to cut subsidies and soft credits. He is quoted as saying that it is not the job of the Central Bank to save production, it must concentrate on saving the currency. *The Russian Bank of Reconstruction and Development* has been created by a decision reported on 6 January. Its remit is to finance investment in priority sectors and in infrastructure. (Is this Fedorov's idea, or another channel for excessive credits? We must ask him. Of course, they *do* need an investment bank; the existing commercial banks do not fulfil this function.) Short-term prospects look disastrously bad.

21 March 1993, Glasgow

First reactions to Yeltsin's attempt to establish control. His claim to exercise power has been challenged by his own vice-president, Rutskoi, *and* by the president of the Constitutional Court. And of course Khasbulatov will speedily organise a counterblast from parliament. No doubt many moderate deputies will have been enraged at being described as Bolsheviks. So we must expect any decrees now issued by Yeltsin to be challenged, ignored, or both. If, as has been reported, he dismisses a provincial chief, the dismissed man could simply stay put. Yeltsin asks the army to 'stay out of politics'. But unless he has got a united and active KGB (whatever they now call themselves) on his side, he would need the army behind him if his orders are to be obeyed. And if he did not ensure himself of army support, his orders will hang in the air. What if he is impeached? In any case, his pleinpouvoirs are only supposed to last until the referendum at the end of April. If parliament and the constitutional court rule that the referendum is illegal (or even if they don't), how many would vote? Perhaps the least bad way out is new elections, for both president and parliament. It is a long time since Yeltsin had a popular mandate, and it was before the consequences of shock therapy hit the ordinary citizen. It seems to me possible that Yeltsin will have achieved the worst of all possible outcomes: stirring up intense opposition (and giving it a sort of legal legitimacy by acts that look unconstitutional), and this without in fact acquiring power to act. There is indeed need for a state of emergency, under which to implement a recovery programme, for example, on the lines of the Fedorov plan. But instead the danger grows of more conflict, disintegration, confusion. I sure do hope I am wrong. Meanwhile I do hope that Clinton and Major will avoid publicly committing themselves to Yeltsin. To many voters this would look like improper intervention in internal affairs at a very embarrassing moment. Even if it is true that a Yeltsin victory is, in the circumstances, best for us (and for Russia), we could help by not saying so.

What is Yeltsin Up To?, 25 March 1993, Glasgow

It was almost a comedy, but it is less than clear if this was a comedy of errors or a sort of clumsy clever ploy. First to announce a decree giving himself emergency powers, stir up opposition even among many moderates in parliament (thereby increasing the danger of an impeachment vote), getting an adverse ruling from the Constitutional Court (whose chairman did complain that they were not supplied with the text of the decree, despite several requests). And then, after all that, the text is issued and it contains nothing about emergency powers! Which leaves everyone in a daze. Admittedly, the Court is made to look a bit silly, but what of Yeltsin himself? One is left guessing: did he draft a tough emergency powers decree and then deliberately hold back the text until he felt the temperature of the political water, and then toned it down before publication? All this does nothing to enhance his reputation for wisdom. The net effect may be to help ensure that the Congress will not have a two-thirds majority needed for impeachment. We shall soon know. If there is such a majority, then Congress will declare that Rutskoi is acting president, Yeltsin would refuse to recognise the vote, there would then be two presidents, with the army and security police uncertain whom to obey. Clearly, *pessimum pessimorum*. Surely the protagonists (and enough members of the Congress) will shy away from the road to instant chaos. Suppose, as is more likely, there is no impeachment vote and he stays. Yeltsin demands a referendum. The probability as of now is that it will be blocked, both by Congress (or by the smaller working parliament) and/or by the non-cooperation of the provincial leaders who would have to administer it. Meanwhile the chance of implementing any government recovery programme is slimmer than ever. Effective authority to do anything is lacking.

I see that Gorbachev, on a visit to Canada, has called for new elections, presumably for both president and parliament, the latter possibly in the form of a Constituent Assembly. I do not think that Gorbachev himself has the slightest chance of a comeback, but in the end there may no alternative to new elections, despite the risks involved. I still think that it is counterproductive for the West loudly to back Yeltsin, even though his survival is indeed in our interest. But he certainly has grounds for complaint about the aid Russia has not been getting. Admittedly there is dilemma here, or a vicious circle: without large-scale aid everything is likely to go down the drain, but in present circumstances the aid may go down that very same drain. They do need a strong government, with public backing for emergency powers. Has Yeltsin the skill and the decisiveness to impose a recovery package (for example, the one drafted by Fedorov and his group)? And even given both skill and decisiveness, can he (or anyone in his place) acquire the power to act? Prospects are not promising if the government asks the army and police to be neutral. Then we can be sure in advance that decrees will not be obeyed.

What after the Congress – Some Preliminary Impressions, 28 March 1993, Glasgow

Yeltsin survives. His supporters hope to drum up a referendum majority, though it is not yet clear how the question(s) will be phrased. The Congress may add a question or two, so a possible outcome is support for Yeltsin *and* opposition to some of his key policies. Yeltsin's own performance, first confrontational and then conciliatory, must be confusing to friend and foe. A feature of the Congress is the emergence of Chernomyrdin as a politically significant force. In his speeches he seemed to me to be bidding for a key role as the leader of a government of national salvation. Some deputies are clearly trying to transfer some power from the president to the *government*. One of the proposed resolutions sought to get both Yeltsin and Khasbulatov to step down. Two 'reforming' ministers, Nechaev (Economy) and Barchuk (Finance) are out, but reformer Boris Fedorov takes over Finance. Chubais (Privatisation) is still there, but maybe only because (so I am informed) Fedorov threatened to resign if he was sacked. The more naive foreign commentators (including, I fear, those who advise Western governments) just see a struggle between 'democratic' pro-market Yeltsin and anti-market 'hard-liners' or just 'communists'. The government itself is divided (with Yeltsin changing as the mood takes him), with Chernomyrdin representing the trend away from laissez-faire towards a 'regulated' market and caution. While a segment of the real 'hard-liners', including some military, may favour marketisation under martial law à la Pinochet. Real communists are very much in a minority. But the basic problem is lack of effective political authority, in the absence of which any recovery plan will remain on paper while chaos grows. While Yeltsin may think he can get that authority in and through a referendum, a strong current of opinion (for example, reflected in speeches by Chernomyrdin and the head of the Constitutional Court) favours early elections, of the president and of parliament, the latter in the form of a Constituent Assembly. It is not yet clear whether Yeltsin can be persuaded to accept this, and even less clear what the outcome of such an election may be. Meanwhile in his speech Skokov warned: 'It would horrify you if I told you of the position inside the army.'

A special edition of *Voprosy ekonomiki* (No. 2, 1993) is wholly devoted to a sort of inquest into the reform process. Many well-known names contributed. Abalkin deplored the lack of any development strategy. Gaidar attributes failure to control inflation to the weakness of government; the reaction of state enterprises to restrictive monetary policies (pile-up of unpaid debt) occurred also in the Czech lands and was not foreseen. Petrakov and Yavlinsky strongly attacked the policies pursued in 1992, while Yasin is more moderate in his criticisms, though worried by the effect on the future of the collapse of investment. Layard (LSE, influential adviser) urges more rapid deregulation and privatisation, but also stresses the importance of structural change (does this make for a consistent package?). The editor, Gavriil Popov (ex-mayor of Moscow) attacks the IMF strategy (designed, he says, to reduce Russia to a raw-materials-producing satellite of the developed world, a line which also follows Abalkin's fear of deindustrialisation). Popov and some of the others are unhappy with privatisation in its present form. The wide range of views is notable. Meanwhile it is reported that inflation over the two months January–February reached 60 per cent. (not as bad as 40 per cent a month, but bad). On 12 March the Ukrainian karbovantsi stood at 1233 to the dollar.

The latest from Moscow suggests a total shambles, with parliament (or rather the Congress) refusing to endorse a Yeltsin–Khasbulatov deal. On top of that they voted to index (backdated to last year) savings bank deposits, i.e., print still more money. The net effect is to discredit all politics. Paralysis continues.

14 May 1993, Glasgow

Met the Swedish economic adviser to Russians, Anders Aslund. He is a committed 'laissez-faire' man, and considers that Russia is making adequate progress towards a deregulated market economy. He hopes that the political balance in the government has shifted towards the radicals again, despite the appointment a month ago of two 'moderate' first-deputy-premiers, by the dismissal last week of Skokov (potentially powerful secretary of the Security committee) and of Khizha (said by Aslund to be the most 'conservative' of the ministers). However, the same source is very uneasy about premier Chernomyrdin, who, he said, plots against Chubais and has rows with Boris Fedorov. An important battle is raging over privatisation. A gathering of managers and officials concerned with the military–industrial complex has argued that a national 'conversion' scheme is needed, that if each factory tries to switch to civilian production without either the resources or the market knowledge, results are frequently nil. Example cited: one plant went into colour TV, but, at prices that cover costs, most citizens are now too poor to afford anything other than a small black-and-white. Proposed solution: the creation of large autonomous corporations within the complex, directly linked with financial institutions, endowed with a sort of plan bureau. Others too have argued for a new form of corporation, whereas the logic of Chubais's 'voucher privatisation' is to disintegrate into small independent productive units. Which could be useful to combat monopoly, but has disadvantages where there is an established vertical structure. Danger is also seen in segments of an integrated whole 'opting out' with privatisation. Chernomyrdin is also said to be interested in a recreation of a sort of 'Gosplan' to help run coherently what remains of the state sector of industry. This, in my view (but *not* Aslund's), may well be the sensible thing to do for the big heavy-industry complexes. Whether they will be able to implement this (or any other) policy is another question. Meanwhile Yeltsin's idea of a constitutional convention, bypassing the existing parliament, is a challenging ploy. I see from the papers that several of the players, in both the economic and constitutional conflicts, are men I know well, Evgeni Yasin and Viktor Sheinis. I would get a much clearer picture by talking to them. There is danger of having two bodies drafting two constitutions, as well as different ministers following different economic policies. Rumours about Fedorov perhaps replacing Gerashchenko at the State Bank are still unconfirmed. As you know, ministers blame him for printing money *and* adopting policies which compel the State Bank to print more money.

Ukrainian Mess Continues Messy, 21 May 1993, Glasgow

So Leonid Kuchma resigns, or tries to resign. He is not the first. Vice-premier Yukhnovsky resigned (or was pushed) a few weeks ago. It is not clear whether Kuchma's failure to get parliament to vote him special powers was or was not complicated by his own power position *vis-à-vis* President Kravchuk. Maybe Kravchuk is about to become his own premier. Nor is it clear whether parliament's reported reluctance to give sweeping powers to Kravchuk is an aspect of power-struggle or is based on policy differences. Meanwhile reform, and privatisation, is proceeding at a snail's pace. But who is the snail? How much of the slowness is due to divisions at the centre, how much to the power position in the provinces of the former apparatchiki? Ukraine's inflation rate is just about double that of Russia. So is the reported budget deficit. The very big increases now being imposed by Russia for deliveries of oil and gas helps to make a critical situation catastrophic. And if the Russian government lacks power to enforce its decrees, the Ukrainian government has even less. We are likely to land in the middle of a chronic political–economic crisis.

1 June 1993, Glasgow

Here are a few fairly relevant snippets.

1. *Ukraine.* The president, his government and the parliament are locked in a three-way confusion. There are now well over 3000 karbovantsi to the dollar. Political paralysis requires a solution. We are likely to arrive in the midst of all sorts of crisis.
2. *The rouble* has passed the 1000 to the dollar mark even sooner than I expected. One reason is that there is still no sign of the tough polices needed to deal with the inflation – though it was only 16 per cent (over the previous month) in April. Fedorov, in a tough-sounding article in *Izvestiya*, spoke of the urgent need to reduce subsidies to essential imports and to the coal industry, the latter amounting to 2 trillion roubles, this being 20 per cent of the budget revenue!! Some loss-making pits must close. He accused Gerashchenko of a credit policy which undermines the rouble. Vice-premier Shokhin, a reformer, had an article published in which he proposed recalling Gaidar as vice-premier and minister of finance, and moving Fedorov to head the Central Bank.
3. But the political balance in the government is not too favourable to such schemes. Chernomyrdin has been reinforced by the appointments of Lobov and Soskovets to key economic posts. Yeltsin seems uncertain what to do next.
4. Meanwhile Gerashchenko has accepted that credits to industry be the responsibility of the Ministry of Finance (that is, Fedorov), no doubt convinced that the government will find it politically impossible to pursue a restrictive policy (and stop using him as a scapegoat). Yeltsin has gone back on several of his referendum promises, for example, restoring a sharp rise in gasoline prices and postponing some social benefits. But the claims of agriculture, of 'conversion' of the energy sector, for credits and investment will surely prove irresistible. However, they are trying to cover

at least part of the budget deficit in a less inflationary way: exchequer bonds have been issued repayable in three months at 60 per cent interest (for 650 billion roubles).

5. Vice-president Rutskoi continues to campaign vigorously against the government, denouncing Yeltsin. One wonders how much support he can muster among the military. Many officers have been put into an impossible position. And the quarrel with Ukraine over the Black Sea fleet is boiling up again. And in seeking provincial support for his version of the new constitution, Yeltsin is being forced to concede too much to the regions and national republics. There is no imminent danger of a coup, the army is demoralised and divided, but . . .

11 June 1993, Glasgow

Quite a lot to report, having met in London and Paris interesting individuals from Ukraine, and also the Russian Minister of Labour (Gennady Melikyan), the Czech deputy-Minister of Finance (V. Rudlovcak), a Romanian reform adviser (Cristian Popa), an old economist friend who is now a leading Hungarian politician, plus assorted Poles. This letter will be concerned first with Ukraine, then with Russia.

Three Ukrainians seen were: Vladimir Lanovoi (or Lanovyy), former minister, once seen as the 'Ukrainian Gaidar', Oleksandr Savchenko, now with EBRD in London, and Elena Skliarenko, of whom more in a moment. Points gleaned from discussion with them were: One reason for slow progress is that Ukraine, when cast adrift by the collapse of the USSR, had had no revolution, and most of the old leadership was still in place. Privatisation has been effectively blocked so far by a combination of ambiguous laws and local bureaucratic pressures. If a private firm is set up, it is likely to have trouble getting a credit, fuel deliveries, and so on. Non-state would-be exporters pay export tax, from which state enterprises are exempt, and so on. Foreign trade is in a parlous state, the volume in the first four months of 1993 (according to Lanovoi) being only 33 per cent of the analogous months of 1992. The payments situation with Russia is confused, with clearing arrangements inadequate. Lanovoi had negotiated about this with Gaidar, but they were both sacked! Kuchma, still premier, is trying to recreate state industrial-sector committees to run the big state industries. Lanovoi sees him as representing the interests and views of state managers. (Not very different from the views in Russia of Lobov, and probably Chernomyrdin too. A.N.) The karbovanets continues to depreciate, but new Russian rules concerning the validity of rouble banknotes held outside Russia has reduced the attractiveness of the rouble to Ukrainians.

The huge rise in prices of energy supplied by Russia has naturally worsened a bad situation. Both Lanovoi and Savchenko see no grounds for optimism and expect political troubles. The Moscow *Ekonomika i zhizn'* (No. 20) printed a long survey by its Ukraine correspondent. A gloomy picture. Social tensions, 85 per cent of population below poverty line. 4.5 million unemployed. Many shortages. Sugar and butter rationed. In the single month of January prices of basic foods quintupled. (Presumably some controls were lifted. A.N.) Kuchma favours marketisation, but wants to precede large-scale privatisation by macro stabilisation. State enterprises are to be commercialised, but with the state retaining majority shareholding. Meanwhile his aim is to retain control over prices and incomes, and to subject a part of output to 'state orders'. The correspondent paints two alternative scenarios: one retains 'socialist' verbiage, tries for a deal with Russia and puts off radical reforms except in trade and services. The other combines more radical marketising policies with a dangerous worsening of relations with Russia, whereupon it will all come unstuck. *But* note that the tone of the correspondent is one that suggests an anti-Ukrainian bias. Another report concerns the Ukraine's draft budget for 1993. The deficit 'limit' is given as 983 298.1 million karbovantsi (I do not like the 0.1 A.N.). VAT is up at 28 per cent, and there is a revenue tax (and not a profit tax) on enterprises. There is an anti-inflationary programme, but surely the line will not be held.

Now a few points about *Russia*. The minister, Melikyan, proved to be moderately gloomy. He is alarmed by the political consequences of the extremes of income inequality. He realises how important it is to reduce subsidies and soft credits, but a rigid monetarist policy would lead to massive unemployment and social-political convulsions. He took the view which I have often expressed: there must be selective support linked with an industrial strategy, while some chronic loss-makers must be bankrupted. Once again there is a mountain of mutual inter-enterprise debt. Western advisers tend to assume that there can be market-type responses in Russia when markets are either highly imperfect or non-existent. Another of the Russians, V. Naishul (an old friend, but with a Friedmanist ideology, A.N.) insisted that *the* decisive problem was the lack of legal order or proper commercial law. It is this above all else that prevents or distorts the functioning of the market. He was more optimistic than the minister. But both he and some of the East Europeans stressed one point: before the collapse of communism the party was where the power lay. The state machine was weak. It still is weak. It is wrong to expect governments to do things which they are incapable of doing. (Fair point! A.N.) Two recent issues of *Ekonomika i zhizn'* are full of interesting material. An editorial argues (as did Melikyan) that weak or non-existent markets cannot cope with needed reconstruction, that the Russian government is right to be drafting a restructuring plan. 'It seems that state enterprises will be divided into two. Some will be under direct government control, others will be granted full commercial independence.' A major article is devoted to the vital issue of investment.

The collapse of investment, to a level well below physical depreciation of basic capital, led to 'direct degradation of the productive apparatus.' Output of capital goods is falling steeply, most construction enterprises are on the edge of bankruptcy. 'The restoration of Russia's productive potential requires a gigantic volume of investment resources. If the aim is to slow down the decline of GNP in 1993, stabilise it in 1994 and to grow by just 2 per cent in 1995, this would require a doubling during 1993 of investments over the level of 1992.' In fact 'we need to double our investments just to reach the level required to replace worn-out capital.' Clearly, argues the author, this requires government interventionism. 'Commercial investments are impossible during high inflation.' And 'it is clear that foreign capital will not come to a country where internal investment activity is paralysed.' This sort of issue underlies my own pessimism. It is nice to see a flourishing market in French perfumes and American panty-hose, and presumably someone responds to advertisements for Mercedes cars at $34 000 and up ($34 000 is about a hundred *years* salary for a civil servant!). But how can they recover if investment is negative? The same journal speaks of a railway crisis. Rail wagons used to be imported from Eastern Europe, the Ukraine, Latvia. Rails are worn out; 'investment in rail has collapsed'. Meanwhile oil is being increasingly moved by rail, because 'in a pipe no one knows whose it is'. And the demand for mineral fertiliser from Russian agriculture appears to be 75 per cent down on 1991 levels, because the farms cannot afford the high prices. Many rail wagons are full of fertiliser and creating bottlenecks at border stations, as attempts are made to export, including to China. *Finally, Ekonomika i zhizn'* estimates that the (real) budget deficit in 1993 will be 20 per cent of GNP, the same as in 1992. Well, and so on . . .

Russia: Is the Worst Over?, 6 July 1993, Glasgow

This is a question which has no simple answer. The signs are contradictory. Some assert that the corner has been turned, that a market-based recovery is gathering momentum, though no one denies that there remain unsolved problems and that many suffer hardship. Others point to the hardship and the problems, and forecast continued decline, with inflation in four figures. Who is right?

Let us look at the negative signs. First, GNP and industrial output are 20 per cent down on a year ago. Some forecasts insist that the fall must continue at least into 1994, because of the collapse of investment, which is down between 60 and 70 per cent in volume in the last two years. This has a double effect: (1), it causes a decline in demand for and production of building materials, machinery and equipment, affecting particularly the high tech. end of the range; (2), such industries as oil extraction and refining, ferrous metallurgy, chemicals, transportation, all report failure to replace worn-out or obsolete equipment and cite this as a cause of continued decline in productive capacity. Conversion of the military–industrial complex is also slowed by lack of needed investment. A combination of budgetary stringency and ideological reluctance has greatly reduced the state's role in investment, while in the present inflationary and political uncertainty private long-term investment is very small. The government has now published a recovery plan, with priorities, but it may not have the clout or the resources to implement it.

Second, while any visitor can observe the vast range of private commerce, and also the appearance of elements of market infrastructure and financial services of many kinds, a Russian critic wrote: 'among the new rich I cannot recall a single producer of material goods.' Tension (and corruption!) arises from the fact that, for instance, Mercedes cars are on sale at a price equal to a *hundred years' salary* of a fairly senior civil servant! Third, curbing inflation is proving very difficult, despite the cooperation of the State Bank in the effort to reduce the flow of soft credits. There are still large subsidies to the coal industry and to agriculture. The budget deficit may stay at 20 per cent of GNP. No state firm has yet been bankrupted. Sectoral and regional lobbies are powerful. Inflation could well remain close to 20 per cent a month, though admittedly worse was expected. Finally, all is far from well with *agriculture*. The number of would-be private farms is still small. Collective and state farms suffer from reorganisation and uncertainty, and prices fail to cover soaring costs. Purchases of fertiliser have slumped by 75 per cent. Meat and milk production has fallen sharply, despite the subsidies. All this can be cited by the gloom merchants.

But there is also a positive side. Yeltsin's position has been strengthened by the referendum, and by the confusion and splits among his enemies, though it should be noted that his own ministers are at odds with one another (for example, vice-premier Fedorov versus Lobov, with premier Chernomyrdin closer to the latter). Privatisation has made considerable strides, in various forms (employee buy-outs, managerial take-overs, purchases through share auctions, and so on.). The 10 000 rouble investment vouchers, which recently sold at half-price, have risen in value in the last months. While no one denies that crime and fraud are prevalent, a commercial 'market' climate is developing, and would develop faster if there were greater confidence in the legal system and in a consistent government policy. Some regions and some cities (for example, Nizhni Novgorod, St. Petersburg, Kalningrad-Königsberg, parts of the Far East) have taken initiatives to develop a healthy private enterprise in association with the local government and with foreign interests – though so far the commitment of foreign money has been small. While, true enough, the lower-paid and the pensioners are suffering hardship, many have found ways and means to supplement their income, and even to earn some dollars, which help to explain the absence of politically-motivated disorders. Alarmist talk of civil war, of disintegration of the Russian federation, has proved to be alarmist talk. While it is true that investment is too low, there is considerable underused productive capacity which can be brought into operation. Low wages ($25 a month!) and good technical training can attract foreign capital, and a recent deal involving civil aircraft may prove a promise of things to come. Export potential is there, if it can be properly organised, managed, financed. The large sums kept abroad by Russian firms and 'new rich' represent an investment potential, which could be realised as and when stability is achieved. Furthermore, while it is true that GNP and industrial production both fell by 19 per cent in the first quarter of 1993, this was over the first quarter of 1992, there was no significant fall from the *last* quarter. This is some evidence of levelling out.

So – is the worst over? On two conditions (in my view) it could be. The two conditions are: a strong government capable of enforcing the law and an anti-inflationary policy, and substantial foreign aid and investment *targeted* to strategically key areas. Unless it is targeted, there is danger that foreign aid will finance luxury imports for the new rich and/or find its way into bank accounts in the West. It is both politically and economically important that the aid and credits be large enough to make a visible difference. So far the large figures bandied about remain, in people's minds and in reality too, devoid of meaning. Thus to talk of $47 billion when no such sum is in prospect begins to look like a bad joke. An important priority is to ease the situation of the very numerous new poor. They derive no benefit from imports of BMWs and French perfumes . . . Conclusion: we are at a turning-point, political as well as economic. Disaster *can* happen, but disaster has become less likely as 1993 progresses.

26 July 1993, Glasgow

The Russian monetary 'reform' looks like a combination of incompetence and deliberate provocation. I suspect our old friend Gerashchenko, probably in cahoots with Chernomyrdin, taking advantage of the absence from Moscow of both Yeltsin and Boris Fedorov. You have doubtless read of the latter's cries of distress. What was it all for? Not just mischief-making, of course. The intended principal targets were those ex-Soviet republics which have accumulated large stocks of roubles, and that (despite its leaving the rouble zone) includes Ukraine, since many of its citizens and traders preferred the rouble to the even more rapidly inflating karbovanets. But equally hit are ordinary citizens. Perhaps the authorities had in mind to hit those of the new rich who had hoards of many million banknotes and now face having to explain their provenance. But in prac-tice millions of common folk, indignantly queuing outside banks which, not having been forewarned, do not even have stocks of new notes, are cursing the authorities. What a shambles! Of course a monetary reform is needed, but as part of a prearranged package of anti-inflationary intent. Of such a package there is no sign. In fact the 5 July issue of Moscow's *Kommersant* notes the temporary stabilisation of the rouble–dollar rate (around 1100), but 'the rise in prices does not slow down; the emission of roubles is stronger than the stabilisation of valuta', and the latter is not expected to last long. The cost of living index in June showed a rise of 23 per cent in the month (May also +23 per cent). But personal incomes grew faster, inventories in the trade network are low, agricultural prices rose rapidly, from 1 July coal prices have been freed (with the expectation of a price rise which will reach 500 per cent), there is irresistible pressure for still more credits for the agricultural sector and for the needs of the Far North. In all, *Kommersant* forecasts a 35 per cent increase in prices in July, *and* that attempts to limit the growth of money supply will lead to another big growth in inter-enterprise debt.

The Russian Situation in Mid 1993, 10 August 1993, Glasgow

The journal *Kommersant* has produced an analytical supplement, concen-trating on industrial output and prospects. The output index looks as follows: 1990 (100), 1991 (91.04), 1992 (73.3), 1993 (64.0 – forecast). Because of statistical problems of measuring in terms of prices at a time of very high inflation, the analyst uses physical output data to measure rates of decline, which vary greatly by industrial sector. The figures are for May 1993 (September 1991=100): Electricity, 92.5; All fuels, 88.8; Iron & steel, 85.2; Chemicals, 82.9; Timber & wood, 72.7; Machinery, 68.6; Bldg materials, 68.0; Food industry, 74.4; Light industry, 58.8. The rate of decline varied widely by periods. Thus in the second half of 1992 the relaxation of monetary policy did bring about a slower decline, even though it was noted that many of the soft credits were shifted into trade deals. The sectoral shift was 'regressive', that is, there was a particularly large fall in what should have been high value-added processing, explicable by the fact that prices of materials and energy now approach world levels, and with these hugely increased costs the (comparatively inefficient) manufacturing sector becomes lossmaking. Thus light industry (textiles, clothing, and so on) is squeezed: deflation of consumer demand combined with ballooning costs of inputs drives it to the wall.

Average real incomes have plummeted. This has also affected the food industry, and the decline can best be measured by the decline in one year of consumption of animal products by between 20 and 35 per cent. 'The sudden and unprepared shift to medical insurance has led to a catastrophic decline in medical services. Ill-health grows, death rates are up, the population numbers are falling.' Unemployment remains very low, despite the fall in production since 1989 by some 35 to 40 per cent. Obviously productivity is way down, and the expected unemployment did not (yet) happen. 'No lockouts, no bankruptcies. Why sack people when the mighty inflation writes off everything, ever more money is printed, enterprises managed to stay afloat with the help of credits, especially as money is worth so little . . . If average wages are a dollar a day, even an economy in crisis can pay.' But this autumn it may be different. Enterprises face a shortage of cash, and then there are school-leavers and demobilised soldiers. So up to 8 per cent open unemployment by the year's end is a real possibility. This would be a further burden on the budget, and nothing serious is being done to retrain the labour force. In fact education, like medicine, is in dire trouble. New tax laws are intended to stimulate investment, with exemptions from taxes for reinvested profits, and this applies to state, private and foreign enterprises. Unfortunately, tax evasion is widespread, so that the incentive to invest functions 'only on paper', and the commercial banks 'successfully coordinate their tax avoidance work'. All this despite the formidable multiplicity of taxes, levies, fees, central and local, about which honest business complains.

The *foreign trade* picture in the first half-year is extraordinary. Exports reached $18.3 billion, up by 3.2 per cent over the same period last year, imports were a mere $9 billion, so there seems to be *a record trade surplus*! What happened to it, asks the author. Have reserves increased? Has more foreign debt been repaid? Or has the money been left in foreign banks? No one knows. But so-called 'essential' imports fell extremely fast: medical drugs by 79 per cent, meat by 78 per cent, grain by 49 per cent, machinery and equipment by 75 per cent. Total imports fell by 48 per cent. It all looks strange and unhealthy, the more so because the rush to export has been associated with underpricing by incompetent newly-baked traders. Frankly, all this does not add up to an optimistic scenario . . .

Oil output fell by 13.7 per cent in the first six months of 1993. Prices have been freed, but with a limit set to profit margins. The internal price of oil increased 600-fold since 1990, but since the exchange rate has depreci-ated 1300-fold in the same period, the internal price as at April was further below the world price than it had been in 1990! A ton of oil in 1990 equalled 10 per cent of the average monthly wage. It is now 80–90 per cent of the monthly wage. (Source, *Ekonomika i zhizn'*, No. 28, states that in USA it is 5–6 per cent of the American wage.) A table shows the fall of oil deliveries to former Soviet republics: from 117.5 million tons in 1990 they fell to 75.5 in 1991 and are expected to be 56.9 in 1993. (Deliveries to Ukraine: 49.3, 33.5 and 22.6 million tons respectively.) The same journal prints a Declaration of a National Economic Agreement, the result of a round table called jointly by government and parliament. It is similar to other past declarations, adopted in both Russia and Ukraine, but which may remain on paper. It is rightly described as 'centrist', that is, represents a mixture of marketising, caution and regulation, à la Chernomyrdin. This may be the basis of his recent policy declaration, which I have yet to see and study.

The currency withdrawal was less drastic than it seemed from earlier reports. What was withdrawn were banknotes issued prior to 1993. But in 1993 there had already been issued banknotes to the value of 3.25 tril-lion, and at most 1 trillion of the old notes were still around, and part of them were in the hands of the banks. All of the 1993 issue remained valid. But, according to *Kommersant*, the central bank failed to inform the Ministry of Finance what it was up to. *More on Currency Withdrawal.* *Izvestiya* (30 and 31 July) stresses the damage done to those republics which had been lavishly supplied with the old rouble notes by the Russian central bank in recent months, with Gerashchenko taking care that they be not supplied with the new (1993) notes. Fedorov demanded Gerashchenko's resignation, both because he was neither informed nor consulted, and because CIS partners 'were cheated'. Anders Aslund is quoted as supposing that the whole business is connected with money-laundering, but this is thought unlikely. (I know that Aslund considers Gerashchenko to be a villain!) The well-informed political editor Otto Latsis (whom I know well, A.N.) explains the fiasco by 'incompetence, plus indifference'. Gerashchenko did apologise to 'northerners on holi-day', who were caught far from home with sackfuls of roubles, but many others, including refugees from other republics, were severely penalised, as they could only have had old rouble notes. And then there were private entrepreneurs and traders, but probably Gerashchenko had an ideological predisposition to penalise them . . . Chernomyrdin is also to blame for approving the measure, Yeltsin for not stopping it earlier.

Parliament's efforts to sabotage the privatisation process, by diluting the powers of Chubais's ministry, is causing much confusion. One possible proposal ('not impossible', according to *Kommersant*) is 'to take back all that has already been privatised, in order to then reprivatise it fairly'. Meanwhile the Economic Ministry (Lobov and co.) tries to achieve control. *The budget*. Fedorov stated publicly that 'so long as I am minister, I will not implement the crazy budget deficit approved by parliament.' And indeed the figures are: Revenue, 28.38 trillion; Expenditure, 44.65 trillion. Deficit would be at least 25 per cent of GNP. *The All Russian Economic Consultative Group* met in Moscow on 27–29 July. This included senior officials, managers, regional representatives. They denounced the irresponsible budget and the currency exchange scheme, were gloomy about prospects: machinery and equipment in civilian industry is worn out, 26 years old on average, is not being replaced, investment is far too low, the defence industry produces non-military goods at excessive cost. Energy and materials are being dumped on world markets, and four-fifths of the proceeds are not repatriated. There are too many heavy taxes, yet 'tax avoidance is a national sport'. Regional separatists retain revenues and valuta. There are no policy successes to report. 'But the most frightening is that state-power is paralysed, so that even the most brilliant economic programme has no chance of being implemented.' (Their words, not mine! A.N.)

The Yeltsin 'Coup', 23 September 1993, Glasgow

The Background. Political paralysis, the stand-off with parliament, could not long continue. The St. Petersburg daily, *Nevskoe vremya* wrote, on 15 September, that 'in September–October the destructive influence of dual power must end'. The government itself was divided, with Lobov and Soskovets supporting lavish credits to industry to 'save production', and Fedorov and Chubais stressing the need to limit inflation. Yeltsin had been persuaded to support Lobov's plans, but cancelled his signature when Fedorov counter-persuaded him. Meanwhile, parliament had adopted a highly inflationary budget, with revenues covering less than half of expenditure, apparently in the belief that a 30 per cent a month inflation would be better than the imposition of a hard monetary policy. Yeltsin vetoed the parliament's budget bill, *but* his veto was about to be overridden, with consequences (political and economic) which would be deplorable. And if Yeltsin refused to implement the bill, then impeachment would follow. Both vice-president Rutskoi and 'speaker' Khazbulatov were becoming increasingly intransigent, and talk of compromise began to evaporate. It is not that parliament is communist-dominated. It contains few organised parties, and represents all kinds of industrial and regional lobbies. 'Populism' dominates, that is, irresponsible voting for subsidies, higher pensions, and so on, with no serious concern for tax revenue. Paralysis and drift were widely criticised. But what could Yeltsin do within the constraints of the existing constitution?

An important first policy step was taken on 16 September: Gaidar was brought back as first vice-premier, and Lobov shifted out of economics and onto the Security Council attached to the presidency. This move had two consequences: first, it shifted the balance *within* the government towards the radical market reformers (and it is significant that Chernomyrdin stated that *he* proposed Gaidar's return). Second, Gaidar was *the* bête noir of the parliamentary majority, and of Rutskoi and Khazbulatov, so his appointment was a clear signal that there would be no more attempts at compromise. Both men so saw the move, and stated that a 'coup' was imminent. Yeltsin had been blamed for hesitating too long. His support reached its height at the time of the April referendum. It has slipped since. One way of bypassing parliament was by setting up the 'Council of the Federation' as a kind of upper house. The Council duly met in the first days of September, but failed to agree. Meanwhile Khazbulatov was calling an 'all-union economic consultative council' to meet in Moscow on 20 September, to call for the resignation of Fedorov and Chubais and Gaidar. The political situation was further complicated by a split in the Civic Union, with Volsky apparently reaching some understanding with Gaidar and with Yavlinsky, while part of his former team, led by Lipitski, moved towards hard-line opposition. Gaidar now leads a political party, 'Choice of Russia' (*Russki vybor*). His differences with Yavlinsky today are seen as one of personal rivalry rather than of policy. Another important political move by Yeltsin, which took the wind out of the sails of the moderate nationalist opposition, was his overtures to most of the other ex-Soviet republics. Leaders of Armenia, Belarus, Azerbaijan, Kazakhstan, Uzbekistan, Georgia, Ukraine, were courted with offers of a trade and payments union. Khazbulatov tried to go further, publicly proposing an elected CIS assembly, but that was plainly impracticable. Yeltsin was able to announce that 'on 24 September a CIS economic union was to be formed'. (It still has some way to go, and Kravchuk did not sign as a full member, fearing nationalist backlash, but serious foundations were laid that day in Moscow.)

How? – And What Now? Although they must have expected action on such lines (the dissolving of parliament had been discussed and anticipated for months), Yeltsin still managed to catch his opponents on the wrong foot. They had hopes of the constitutional court, and Yeltsin suspended it, so it could not even decide whether its own suspension was unconstitutional! Parliament found itself isolated behind its own barricades, with phones and electricity cut off, its daily paper stopped from publishing, TV and radio firmly held by Yeltsinites (and broadcasting and appropriate propaganda). A smallish crowd did gather by the White House, but what was striking to me (and I travelled daily by packed public transport . . .) was the passive indifference of the population. Given this fact, and the unwillingness of the bulk of even the discontented army officers to intervene (for that would mean civil war), Rutskoi and Khazbulatov had no effective cards to play. No doubt they hoped that Yeltsin would order troops or security police to attack the White House, but surely he will do no such silly thing, he will just let them stew in their own juice. He offered reasonable social benefits to the deputies. Many will go home. So he has won? Not quite. In Moscow, yes, but Russia is vast. What of the regions? On the eve of the coup, Boris Fedorov spoke on TV about regions and republics retaining tax revenue, contributing to the federal financial crisis, and he reminded his audience of what happened to the USSR budget in 1991. Many regions in varying degrees deplore the unconstitutionality of Yeltsin's actions, and even the controlled TV reported that some have decided 'to obey neither side, to look after themselves until things get sorted out in Moscow.' Yeltsin may have dealt a blow to 'dual power' (*dvoyevlastiye*), but there is still danger of powerlessness (*bezvlastiye*). A gathering of regional representatives met in St. Petersburg on 24–25 September and proposed a sort of compromise: simultaneous elections for parliament and the presidency, a proposal Yeltsin has rejected (for no very convincing reason, I would add), but which may resurface.

There are still a great many potentially explosive unknowns. Thus there is still no electoral law, or constitutional principles, for the forthcoming election. What should be the basis of representation in the upper house of what it is apparently proposed to call the Duma? How is the lower house to be elected – by constituencies, first past the post, party lists, or some permutation or combination of these? Can all this be sorted out by December? And can the government pursue harsh policies (Gaidar, in an interview, used the words 'starvation budget') in the run-up to the elections? With so many people impoverished, how will they in fact vote? I discussed public opinion with Academician Tatyana Zaslavskaya, who runs a highly sophisticated and independent sampling procedure. According to her, Rutskoi had a clear majority in the rural areas, Yeltsin, in the large cities. Khazbulatov came a respectable third. But there may be dark horses: Yavlinsky, Shakhrai, for instance (both would be reasonable reformers, whereas Rutskoi is described by Zaslavskaya and others as at best 'confused'). It is important to realise that, apart from the stratum of nouveau-riches, most find life very hard. A full professor of mathematics at Moscow University (and a cousin of mine, A.N.) tells me his salary is now 50 000R, £95, a month, about to be raised to 70 000R, and he also has a war pension, and his wife works, so they just about manage. A tolerable restaurant away from the centre served me a tolerable meal which, with one beer, cost me 11 000 roubles, that is, almost a week's professorial salary! He and others speak sadly of disastrous decline in science and research, the emigration of key scientists. So, assuming Yeltsin holds on, and Gaidar, Fedorov and Chubais retain the support of Yeltsin and Chernomyrdin, where is the economy going?

The two heavyweights with whom I discussed the matter were Evgeni Yasin (a leading government adviser and a most able man) and Leonid Abalkin (Director of the Institute of Economics and former 'reform' minister under Gorbachev). Yasin took a line similar to that of most of the young members of Gaidar's team. Despite serious problems of controlling inflation and establishing a legal order, the way to the market exists. Enterprise managers have learnt to calculate, to study markets, to rely less on handouts. Interest rates on bank credits now reach 15 per cent a month, so demand for credits has fallen. Many now ask for prepayment before delivery. New breeds of entrepreneurs are appearing. Extremes of wealth have been a result of a distorted economy, and, yes, some ugly features of crude early capitalism can shock, but one cannot rely on the state machine to correct or allocate, as it is rotten with corruption. While investments are indeed far too low, it is necessary to wait until inflation is brought down to a tolerable 30 or 40 per cent a year. The existing capital (including that held in foreign banks) will be invested, as profitable opportunities (including for foreigners) do plainly exist. There are some opportunities to increase budget revenues: for example, the excise and/or import duty on imported liquor and other luxuries is far too low: cognac, whisky, Smirnoff vodka, sell in street stalls far lower than in London and Paris, and far lower than a kilogram of sausage! All this calls for cautious optimism.

Abalkin does not agree. He points to decline, impoverishment, collapse of R&D, worn-out equipment, the certainty that decline can only continue. He accuses Gaidar of having no recovery programme, concerned for monetary stabilisation and not production. He pointed out that, at the macro level, accumulation is astonishingly high, but it consists mainly of stocks, inventories. Import competition, with the appreciation of the rouble in real terms, can have disastrous deindustrialising consequences. Thus a Russian TV set sells at 250 000 roubles, a Samsung at 280 000.

Abalkin is more pessimistic in his political prognostications too. I would
not discount his arguments. Could Yasin's view prevail as against his in
the proportions of, say, 60–40? There is no choice but to wait and see –
though Yasin argues that this could forego big profit opportunities. I was
told that a big factor in the rouble appreciation after June was central
bank intervention, made possible by the huge export surplus in the first
half-year, plus a change in rules governing compulsory sales of export
proceeds. But a nervous market sent the rate tumbling on 21 September
from about 1050 to 1500 roubles to the dollar. Yet a week earlier I had
read that one could buy dollars in the futures market for delivery on
3 January 1994 for 1650.

Conclusion. Despite Yeltsin's victory, much remains uncertain. One
danger is political disintegration, as regions go their own way. Another is
continuing high inflation, especially if the presidential election is not due
until next June: how can Yeltsin meanwhile avoid making concessions, to
regions, to lobbies, to wage-earners, to agricultural interests? Gaidar will
have a very difficult task, even though the 'populist' parliament will not be
there to trouble him, yet. (N.B.: There is in fact a danger that a free election will actually increase the number of semi-communists in parliament,
as it has done in Poland.) When asked by an interviewer about the danger
of unemployment, Gaidar replied that Russian management is 'paternalistic', more like the Japanese, and that the danger of mass sackings is
overstated. This surprises me. It suggests the continuing of the 'no bankruptcies' policy, the retention of surplus staff. Surely, if Gaidar's own
tough recipes are followed, unemployment must swiftly rise. Yasin's policy
draft did recommend a sort of industrial policy, supporting some key sectors of the economy. But his proposals went much less far than those of
Lobov, who combined the notion of tight ministerial control over the state
sector with a huge infusion of funds from the budget; a policy described
by one of Gaidar's team as 'populist protectionism'. He also tried to block
privatisation. Gaidar announced the intention to lower taxes and interest
rates, but not until stabilisation is achieved in maybe 1995. His statement
of aims made no mention of either production or investment, which did
seem an odd omission. (He may still be listening to Sachs!)

My own view remains one of caution tinged with pessimism. The government still lacks power to administer. For example, many workers in
the Far North, which includes the oil and gas areas, are migrating south
because in the short summer months the needed supplies have not been
sent to see them through the winter. When I pointed to the large budgetary sums voted for just this purpose, the reply was: yes they were
voted, but only part of the supplies were sent, due to payment delays and

other reasons. As argued earlier, elections, if they take place, will provide a powerful impetus for unsound vote-gathering concessions, and if they do not take place there could be major disorders – which indeed could accompany the elections. Investment remains very low, well below the needs of replacing worn-out track, pipelines, machinery. Ecology is a disaster area. Agriculture continues to absorb subsidies on a big scale. The potentially very promising agreement to create an economic union within CIS can only be made a reality if there is a joint stabilisation programme, which is not very likely. Ukraine is in a much worse state than Russia. Georgia is, literally, a bloody mess. Kazakhstan is stable, and a commentator referred to president Nazarbaev as 'the reuniter of the lands of Russia'. (He has long advocated such an economic union.) The streets are full of kiosks selling imported liquor and Snickers, and the new rich buy Mercedes, BMWs and Volvos, but production looks set to decline further. Privatisation of the larger enterprises has (so far) changed little: management is the same, the 'shareholders' play hardly any role – though some insist that there is now a much tougher line on credits, which compel management to think seriously about money, prices, costs, demand. Some genuinely enterprising entrepreneurs are beginning to appear. Beggars abound. So do protection rackets, so does corruption. The gap between rich and poor is immense. This affects the markets for cars. BMWs, Volvos, Mercedes, even a few Rolls Royces, are status symbols for the new rich. Below the new rich there should be a market for Hondas and Toyotas, but very few are to be seen, because there is a wide gap separating the new rich from those who can afford Ladas or no car at all.

This market pattern reflects the absence of a *middle class*. And that, in turn, affects the political balance and economic prospects. On what social stratum can the reformers rely? What grounds have we for supposing that democracy and market reform in Russia are mutually compatible? To repeat: if parliamentary elections take place, the result may not be helpful to Yeltsin. He might well find reasons for postponing them. Even if Rutskoi and Khasbulatov are discredited, a new populist–nationalist opposition (*and* regional power-centres) could cause chronic troubles. Nor could we have heard the last of the nationalist army officers' organisation. The most hopeful alternative to Yeltsin is in fact Yavlinsky, surprisingly popular in opinion polls, popular also in Nizhni Novgorod, where the local authority subsidises the poor. There *are* grounds for hope, but for disaster scenarios too.

Another October Revolution, 3 October 1993, 10 p.m., Glasgow

When I left Moscow just a week ago, the situation in the capital seemed under control, with the bulk of the population apathetic, almost uninterested. Opponents of Yeltsin could muster a crowd of a few thousand. Trouble there would be, especially when the regions would go their own way, but my Russian colleagues thought that Yeltsin and his government could hold on (but there was doubt whether the promised elections would or could be held). Today's events, however, are threatening and dire in the highest degree. *The* direst event, seen on our own TV, was the crowd of some thousands, some armed, storming the Moscow town hall – and the security troops guarding it hastily broke downstairs windows in order to abandon the building without firing a shot. The same seems to have happened at the TV station at Ostankino. Who, then, will defend the Kremlin? Whatever the declarations of the ministers of defence and security, will their troops fight? If they will, blood will undoubtedly flow, and we are well into the possibilities of civil war. If they do not shoot, Rutskoi could take over. Another civil war scenario is a clash in, say, Red Square between rival crowds. Rutskoi having called the mob to storm the Kremlin, it is difficult to see how a peace formula can be patched up by Patriarch Alexei. All my economic reports are irrelevant now – until we know who wins and whether whoever 'wins' will have effective control over Russia. In 1918 the great poet Alexander Blok wrote: *My deti strashnykh let Rossii*, 'we are the children of Russia's fearful years'. There would seem to be more fearful years to come.

4 October 1993, Glasgow

A victorious Yeltsin must now devise an economic strategy. Earlier in September he signalled a harder market-and-stabilisation line by appointing Gaidar and sidelining Lobov. He had before him a proposal from Fedorov which, according to good sources, was opposed by Chernomyrdin. This included a wage semi-freeze (any increase exceeding 70 per cent of the previous quarter's prices rises would attract a penal tax; a 7 per cent special VAT would go into a fund used to finance agriculture and the coal industry, a proposal to introduce a local sales tax of up to 10 per cent, and so on.). If these proposals are not adopted, the budget deficit for 1993 will exceed the 30 per cent a month rate, given the rise in energy and farm procurement prices *and* continued decline in output. The

IMF would continue to be displeased. But what can be done in the short run to raise revenue and cut expenditure?

A report in *Ekonomika i zhizn'* (No. 38) states that the *gold reserve* of Russia barely exceeds 300 tons, which is 2000 tons down on the 1985 figure. Total gold production in 1992 was 129.5 tons. The two largest producing areas were Magadan and Yakutia. The Australian firm 'STAR' has invested in the firm Lenzoloto, overcoming bureaucratic obstacles. The journal *Kommersant* reports on the appearance of a sort of surrogate money, the LIAL, a 'paper litre of vodka'. Bills of exchange denominated in vodka (obligation to deliver stated quantities of the liquor) are now in circulation. At wholesale level such a liquid bill of exchange is usually 500 boxes (10 000 half-litre bottles). It rises in value with the rouble price of vodka. As at mid-July, one LIAL equalled $1.23. What would monetarist theorists make of that sort of liquidity preference?? The same journal printed a report from Nizhni-Novgorod, where Yavlinsky's advice is being followed. Interestingly, 'privatisation' there gives emphasis to employee shareholding, with employees of successful firms rewarded with sizeable dividends. As Yavlinsky may become a serious political contender nationally, this is worth noting. Machinery and equipment output continues to fall (for example, forging and stamping machinery by 43 per cent over last year), but there are exceptions: vehicles and materials handling equipment are beginning to do better.

6 October 1993, Glasgow

The news from Moscow is most disturbing politically. Yeltsin is today addressing the people on TV, and right now I do not know what he will say. But almost every independent newspaper has been closed, and the mild *Nezavisimaya gazeta* appears with censored blanks. (They say censorship will not continue . . .) I would bet a whole number of bottles of authentic vodka that there will be no elections in December. My guess is that he will have a plebiscite or referendum vote instead with no alternative (that is, 'vote for me, or else face chaos and disorder'). But my supposition could be proved wrong within hours. And if no authentic election is due in the near future, Gaidar's tough budget plans could go ahead without any populist concessions. But then the political sky may turn stormy, and the notion that now is the time to rush Western aid to sustain Yeltsin (Sachs was urging this) might be queried, if 'democracy' is dumped. Maybe I am influenced by the fact, just reported by colleagues, that Boris Kagarlitsky, a left-wing activist totally unconnected with the Rutskoi camp, has been arrested and badly beaten.

12 November 1993, Glasgow

Nothing sensational to report about Russia. Yeltsin's decision not to have a presidential election after all, or not until 1996, may not be very 'democratic', but does give Gaidar and the government more freedom of action. Except that presumably unpopular measures may be postponed until after the parliamentary elections in December. There is a multiplicity of parties, and a complex electoral procedure, making any forecast hazardous. The ban on some of the more extreme parties may help the vote of the Communists headed by Zyuganov, who could turn out, like in Poland, to be the largest single party in a fragmented parliament, but Yeltsin has tight control over the media. My instincts tell me that this is not the time for Western statesmen to blow pro-Yeltsin trumpets publicly. It could be counterproductive. Inflation is still high. But there are numerous regional variations. Thus according to *Ekonomika i zhizn'* (No. 44), the average price of a kilo of cheap bread was 127 roubles, but in the town of Orel it was 23 roubles, and in Blagoveshchensk (East Siberia) it was 500 roubles! The market price of vegetable oil averaged 1292 roubles, but in Moscow it was 2000, in St. Petersburg – 3200. We are far from a perfect market! Local subsidies, transport problems and local mafias no doubt help to explain huge price differentials. It is being confidentially forecast the industrial output in 1993 will fall between 16 and 18 per cent compared with the year 1992, which in turn was 18.5 per cent below 1991.

Russia: Exchange Rates, Inflation, Prices, Costs, Wages, 16 November 1993, Glasgow

A complete transformation has occurred, as a result of the relative stability of the rouble–dollar exchange rate at a time of rapid rise of rouble prices and incomes. On 3 November there were still 1179 roubles to the dollar. This despite a 20 per cent rise in prices in October (*Izvestiya*, 5 November). Similar or higher inflation rates per month were recorded in July, August and September. Wages per month now average between $70 and $75, while just four months ago they were close to $30 at the exchange rate then ruling. Though foreign trade is expected to be in large surplus in 1993 as a whole (imports –44 per cent, exports +1.4 per cent over 1992), drastic changes are likely because soaring rouble costs *and* a soaring (real) exchange rate has made most Russian goods uncompetitive even in Russia. Thus the internal price of a Zhiguli (Lada) car is now reported to be *double* that of a similar imported car, the same is true for most farm machinery, many durables, and so on. 1994 could spell disaster for much of Russian industry unless protectionist measures are taken. The same issue of *Izvestiya* notes a speed-up in industrial decline, a fall in GNP in 1993 (over 1992) of at least 10 per cent, with continued if slower decline in 1994. New taxes are expected to include a sharp rise in the rate of VAT. Low-interest credits have been largely eliminated, depreciation allowances greatly increased via the revaluation of capital assets, there are tax concessions on reinvested profits. But inflation roars on, with reported increase in velocity of circulation as a response to tighter money. *Moskovskie novosti* (7 November) reports a criticism of government economic policy by Yavlinsky, Shakhrai and Volsky. According to them, the anti-inflation measures of Gaidar have deplorable effects: 'When manufacturing is in a state of collapse, and even the sectors capable of export, and output of materials, are also in decline, it is wrong to slaughter them by tightening the financial noose.' Investment is far too low, the decline in high tech is particularly great. The policies actually followed have failed to slow inflation. And so on. Another (predictable) breakdown: the privatisation and fragmentation of repair workshops have led to the collapse of guaranteed repairs and maintenance of Russian-produced durables. Another reason to buy foreign!

Ukraine. As at 5 November, the official karbovanets exchange rate to the dollar was 5970, the free market rate 31 000 (!!). Ukraine has tried to issue bonds at $25 million each, at 7 per cent interest, 'guaranteed by the republics property and assets'. My friend Chernyak has claimed publicly that president Kravchuk has no right to pledge the republic's property in this way. Anyhow, exports are low, currency reserves zero, disastrous lack of policy continues.

18 November 1993, Glasgow

I see today that the 'capital flight' from Russia has taken the form of bags of valuta worth £1 million stolen from a London-bound plane (at Sheremetyevo? En route? At Heathrow?). Also today I read an excellent article by David Remnick in the current *New Yorker*. I fear that the following extract rings true: 'The dulling realities of Soviet society have come unwound, and now Russia is a scene of radical polarisation. The fondest wish of the Russian reformers in 1991 was that out of economic change would emerge a large middle class and business elite, which would become the main constituencies for further change. There are no signs of this happening. Instead Russians have watched with fury and envy as a small percentage of people have grown rich – gaudily rich – in an environ-

ment of almost general chaos and criminality. Capitalism in Russia has
produced far more Al Capones than Henry Fords . . . In fact the economy hardly merits the name of capitalism at all, since it operates largely
outside the framework of law. There is not a single field of activity, not a
single institution free of the most brutal forms of corruption. Russia has
bred a world-class mafia. According to Luciano Volante, the chairman of
Italy's parliamentary committee on inquiry into the Mafia, Russia is now
'a kind of strategic capital of organised crime from where all the major
operations are launched'. He said that Russian mob leaders had held
summit meetings with the three main Italian crime organisations to discuss money-laundering [I wonder which laundry that £1 million was
destined for, A.N.], the narcotics trade and even the sale of nuclear material . . . The new Russian mobsters, who are involved in everything from
arms sales to banking, have learned to work with former officials in the
highest ranks of the communist party and the KGB . . . There is little
doubt that the ministries of Yeltsin's government – especially in areas like
foreign trade, customs, tax collection and law enforcement – are also
thoroughly corrupt. According to Yuri Boldyrev, who was until recently
the government's chief investigator into corruption, the decay in state and
public institutions now "goes beyond the limits of imagination".' I am
sorry to say that this seems true. The question is: who can clean it up?

Russia on the Eve of the Elections, 8 December 1993, Glasgow

Coal Strike Averted. But at what cost? As with a recent stoppage in the
gas industry, a major cause was that the workers had not been paid, this
being due to customers (including the state budget itself) not paying their
bills. *Finance Minister Fedorov* gave a long interview to his critics in the
journal *Kommersant* (26 November). He argued that top priority must be
given to moderating inflation and then reducing interest rates, and this
would benefit accumulation and so investment. He opposed budgetary
financing of investment, despite arguments that, unless some investment
projects are devised with government help, no restructuring could take
place. Fedorov declared his opposition to protectionism. He also stressed
the unreliability of published statistics. However, when he answered questions on the real budget deficit, everyone was bemused. The 1993 deficit
will be 11 trillion roubles, or 13 trillion if one excludes the proceeds of
foreign credits, but agreed that he himself had put forward an estimate of
17 trillion, or 18.5 trillion excluding IMF credits. He also yet again
demanded that Gerashchenko resign. Clear? *Chelnoki* is the Russian word
for thousands of cross-frontier traders, who go to Germany, Poland and

even the Arab Emirates. Example: lively trade in second-hand cars driven from Germany: a car bought for 2 to 4000DM sells in Russia for $4000. But many cars are also stolen. *Real estate advertisement* offers, for example, villa in Montebello, USA, for $369 000. Four hundred times the annual salary of an unbribed minister? Is this not evidence of a sort of haywire free-for-all (for the new rich)?? *Gaidar interview in Ekonomika i zhizn'* (No. 49) attributes reform hiccups to the need to make compromises with parliament and others, including members of the government. But he insisted that commentators overdo the gloom. Forecasts of mass hunger and freezing have proved wrong. Though of course people are very poor, there has been an improvement since January 1993. By the end of 1994 the reduced budget deficit will (he claimed) be financed by bond sales, and money supply will rise by no more than 3 per cent a month. On privatisation, he regretted that so much has taken the form of employee buy-outs, often at nominal prices, 'We are ceasing to give property away, we will sell it, and make sale conditional on further investments.' He claimed that restructuring is in progress, despite widespread beliefs to the contrary, and that much of the decline in output affected goods of poor quality and high cost, goods not in demand. Unemployment is still low, and he hopes will stay that way.

Currency Depreciation and Inflation Forecast. Kommersant cites the government's declared intention to reduce monthly inflation rates to 10 per cent in March and to 1 to 3 per cent by December. (In recent months it was 22 per cent). This would imply a price rise of 2.9 times between Oct. 1993 and Dec. 1994. It is supposed that the exchange rate will depreciate at half (or less than) this, so this suggests 1700 roubles to the dollar in mid-year, 2500 by December next. However, if 22 per cent a month inflation continues into the first part of 1994, as is more than probable, 3000 roubles per dollar at mid-year is a more realistic forecast. 'The next two months will tell'.

The Russian Elections, 13 December 1993, 9 a.m., Glasgow

In the night I was making comments on the BBC Russian Service as the results came in. Except that they stopped coming in, suddenly. The Russian radio five minutes ago was avoiding the subject. Of course, the count is not yet completed, but the scene of as now looks something like this:

1.   The constitution seems to have been adopted, but on a poll that only probably just tops 50 per cent of registered voters, though by a comfortable majority of those that did vote.

2.   Zhirinovsky's Liberal-Democratic (that is, neo-fascist) party did well, better than the Communists, but (so it is claimed) not as well as Gaidar's Russia's Choice. At 4 a.m. our time I heard an unofficial estimate that did get broadcast by Russian radio's world service (but not their internal one) giving Gaidar's party 25 per cent, Zhirinovsky 13 per cent, Yavlinsky's group 12 per cent, the Communists 8 per cent, Shakhrai's (moderate-reformist) group 7 per cent, the Agrarians just above 5 per cent, while none of the others (including Volsky's Civic Union) got above the 5 per cent barrier which must be crossed for the national lists. However, I strongly suspect that the reason they stopped broadcasting results is that Zhirinovsky and the Communists did better than this, and also that, if the announced results are anything like those just cited, Zhirinovsky will cry foul. Despite the presence of foreign observers, many suspected all along that the results will be fixed.

3.   It is important to bear in mind that Yeltsin acquires so much power under the new constitution that in most respects he could ignore parliament. But can he? For example, suppose they refuse to adopt the budget, vote to increase pensions, pass a vote of no confidence in the government, try to stop land privatisation, will this not matter? Also of great importance is the 'constituency' composition of the Duma. Only half its members will be provided through national party-grouping lists, the other half are via constituencies, and a large proportion of the candidates have no unambiguous party labels, represent local interests, their behaviour as deputies unpredictable.

4.   It is reasonable (until we have the final figures) provisionally to conclude that, firstly, in the words of my old friend and well-known publicist Alexander Tsipko, 'democracy is the main loser' and the likely composition of the new parliament will be 'worse than the previous one'. Secondly, Zhirinovsky moves centre-stage in Russian politics, instead of being an insignificant clown-demagogue-extremist. For such a man with such a programme to move centre-stage, with serious ideas of actually collaborating with Yeltsin, sends shivers down many spines.

It is essential to bear in mind that we do not have the real results yet, and I shall obviously be able to find out much more when I get to Moscow later this week. But all one's vibes are that this is bad news, on balance, and that the outlook remains stormy. It will be very revealing to discover what the young men in Gaidar's institute think will be the effect of all this on the reform programme, inflation, and so on.

13 December 1993, 3 p.m., Glasgow

Clearly the worst has befallen, the earlier figures I cited this morning were overoptimistic, the reason why the TV and radio coverage of the elections was abandoned has become depressingly clear. Parliament will clearly be a major problem. Especially if, despite the greater powers of the president, there is a constitutional court that functions, replacing the one dissolved by Yeltsin in October. Even worse is the thought of Zhirinovsky as a credible presidential candidate in 1996. One sense of déja vu: in 1906 a Duma was elected that displeased the Tsar Nicholas II. He dissolved it after 70 days. New elections produced one just as radical. So the Tsar changed the rules, and a more acceptable Duma was elected in 1907 on a much narrower franchise. What will Yeltsin do now? One model, which was drawn for Ukraine and clearly also applies to Russia too: the neo-liberals cannot expect to be elected if they present a neo-liberal shock-therapy anti-populist programme. At the very least they have to disguise themselves as social-democrats. Free market policies and democratic voting are incompatible in Russia, it would seem. Zhirinovsky's successes, especially if he teams up with the Communists (whose vote is not yet clear), can do serious direct and even more indirect damage, internally *and* in external relations, particularly with ex-Soviet republics. And it seems as if soldiers voted for him in large numbers. Gloom deepens.

26 December 1993, Glasgow

I'm now home from Moscow. There I participated in a long radio discussion with Yavlinsky, participated also in a three-day conference ('Where is Russia Going?'), and in a discussion at the Gorbachev foundation, lunching with its effective head, Aleksander Tsipko. Discussions also with Otto Latsis (political–economic editor of *Izvestiya*), the political sociologists Gordon, Levada, Tatyana Zaslavskaya, plus Satarov (member of the President's Council), Viktor Danilov (leading expert on peasants), the excellent Evgeni Yasin, Mau, Sinelnikov (of the 'Gaidar' institute), Yuri Goland (whose special subject is hyperinflation and its cure), plus one of the BBC's correspondents who was once one of our students in Glasgow, etc. Key impressions include: Shock waves from the bombardment of parliament are still reverberating. Election results demonstrate deep unpopularity of Gaidar policy which, if left unmodified would result in a future president Zhirinovsky, who counts on this and therefore told his supporters to vote *for* the Yeltsin constitution. He is an irresponsible demagogue rather than a 'fascist'. Despite Yeltsin's statements to the contrary, a new economic policy detailed to me by Yasin and supported by Chernomyrdin is likely to include a more active investment strategy and greater concern for the new poor (half the population!), to mobilise social consensus for recovery and to avoid conflict with the new parliament. But economic decline is set to continue and prospects are, I fear, grim.

Russia in December: What's for 1994?, 28 December 1993, Glasgow

What follows is the result of numerous discussions in Moscow in the period 14–22 December, and the study of a number of reports, official and unofficial. There is a very unhappy Christmas in prospect (Orthodox Christmas is on 7 January). Though this note intends to concentrate on matters economic, these are so closely linked with the outcome of political conflicts and manoeuvrings that the political dimension cannot be avoided.

The bombardment of parliament still reverberates. Its after-effects affected the election result (of which more in a moment) by removing some parties from the ballot and so clearing the way for Zhirinovsky. And while those yearning for a firm hand may have been impressed by 'Yeltsin the strong man', many others of various political hues bitterly protest at apparently needless slaughter of Russians by Russians, and suspect Yeltsin of 'provocation'. It would seem that there was difficulty in finding tank crews willing to do the dirty work: eight officers agreed, with the help of a few thousand dollars each. I am told that two of them have been killed, the other six are in hiding. Several of my Russian friends show contempt for Yeltsin, his limited intelligence, drinking bouts, unpredictability, lack of flexibility. They doubt his ability to work with the new parliament. What if he cannot? The new constitution has given him extensive powers, so maybe he can ignore it and rule by decree? Maybe. But many decrees in the past year or two have not been implemented, and some regions may ignore those decrees that parliament – the new Duma – wishes to countermand. What then? He cannot rely on the army, if, as has been reported (and denied, and again reported) that 63 per cent of the officers voted for Zhirinovsky. It is significant that Yeltsin has just dissolved the Security Ministry (the successor of the KGB) and subordinated its successor – the Counter-Intelligence Office – directly to himself, that is, removed it from within the government. What premier Chernomyrdin thinks of this is not known. Anyhow, any economic policy can only be carried out if there is a minimum of political order, a clear demarcation of powers, laws that are obeyed. Yeltsin did win the constitutional referendum. Yes, but not only did many abstain, he won it also because Zhirinovsky told his supporters to vote and to vote 'for'. He favours a strong presidency because he wants to be president! He now claims that he saved the day for Yeltsin.

The election result, now that the constituencies as well as the national lists can be taken into account, is not quite as bad as it first seemed. Gaidar's Russia's Choice has more deputies than Zhirinovsky's party, apparently because the latter has few attractive constituency candidates (though a few suspect the count). But quite plainly the reformers have no reliable parliamentary majority, and the Communists came a credible third. Rumours of a Yeltsin–Zhirinovsky deal seem unfounded, but some speculate that there could be negotiation with Zyuganov's Communists. Anyhow, Zhirinovsky's remarkable performance on the national party lists has sparked off alarm, even panic, here and there. Exaggerated? Is there a 'fascist' danger? Will economic policy be affected? Opinions vary. Zhirinovsky is a demagogue who knows how to appeal to the various discontents: loss of empire and a sense of national humiliation; breakdown of law and order; widespread impoverishment; the new rich that produce nothing and have everything. Perhaps it is not appreciated how television advertising irritates the ordinary citizen: luxury cars, holidays in Thailand, BMWs, even villas in America for $350000, this at a time when the official minimum wage represents half the costs of food for an adult male . . . Since official policy threatens more of the same, there is bound to be a protest vote. How to register it, other than by voting for the communists or abstaining? So many chose Zhirinovsky, without being 'fascists' or ultra-ultra-nationalists, though no doubt some of these did vote for him too. Talk of urgently creating a new 'anti-fascist front' may be premature or unnecessary, but clearly there are serious grounds for concern in the ex-Soviet republics (which he wishes to reincorporate) and in the West generally. (He cashes in on anti-American sentiment, aided by tactless pro-Yeltsin declarations by Clinton and others, declares support for Iraq, opposes the rundown of the military–industrial complex.) He would support protectionist-isolationism, and would make foreign investors unwelcome. So I do not deny that he is bad news. However, it does not follow that it would be helpful for us to say so, as that would help him.

The Economic Situation continues to deteriorate. I acquired two recent reports, one by the Forecasting Institute of the Academy of Sciences, the other by the 'Gaidar' Institute, and there is no difference between their evaluation of existing trends. It is expected that GNP and industrial production will have fallen in 1993 by 15 per cent, after falling by 19 per cent each in 1992. Aggregate decline in three years is of the order of 40–45 per cent, which is frankly dreadful, though some allowance has to be made for unrecorded transactions. Investments fell by 45 per cent in 1992, by a further 12 per cent in 1993. A further fall in 1994 is 'confidently' forecast: the Academy's Institute expects GNP to fall by between 8–11 per cent, industrial output by 10–12 per cent, agricultural output by 11–13 per cent. 'In the year 1994 any significant rise in investment activity is improbable.' Yet without such a rise the huge problems of restructuring cannot be tackled, and so decline must continue, since net investment has become negative. While the Academy's report accepts that there has been a trend to a more balanced stagflation, with supply and demand at closer balance and the rouble acquiring real purchasing power amid 18–20 per cent a month inflation, there is a warning: the huge fall in output 'places the economy in a critical zone of both consumption and investment. So 1994 promises to be another year of strain, in both economic and social aspects.' The election result and prospects of further decline justify reassessments of policy.

Inflation and Public Finance. After exceeding 20 per cent a month since midsummer, the inflation rate dropped to 15 per cent in November. It is also claimed that the budget deficit in 1993 will be below the worst expectations. In fact, according to several sources, Fedorov refused to implement the budget adopted by parliament in the summer, which would have represented a deficit exceeding 24 per cent of GNP. There has also been a sharp cut both in low-interest credits and in import subsidies as well as in state-financed investments. Unfortunately, the harsher policy of the most recent months has taken the form of simply not paying the state's debts to suppliers, not keeping promises previously made, and so on . . . In this way, while keeping the budget deficit within bounds, the state contributes to enterprises' insolvency and to the mountain (high again) of cumulative inter-enterprise debt, as well as adding to commercial uncertainty and setting a bad example to business. When inflation is of the order of 20 per cent a month, payment delays equal lower payments! When I pointed all this out, I had the following reply: yes, but it was necessary to keep the budget deficit down, and anyway many enterprises (and regions) delay making *their* payments into the republican budget . . . There are major uncertainties in the way of estimating what will happen to inflation in 1994. Gaidar speaks hopefully of a much lower inflation rate in the second half of the year. Against this there is the expected cost of populist election promises, the need to pay debt already incurred, plus the monetary and fiscal consequences of the policy modifications which will be discussed below. The rate for the dollar reached 1250 while I was there. It still declines by much less than the inflation rate. Given the high and rising level of internal rouble costs, most Russian manufactures are or are about to become uncompetitive in Russia, which will contribute to further industrial decline, or call for vigorous protectionist measures. Or the rouble will fall steeply. Or, of course, all these at once.

Law, Illegality, Kleptocracy. Everyone agrees that a healthy market economy requires a legal order, the observance of contracts, a minimum of trust. Everyone agrees that these are serious 'lacks'. Some go much further. Here, for example, is E. Starikov, of the Institute of Social Problems of the Russian Academy: 'The government apparatus, covering all spheres of commercial activity with a tight network of licences (and with us the words "licences" and "corruption" are synonyms) lives on the criminal extraction and redistribution of bribe-taxation, analogous to rent-extraction. However, the "capitalisation" of the power of the apparatus takes not only the form of vulgar robbery and bribe-taking, but also more "civilised" forms of the participation of officials in the profits of firms. Some officials, on the basis of stolen state property, create their own commercial undertakings, granting to them various privileges.' After some remarks about the power and scale of the financial mafia, and those whose billions of profits from the legal and illegal exports of materials remain abroad, he also writes of 'gangocrats' (that is, kleptocrats) who 'benefit from the paralysis of state power and growing anarchy', 'organised crime' supported by private armies achieving real power. Dramatic exaggeration? Alas, most of the audience (at the conference I attended) seemed sadly to acquiesce. And in a recent report by a prominent American specialist there is a vivid account of how would-be small businessmen had to pay mafia-like structures and also the police, in order to continue in business. No one suggested that this was exceptional.

Privatisation has, unfortunately, to be seen also in the context of semi-fraudulent appropriation. There has been a substantial increase in the rate of privatisation of enterprises large and small, but most are under the same management (with or without the nominal ownership of shares by the workforce), with little change in behaviour. Very few instances are encountered where there is an identifiable owner–entrepreneur. Many instances are cited in which management acquires assets which are grossly undervalued. Vouchers (now valued at roughly 10 000 roubles, that is, at face value) are seen as a political rather than an economic measure. Some of the newly-hatched investment (mutual) funds are said to be in poor financial shape. Some participants at a conference ('Where is Russia Going?') forecast the collapse of several merchant banks. Two of the participants at the conference, including a leading expert, V.P. Danilov, strongly criticised the privatisation policy as applied to *agriculture*. The effect of legislation has been to weaken or disrupt many existing state and collective farms, creating doubt and confusion, whereas there is neither the human nor the technical (or credit) base for the speedy creation of independent peasant–proprietor farming. This has had negative effects on output. Meanwhile losses remain high in the food chain, for lack of infrastructure (hard-surface roads, storage space, and so on). Many farms and peasants are in dire financial straits, owing to soaring costs of inputs and delays in payment (including by the government itself). One effect has been the collapse of sales of fertiliser, pesticides, most farm equipment.

Foreign trade balance in 1993 looks highly healthy, in that exports are likely to exceed imports by around 20 billion dollars. But: (a) the halving in one year of imports has painful effects; (b) exports consist overwhelmingly of fuel and raw materials; (c) despite the export surplus and debt repayment restructuring, foreign debt has grown and is estimated to reach 84–85 billion dollars, because; (d) capital flight and non-repatriation of export earnings are high, though estimates of the extent of these vary widely. 'The non-repatriation of export proceeds mean that they are not invested in the Russian economy. The principal exporters, i.e., the energy sector, leave their valuta revenues untouched and get soft credits from the state' (cited from Academy Institute report). The same source casts severe doubt on the trade statistics in general: 'Experts of the IMF, basing themselves on statistics from exporting countries, consider that the official figures understate imports by some 50%' (!!). Foreign investments remain 'insignificant'. *Personal incomes* show not only an exceptional and growing gap between the new rich and everyone else, but also vast and apparently irrational (and demoralising) differentials within each and every group, totally unrelated to skill or productivity. To cite a headline from *Nezavisimaya gazeta*: 'The Whip of Beggary for the Majority may be no Way to Reach Civilisation's Heights, but it sure can Lose Elections'. Politicians cannot ignore mass discontent. Average wages and salaries in October were 93 000 roubles a month, 291 000 in the gas industry, but only 75 000 in machinery and engineering, 65 000 in health, 59 000 in education, 52 000 in agriculture. The minimum wage, which some receive, has just been 'raised' to 16 000, less than the minimum pension and much less than is needed to keep body and soul together. By contrast, my driver told me he earned 800 000. Then there are the new rich, catered for by TV advertising and luxury imports. Can one really be surprised at the vote received by Zhirinovsky and the Communists?

So, should there be a New Policy, and if so, What? One of Yeltsin's advisory council told me that he, in common with all other council members, received from Yeltsin a request to answer the above question. On the answer depends much, economically and politically. One possible line, apparently Gaidar's, is that the admitted failures of the past were due to the failure to apply consistently the monetarist-restrictive policy, which was to have led to financial stabilisation. So it must now be consistently and rigorously applied. The weaker enterprises must be closed, the very considerable disguised unemployment made open, the budget deficit reduced by higher taxes and spending cuts. Stabilisation could then be followed by the needed restructuring, and with the end of 'voucher-privatisation' next June it could be possible to link sales of state enterprises in investment in these enterprises. In my view, and that of a number of critics in Russia, this course would spell disaster (and make probable a future president Zhirinovsky). Important though stabilisation undoubtedly is, if production continues to fall, nothing can be achieved, not even stabilisation. Contrary to the view he himself expressed to me four months ago, the senior adviser Evgeni Yasin is now convinced that a change of policy is indispensable. Yes, restructuring must include the closure of some loss-makers, but in the present inflationary and debt-ridden climate the extent of current losses may be no guide as to what should be closed, or to future prospects. Nor can one rely on the capital market to finance the necessary restructuring-investments, since there is no real capital market. Nominal interest rates are so high anyway that no one in his senses would lend or borrow long term.

From all this it follows that the state, the government, simply *cannot* include itself out. Politically as well as economically, it *must* devise and publicise a recovery programme, selecting sectors and enterprises which can give a quick rate of return in the form of usable output. Inflationary effects can be mitigated if, first, a large part of the existing volume of credits and subsidies are specifically targeted towards these investment programmes (instead of being used, as now, to cover current spending, or for speculation). And, second, it must try to involve the private sector, private capital, the merchant banks. Yasin also favours a social policy designed to show that the government cares about the very poor and is aware of the wild excesses of inequality. (Zhirinovsky has cashed in on the failure of the reformers in public relations; they seem not to care, just possibly because they do not!) So: higher taxes on high incomes, and on imported luxuries (thus, for example, imported liquor and perfume cost much less than in the West and incredibly anyone can import one car duty-free, so thousands 'shuttle' to and from Germany, each driving in one car, probably stolen, for resale), to help finance the safety net. But, to cite the Academy report on prospects for 1994, 'can the half-destroyed and largely paralysed system of state power cope with this complex of problems?' Can the government, led by the influential Chernomyrdin, agree among themselves? Chernomyrdin himself has gone on record in favour of a more interventionist policy. Would Gaidar, Fedorov, Chubais go along? Would the new policy lines, if adopted by the government, form a basis for a working relationship with the newly elected legislature, the Duma?

The political economy of reform cannot ignore the fact that, in Russia, laissez-faire at this stage can be counterproductive, figuratively and literally. If, as is stated in a report of a high-level and sophisticated opinion survey, 'the liberal model adopted by the upper echelons of power *enjoys no support in any of the key groups of society*, with the possible exception of the ideological elite', this too helps to explain the election result (the survey was conducted a few weeks before). It is wrong to write off such views as conservative, brown or red. A very senior official told me the following: he was involved in a phone-in programme and got the following question from an old woman. 'I was a skilled worker, worked all my life, had accumulated adequate savings. Now my savings have been destroyed by inflation, and on my pension I can afford to eat just bread, and occasionally milk. Please explain: *Why?*' What answer could he give? And in this context advertisements for villas in Florida, BMWs, holidays in Thailand, become politically explosive. Any recovery strategy can, of course, come unstuck, involves risk. But a stabilisation programme unaccompanied by any such strategy involves a high probability of political and economic disaster. One hopes that Western governments, Western advisers, the IMF, appreciate this. Some may recall that Marshall Aid to Western Europe was targeted, formed an integral part of recovery and reconstruction programmes. But this was before the dominance of 'Chicago' ideology.

Relations with CIS. Has this semi-stillborn 'Commonwealth' a future? And what is Russia's attitude towards it? Will there be reality behind all the talk of customs and monetary union? Russian policy has been, and remains, contradictory. On the one hand, a union could be the best route to establishing a sphere of influence and security of markets and supplies. On the other most of the republics are seen as an economic burden to Russia and several (Ukraine especially) are in an economic (and political) mess. There seems no basis for effecting a joint monetary or payments policy. Then there are nationalist pressures – in Ukraine against deals with Russia, in Russia to intervene in favour of Russian minorities, and the row with Ukraine over the Black Sea fleet and the Crimea could boil up at any time. Not only Zhirinovsky but some elements in the Russian military, and perhaps also in the government, see advantages in destabilising several of the republics and then picking up the pieces. (Examples: military supplies to the Abkhaz in Georgia, or cutting gas supply to Ukraine.) The present political balance in Russia could lead to tougher attitudes, all the way from Estonia to Tadzhikistan, and on both sides. This would do economic harm to both sides, but plainly would harm the other republics more than Russia.

Finally, what possible scenarios for 1994? (1) Gaidar, with Yeltsin's backing, carries through his tough 'monetarist' stabilisation policy. Unemployment rises sharply. Inflation falls gradually to 10 per cent a month. Output and investment continue to fall. A majority of the Duma votes no-confidence, is ignored. Disorders, regional disobedience, are firmly dealt with. Presidential decrees rule. (2) Chernomyrdin persuades Yeltsin to adopt some version of the 'Yasin' programme outlined above. Negotiations with the new Duma gain support for a government and programme of national salvation. Selective investment programme launched. Fedorov moves to head Bank. Gaidar either accepts the programme or is honourably sidelined. (Yavlinsky is in the wings, waiting). Protectionist measures adopted. Fall in output is checked by September. (3) Drift, with contradictory elements of both the above scenarios, amid much lobbying and jockeying for position, with corrupt and semi-criminal elements joining in. Chronic conflict with the Duma. Some regions go their own way. Disintegration threatens, amid calls for the Army to intervene to save Mother Russia. Decline in output reaches critical proportions. Inflation takes off. (Asked why he thought Ukraine was in so much worse a mess than Russia, a very senior Russian replied: 'We have oil and gas; they do not.')

So – which of the above is most likely? Are there other possibilities? My own view is that (3) is pessimum pessimorum, but unfortunately it cannot be ruled out. Nor can other possibilities; thus Yeltsin is not immortal, and what would happen then? Anyhow, I would give (3) a 20 per cent chance. I personally prefer (2) as providing the nearest approach to hope. Its adoption as government policy might even be characterised as probable. But this still leaves unanswered a vital question: even if it is adopted, has the government the power and determination to implement it? And a half-implemented (2) can easily slide into the morass of (3). As I write these lines, (1) still seems to be the official policy. I give that a 20 per cent chance, in the sense that, with minor modifications, it accords with the advice of the IMF and of such advisers as Aslund, so they may attempt to stay on that course. The reason for giving it only 20 per cent is that it is likely to be blown off course by the changing political balance (including the need to head off Zhirinovsky), and by the growing realisation that the collapse of industry and of investment calls for selective measures of support. A pre-war American musical contained the line: 'Anything can happen and it probably will!'

1994

Additional Russian Snippets, 11 January 1994, Glasgow

1. *Zhirinovsky.* A more careful reading of his book (his *Mein Kampf*, some call it) and election literature leads to contradictory conclusions: in some respects he sounds like a misunderstood and almost reasonable man, in others he is wild and dangerous to the *n*th degree. First, the 'good' news. He argues for pluralism, a multi-party system, human rights and equal opportunities for all persons of any nationality, religion, race. In these respects he certainly in no way resembles Hitler, and those whom I heard gloomily comparing Russia 1993 with Germany 1933 appear to be off beam. Overt anti-semitism is not visible, his chief dislike being of men from the southern republics of the former Union, allegedly leaders in gangsterism and corruption. Now for the flip side. His book is titled *The Final Leap to the South*. To call his foreign policy programme alarming is the understatement of the new year. Not only are the former Soviet republics to be reincorporated in a unitary Russian state, 'Russian soldiers will bathe their feet in the warm waters of the Indian Ocean', in alliance with 'friendly' India and Iraq. America can have South America; Western Europe is kindly awarded Africa; Japan and China can sort out south-east Asia. But Russia's destiny is in the Middle East! (He served at one time on the Transcaucasian military district, and specialised on Turkey, the one foreign country he knows). Turks, Iranians, Afghans, Arabs, should be incorporated into a new Greater Russia, which will keep order and prevent them all from killing each other. To quote him: 'Medicine is not always palatable. Maybe this will not please everyone in Kabul, Teheran and Ankara. But millions would live better.' So – 'the final leap to the south.' 'Our army will carry out this task.' So – war. Haywire? Direct route to Armageddon? Or too daft to be taken seriously? What is the view of the Army's general staff? Is it true that two-thirds of the officers voted for Zhirinovsky? The answers to such questions matter greatly!

2. *The military.* What deal, if any, did Yeltsin make with General Grachev in October? Is it a coincidence that he has been loudly asserting objections to the eastward expansion of NATO and claiming the right to protect Russian minorities in ex-Soviet republics? Both these postures can also represent Yeltsin's own views. So could the reported rise in military spending. Could they also be an attempt to outflank Zhirinovsky? Again, all this matters, and has economic effects too.

3.   *Exchange rates.* Dollar at over 1250. Ukrainian karbovanets at end-year traded in Moscow at 3.34 roubles per 100. This suggests a free rate of somewhere near 40000 karbovantsy to the dollar, probably worse than this by now. Chaos and collapse must be imminent in Kiev. As from January, that is, now, *cash* payments in dollars became illegal in Russia. Credit-card and cheque transactions remain legal, and hard-currency shops are trying to find ways round the prohibition, which in any case may prove unenforceable, so long as devaluation is anticipated.

4.   *Energy's financial crisis.* Unpaid debts to energy providers exceed 2.3 trillion roubles, plus 230 billion owed to nuclear power stations. Non-payers are still supplied with power. A 'state energy programme' includes investments in new oil and gas fields in south-west Siberia.

5.   *New car plant,* with GM participation, is actively being projected on the Volga at Tolyatti, alongside an existing one. Plans are due to be prepared by 31 March 1994. Also *Dupont* is reported as setting up a joint venture to produce and market 'polyhetraftor-ethybene'. Ikarus buses are to be built/assembled in Vologda.

6.   *Budget.* Expenditure in fourth quarter limited severely so as to keep the (nominal) deficit for the year 1993 to 10 per cent of GNP. Revenue includes foreign credits of $1500 million. (This leaves many government debts unpaid.) *Izvestiya* reports disturbing news of a 'tax war' with republics and regions, especially the better-off ones, such as Tyumen and Tatarstan. They spend locally the sums that should be transferred to the federal budget. This 'threatens Russia with disintegration' (*razval*). Will Yeltsin be able to compel payment, especially if he fails to do a deal with the newly-elected Duma?

7.   *Investment projects* have become official policy, which seems (to me) to be good news. Thus Andres Nechaev now heads the 'Russian Finance Corporation', which has the specific task of stimulating investment, directly and indirectly (for example, via commercial banks), with credits on favourable terms granted for programmes seen as priority by the government, both in the private and public sectors. Applicants have to submit 'business plans' and projects for evaluation. The bank will also help set up an export and import guarantee fund. It is also being reported that privatisation, in some regions, is being directly linked with investment: thus in the Urals region the privatisation auction winner can be the one who undertakes to carry out the biggest investment programme. This is also expected to attract foreign investor-bidders. This much-needed emphasis on investment should be seen in the context of the sort of recovery strategy now being considered by the government. It represents a departure from ideologically prescribed rigidity, and about time too! But has the government power to implement such a policy?

Gaidar Goes?, 16 January 1994, Glasgow

The reported motive – Belorussia in the rouble zone – seems trivial. Belorussia is not in serious trouble. It is not as if it were Ukraine! Clearly, Gaidar is out of sympathy with the shift in government policy which I did forecast in the note I wrote on my return from Moscow. There are, I there argued, good reasons for a policy shift, favoured by Chernomyrdin, probably on the lines advocated by Evgeni Yasin. If the government does adopt the policy there outlined, then (to quote myself) 'either Gaidar accepts the programme or is honourably sidelined' – or, of course, resigns. I added: 'Yavlinsky is in the wings, waiting.' I would lay evens that he moves to a key post. (What will Fedorov do?) This is *not* the end of the reform process, to which he (and Chernomyrdin) and Yeltsin are committed. The case for selective interventionism, for some guidance in the process of restructuring the economy is very strong. The political necessity for announcing a new policy and recovery programme is overwhelming. And I am convinced that Western aid – urgently needed – can be more usefully targeted if it is an integral part of a recovery strategy. From what he told me, Yavlinsky favours swift privatisation, but may well disagree with Chubais about method. He thinks that vouchers were a politically inspired irrelevance, and of course he is right in pointing to many dubious transactions, when forms were sold at a fraction of their true value to 'insiders'. Also judging from his past pronouncements, Yavlinsky would favour closer relations with ex-Soviet republics. But of course he has not yet been appointed. We shall soon see.

Meanwhile, a new decree has imposed high import duties on drinks (100 per cent on champagne, 150 per cent on whisky) and also cars, with much higher rates on large cars. This would accord with Yasin's recommendations: tax the consumption of the new rich. It is most important to see what relationship the government can strike up with the new parliament. Gaidar's departure makes conflict less likely, and perhaps Zhirinovsky's foolish antics will help discredit him (Zhirinovsky!). A small example of how measures which work pretty well in some countries have a different effect in Russia: in Poland and Hungary taxis were privatised, and plenty of taxis are in the streets looking for customers. Moscow privatised taxis – and there are no taxis! In a recent interview, Boris Fedorov claimed that inflation in December was only 12 per cent, that since June prices had risen fourfold and the dollar rate rose by only 15 per cent, that average wages are now $100 a month, that real incomes rose in 1993. (*What?* When output and imports both fell? Dubious! A.N.) He urges a positive interest rate on savings which could facilitate investment. Also higher taxes on the rich. However, a critic has pointed to the very high burden that positive interest rates on credits impose on borrowers, making investment unfinanceable, when inflation is high. Finally, to repeat, if Gaidar's departure is associated with a serious recovery programme, it is not necessarily a bad thing, nor does it conflict with continued moves towards a market system. It *may* all get derailed, but let us give the new policy the benefit of the doubt. At least until we know just what it is.

19 January 1994, Glasgow

The following impressions are worth conveying 'soonest'.

1.   *Politics.* According to Vasiliev, it was proposed that Fedorov and Chubais be reduced in rank (that is, cease to be deputy-premiers), while Zaveryukha (who had been elected to the Duma as an 'Agrarian') would become deputy-premier, thus strengthening the agricultural lobby. High expenditures in dollars on the parliament building and on rebuilding the White House, and the cost of including Belarus in the rouble zone while giving Minsk the right (limited, but the right) to issue roubles, all this was too much for Gaidar. Fedorov again demanded the removal of Gerashchenko, and stood down when that was rejected. Chernomyrdin has clearly persuaded Yeltsin of the need for policy and personnel shift.
2.   Vasiliev, and also Vladimir Mau (with whom I had a phone conversation) both forecast what they both called 'Ukrainisation', that is, a rapid speed-up in inflation due to lax monetary and credit policies: 30 per cent a month by May, 50 per cent by September. Maybe (they both said) a period of hyperinflationary disaster is a necessary learning process. Attempts may be made to control prices, leading to shortages and to trouble in relations with the regions. Meanwhile Gaidar intends to lead his party in the Duma. Mau will effectively head his institute.
3.   By contrast, S. Gomulka (LSE, has been an adviser in both Poland and Russia) was far less apocalyptic. He reminded us that Balcerowicz was removed or resigned, but the Polish reform went on. Maybe it was the right moment for Gaidar to go (and Yavlinsky may prefer, given his political ambitions, to stay on the sidelines, pro tem.)
4.   I am of the opinion that we should not assume the worst. Chernomyrdin is not Kravchuk, and he can see the Ukrainian chaos and can draw conclusions about what not to do. And despite your view of Gerashchenko (radio, yesterday) as the worst central banker in history, he

too has no desire to destroy the rouble. In a recent article he, not for the first time, argued for a recovery policy in which credits are targeted to priority investment projects. A speed-up in inflation in the next few months is likely in any case, because of the need to honour commitments already made and to pay debts the budget incurred in the fourth quarter. To illustrate the type of policy that Chernomyrdin has (I believe) in mind, I borrow an example cited by Sir Rodric Braithwaite, who recently visited the gigantic Uralmash factory in Ekaterinburg (Sverdlovsk). The director, described as a first class manager, is in despair. To adjust his production to potential demand (for machinery and equipment) he needs to retool, and for this he cannot raise the capital. Meanwhile he can only pay a pittance to his workforce, and some of his best specialists have left. And of course the demand for modern machinery is low anyhow because of the collapse of investment. To close down Uralmash is surely not the solution. I have no doubt that its losses are covered by subsidy or 'credits' which will never be returned. If these same sums were devoted to financing the needed retooling, which in turn could relate to investment projects requiring Uralmash machinery, the wheels would turn in a positive direction.

5. This would be a part of what I have been calling the 'Yasin' proposals, and not necessarily the wrong thing to do. *If* they can carry it through. It is, however, only fair to add that Mau takes the view that Yasin (for whose intelligence he has great respect) 'always adjusts his policy recommendation to the prevailing wind'. As you know, I take the view that they do urgently need a recovery policy, and investment strategy, that they would be lost without it, and in trouble with parliament to boot. *But* can they implement this, or any other, policy? Can they resist lobbies? Thus Illarionov expects trillions to be poured into agriculture in the spring (for sowing). And in summer and autumn too. And this will be to help cover current expenditure, not for investments in much-needed infrastructure. So there are grounds for gloom, but, in my view, not really more such grounds than a month ago.

Addendum, 20 January 1994, Glasgow

Held this note back until a few more appointments became known. Fedorov remains, and I imagine he at least insisted that he still has the rank of deputy-premier. As Minister of Economics we have Shokhin, reputedly more concerned than was Gaidar with saving industry from mass closures, but that may make sense, unless, of course, every lame duck is given credit crutches. Soskovets, another 'industrialist', has his position enhanced as first deputy-premier. No news of any change at the Bank. Rouble–dollar rate leaps towards 1500. We should await the new government's policy statement to the new parliament before firmly concluding that the worst must now befall. The anti-reformers are *not* in charge – unless Chernomyrdin is so classified, which would be, in my view, wrong.

2 February 1994, Glasgow

Here are a few quotations and impressions. Chernomyrdin gave an interview to *Ekonomika i zhizn'* (No. 4, 1994), which seems to have closely followed his line in Davos. He insists that all along the government followed 'the optimal path between avoiding hyperinflation and avoiding hyperdecline of production'. Today, he asserts, demand inflation has been overcome, the basic problem is cost inflation in the absence of real competition. He considers an agreement with trade unions and entrepreneurs on limiting price and wage rises. He agrees that in 1993 too many promises were given and not kept, and that the fall in inflation in the last two months was 'facilitated' by the non payment of its debts by the government. These and other urgent and inescapable payments he expects to result in 20–22 per cent inflation in January, 15–18 per cent (a month) in the first half-year, falling to 7–9 per cent by the year's end. There is a programme of 'selective support for production', while using the new bankruptcy law to force closure or reorganisation where this proves essential. There will be a 'structural investment policy', but no easy grants of soft credits. A mechanism is being put in place to ensure that credits are used for purposes intended. Yes, the road to hyperinflation can be paved with good intentions, and take on board the fact that most of the inflation-creating factors were inherited from the last year.

The same journal reports a press-conference by Yuri Shafranik, Minister of Fuel and Energy. There are now many joint stock companies producing and processing oil. However, the entire complex faces a payments crisis. While the sector is responsible for 70 per cent of the budget's valuta receipts, it is owed by customers (including the government) the sum of 10 trillion roubles ('over half of all such debt in Russia'). This represents an enormous interest-free credit to all these customers. Can the energy complex be blamed if the energy-intensiveness of industrial production has risen, though it was much higher than in other countries? Can the high industrial costs be blamed on high energy costs, when these are still 30 per cent of world prices, while industrial goods prices are 80 per cent of world prices. He has a

point! And if wages are a fraction of Western levels, how is it that industrial costs are so very high? It tells us much about inefficiency and waste,
does it not? And agriculture is even worse. According to calculations published in *Moskovskie novosti*, for instance, in dollars at the January
exchange rate beet sugar cost $650 (world price $350), vegetable oil 1300
(650), beef 1900 (480), butter 700 (400).

Kommersant of 25 January has editorial feature articles analysing the
composition and policies of the new government. Its views carry some
weight, and here are the essential points. The sudden drop in the rouble
coincided with the resignation of Gaidar, but was due anyway, the more
so when retail prices in December rose not by 13 per cent, as claimed, but
by 23 per cent. The agreement with Belarus makes little difference, since
its GNP is about 7 per cent of the Russian. But, true enough, higher
inflationary expectations pushed up the exchange rate, though it fell
below its peak of 1607 to stabilise temporarily at 1500. Yeltsin decided to
take the election results into account. Yavlinsky offered to form a government, but since he had even fewer votes than Gaidar, he had no chance of
being nominated. Arkady Volsky turned down the idea of joining the
government. He and others (according to *Kommersant*) wish for power to
spend, leaving to others the task of raising the revenue . . . Chernomyrdin
has his eye on becoming president in 1996, and his dominant role in
forming the new government is such that many are asking: what was the
point of the new constitution, which gave so much power to the president, when he allows the premier to reflect parliamentary elections? ('If
there is to be no enlightened authoritarianism, why are Rutskoi and
Khasbulatov in jail?') Gaidar resigned (argues the journal) not least
because he knew that the chickens were bound to come to roost, that
Fedorov shifted 7.5 trillion R. from the fourth quarter's budget into this
year's first quarter, and this, plus the effect of the revaluation of capital
assets, plus credits already being granted, will result in much higher inflation rates 'already in February'. And he could see a speed-up in output
decline too. Fedorov ruthlessly cut spending, 'and Gerashchenko can be
blamed for non-payments, and Soskovets for the fall in output', and it is
best to leave it to someone else to present the budget for 1994 . . . (all
very unkind!). Chubais is still there, but it is noted that while nearly
10 000 large enterprises have been turned into limited companies, most of
the share capital still belongs to the state.

Three scenarios are then discussed. The first, 'unlikely' is: 'Some
unknown spiritual brother of Boris Fedorov will attempt strict monetarism. Output would then fall by 40 per cent, to a quarter of what it was
in 1989.' The second: Chernomyrdin and the lobbyists will lavishly
finance the energy, military–industrial and farm complexes and fill holes,

save lame ducks, and so on, with no real attempt at selectivity and structural policies. Also disastrous, and, alas, 'probable'. The third, 'desirable': an investment programme, financed in large part out of the profits (including in valuta, most of it held abroad) of the energy complex, plus investment-linked incentives for private capital. This needs detailed knowledge of inter-sector links, to assess effects of alternative policies. Gosplan used to have such knowledge. The new Minister of Economics, Shokhin, worked in Gosplan for ten years. In my view, Chernomyrdin will try, following recommendations from Yasin, and now also from Abalkin, Petrakov, Shatalin (all good friends of mine from days gone by!), to avoid scenario two and aim for a variant of the third. But, with Yeltsin *au dessus de la bataille*, a most unstable parliamentary balance, plus strong lobbies and regions, optimism is, to put it mildly, premature.

8 February 1994, Glasgow

Had a visitor here from Kiev, Prof. Sikora. He is convinced that the alarmist headlines about armed conflict with Russia are greatly exaggerated. He also says that Kravchuk cut the inflation rate drastically in December by the simple expedient of freezing prices. I do not trust his economics very much, though he is a decent fellow. He tells me that the de facto acting premier (Ukraine's equivalent of Chernomyrdin) is Zakhilsky, ex-manager of coal mines (and a Jew). The rouble–dollar rate is seriously affected by rumours of a currency reissue, which has caused holders of roubles in (for example) Ukraine to cross into Russia to change them quickly into dollars. This pushed the rouble–dollar rate in areas near Ukraine as high as 2000. *Kommersant* quotes rates of 1708 in Moscow.

E. Starikov, whom I met, sees a conflict taking place between what he calls 'comprador finance-and-trade capital, closely interlinked with the political apparat and criminal elements', with which he would include large state enterprises which have been turned into so-called joint stock companies under *nomenklatura* management, and small and medium-sized businesses, genuinely privatised. The former were alleged, both by Starikov and Sergo Mikoyan (from whom I received a long and indignant letter) to have had far too much influence over the policies of the Gaidar administration. They are said to make money – I quote to give a flavour of politically significant bitterness – 'producing nothing, through valuta deals, dumping-exports of materials and fuel, narcotics, old icons and pretty slave-girls for Western brothels, and imports of firewater, trinkets and secondhand cars, mostly stolen'. Genuine productive business is heavily taxed, has to pay bribes and protection money. The political economy of all this is reflected in votes for Zhirinovsky and even for the communists on the part of what Starikov calls the 'national bourgeoisie', whose survival depends on protectionism in the name of national economic salvation. Chernomyrdin, or anyone else who wishes for support in future elections, must take such sentiments on board. We should recognise that, while accusations of corruption directed at Gaidar and Fedorov are surely false, economic liberalism in Russia is associated in people's minds, not altogether unjustly, with rackets and with a species of new rich who are much more likely to acquire property in London than invest anything in Russia. Finally, the Russian police gazette (*Militsiya*) reports the massive use of falsified bills of exchange, promissory notes, credit guarantees, and so on. Also large scale bribery and undervaluation and other fraud in the process of privatisation. It all helps to discredit the reform process!

9 February 1994, Glasgow

The reason for again communicating is the appearance of an important article by Stanislav Shatalin, now said to have the government's ear. Briefly, here are the essential points he makes, summarising the advice given by the Economics Section of the Russian Academy and the 'International Reform Fund', aiming at setting up a 'socially oriented market economy.' (Soziale Markwirtschaft? Warum nicht? Wie Erhard?).

A.   While there has undoubtedly been some progress in creating the infrastructure and behaviour patterns needed by the market, shock therapy has had some deplorable social effects and is in danger of destroying the country's economic and scientific potential. 'Particularly deep and threatening is the collapse of investment.' At the same time the payments crisis and 'uncontrolled emission' are evidence of loss of control. Purely monetarist measures were helpless to cope with cost inflation under conditions of high monopolisation. 'Financial stabilisation cannot be achieved without halting the decline in production.'
B.   'It is odd that some political leaders in Russia and in the West believe that a change in reform methods is equivalent to a return to the old command system.' A new strategy is necessary. The election results have shown the rejection of shock therapy. A social consensus must be sought.
C.   So, a six point programme. (1) A social plan based on subsistence minimum, plus health and education. (2) 'Reject as naive the belief in the automatic recovery of the economy.' The government must support material production, investment especially. An industrial 'structural policy'

must be accompanied by a legal order, 'stable rules of the game'. (3) 'Combine harsh financial-credit policy with selective support of priority sectors', plus some regulation of prices and incomes (Which? How? Affecting exactly what? I must ask Shatalin! A.N.). (4) More power in the reform process to the regions, but without any barriers to the free movement of goods and people. (5) 'Review the question of external aid', laying more emphasis on Russia's technical and productive capacity, internal sources of accumulation. 'This in no way should be seen as limiting Russia's participation in the world economy, but she has to solve her own problems.' (6) All forms of property should coexist, but it is essential to clarify responsibility. Privatisation should be linked with investment and with efficiency, and 'voucher privatisation' abandoned as useless. 'Particularly dangerous today is the almost total loss of control over and in the economy. The country is in a deep administrative crisis: there is practically *not a single state structure capable of exercising power* . . . Laws and decrees are adopted, but at all levels the governmental mechanism fails to function. *In this situation it is quite pointless to devise any reform programmes* [yea, verily! A.N.], which can only be doomed to failure . . . The present *power vacuum must be filled*, there must be more governmental regulation.' The article is headed: 'The Market Needs State Authority'.

Where is Russia Going?, 12 February 1994, Glasgow

The reason for troubling you with yet another note is the appearance – within a few days in February – of major articles expounding, and criticising, various proposals designed to save the country from disaster. First, a long piece by *Gaidar* in *Izvestiya* (10 February). Looking back, he agrees that they were only able to go half way, that they failed in the task of beginning the restructuring of the economy, 'massive investments, technological renewal, growth in production, the creation of a healthy middle class'. All was blocked partly because the government had no clear and united commitment to policy, and because inflation destroyed the possibility of restructuring. The necessary massive investments required financial stabilisation, but pressures from lobbies wrecked anti-inflationary measures. Lavish credits were diverted into banks abroad. 'Inflation is needed by the parasitic bourgeoisie closely linked with corrupt officialdom and the political elite . . . We have a semi-colonial, comprador regime.' (!!! This is exactly the language used by Starikov, which I quoted in the note I sent you on 8 February, except that Starikov was attacking the Gaidar team!) Gaidar argues that the state's role should be diminished, and that stabilisation would bring forth the capital needed for restructuring the economy. (Here he parts company with all his critics, who see a role for the state in devising an investment strategy, without which output will go on falling and stabilisation will never be). Then there is the so-called 'academicians' programme', devised by *Abalkin, Petrakov*, and *Shatalin*, apparently at the request of deputy-premier Soskovets. Its essentials I have already sent you. These proposals have had a fairly hostile response, not just from Gaidar, who attacked them as backward-looking, but also by Yasin (in the article 'A programme impossible to realise') and the financial journalist Vasilchuk ('Fantasies still remote from reality'). Also Anatoli Chubais described the proposals as 'absurd economically'. I cited *Shatalin*'s ideas in a previous note. *Abalkin* points to the inflationary consequences of decisions taken when Fedorov and Gaidar were in the government, notably the non-payment in the previous quarter of government debt (to farms, to industry, even to the Academy of Sciences) amounting to 7.8 trillion R. Surely 'Fedorov and Gaidar are experienced enough to know that this will now result in a speed-up in inflation, so they cleverly left the government so that others could be blamed.' His proposals do require resistance to lobbyists' pressures, a close link-up of budgetary, credit and investment policies, ending subsidies other than for defined and targeted purposes. He attacks 'monetarist' solutions. (Yasin, in stressing the importance of counter-inflationary measures, attacks Abalkin for 'the false pathos of "down with monetarism", as if it is a foreign invention harmful to the Russian soul'.) But oddly, the same Yasin asserts that talk of 'a social market economy' is 'cheap demagogy'. Only rich countries can afford it. Yasin also regards 1994 as a particularly critical year; the budget, industry, agriculture, are all in trouble.

11 April 1994, Glasgow

I will be in Stockholm on 3 May to receive an honorary doctorate from the Stockholm School of Economics. Not far from there to St. Petersburg, so I am planning a semi-holiday semi-working visit, which will include life in a Russian flat and shopping (with my wife) for food. Might get a more realistic view of how people live. Will be back home circa 20 May. Apropos your remarks in the Bulletin. I certainly concur with your somewhat pessimistic remarks about Russia's prospects. Not only or just because of the government's failure to adopt any positive policy, but also because it lacks the power to implement policies of any kind, or to create the minimum degree of legal order, without which markets cannot function. Finally, may I be permitted a remark concerning your very positive view of Berlusconi's victory. Does it not conflict with your own hitchhiker's report from Asia? There you speak of the desirability of policies 'oriented towards education, health and productive infrastructure', but in Italy you applaud the privatisation of health and education and the slashing of infrastructural subsidies. Or is Italy in some essential respect different?

Russian Economy in 1994: 'Not Hyperinflation But Depression', 24 April 1994, Glasgow

It is worth quoting the views of the analysts of the well-informed *Kommersant*. They note the slowdown in the rate of inflation, but also the continued and alarming decline in output. Some claim that it was a necessary price to pay for restructuring, 'but the sad fact is that there was no restructuring . . . , with almost total collapse of the high tech sectors of industry'. With the onset of depression it is possible that the inflation rate will indeed fall to about 5 per cent a month (after absorbing the recent tripling of electricity prices). However, a large money issue in February may temporarily push up inflation in April over the March level of 11 per cent. The 'industrial' forecast for 1994 is as follows:

	1991=100	1993=100
Electricity	72.4	79.1
Oil	58.2	79.8
Gas	72.8	78.4
Coal	68.4	74.2
Iron & steel	52.7	76.5
Non-ferrous metals	52.4	87.3
Chemicals	45.6	75.4
Petrochemicals	46.6	74.4
Machinery & equipment	54.2	75.5
Timber & paper	50.9	73.3
Building materials	43.4	76.9
Light industry	43.4	76.9
Food industry	50.4	68.3
All Industry	51.0	75.0

It is hardly necessary to stress that these are *catastrophic* figures, with still no sign of a let-up in decline. The same source discusses prospects of specific industries. It is noted that oil exports are impeded by lack of port facilities (rail has become too expensive). Also that major oil companies are shunning investment in Russia. There is reported confusion in the grain market: the government hopes to cut out imports, but (despite promises) has not paid its own debts to procurement agencies and farms, so the internal market languishes.

In *Ekonomika i zhizn'*, Pavel Bunich (Aganbegyan's deputy) makes the interesting point that, having got rid of Gaidar and Fedorov, Chernomyrdin is politically able to pursue a more restrictive monetary policy than they, though he has made promises he may be unable to keep. Meanwhile 'the most important thing today is investment'. The basic capital is wearing out, is not being replaced. This cannot go on. He and others advocate government support, jointly with private capital, for promising investment projects, ensuring that credits are properly used, and not spent on wages and commodity speculation. Unfortunately, 'we all know that our market is 80 per cent criminal.' (Unfortunately, as Illarionov pointed out when we met in London, most officials and bureaucrats are corrupt). 'Stability, a sound legal base for enterprise, guarantees for foreign investors, are lacking.'

28 April 1994, Glasgow

Positively my last note until the end of May, as I will be in Stockholm and St. Petersburg. *Had a word with Mau* who has been in the UK with Gaidar. He confirms that, after Gaidar's departure from the government, Chernomyrdin has been following a tight monetary policy. Mau's explanation: previously he could blame Gaidar while adopting a less severe stance himself. Now has himself to defend the finances against the spending lobbies. Mau believes that Chernomyrdin is basically sound, except that he sometimes does something silly. At which point Yeltsin can restrain him. He does not think that Yeltsin is on the skids, though admittedly he does not do very much. *The first quarter's statistical report*, summarised in *Izvestiya*, shows a decline by almost 25 per cent in industrial production compared with the first quarter of 1993. Analysis shows that 58 per cent of the decline is directly attributable to 'lack of demand', 33 per cent to production or material bottlenecks, 6 per cent to closures. Consumer services are 49 per cent down – people cannot afford the high prices. Imports have continued to fall, with very large cuts in imports of grain, meat, sugar. The first quarter saw a trade surplus of $5.1 billion. The exchange rate has gone above 1800 to the $.

I have been invited to a major conference called by the academicians in September (12 to 15), to be held in a rural location near Moscow. I mention this because a trip in that direction in September may be on your mind. But I have not spoken with you for what seems like many months. Could you possibly phone me – or shall I ask Yana for a number at which I could get you, on Friday or during the weekend? (We leave at the crack of dawn on Monday.)

PART III

A Personal Note

Life's surprises – and some odd memories

In 1955 I was on my first visit to the former Soviet Union since childhood. Foreigners were rare birds then. Particularly in Kazakhstan. Our group, led by a parliamentary under-secretary, was given VIP treatment. We even stayed at the rest home of that republic's Council of Ministers, in the hills above the capital, Alma Ata. Each of us were given a boxfull of exquisite apples, for which the area is rightly famous. Alma Ata – 'father of apples'. Anyhow, our next stop was to see the beginnings of the so-called virgin lands campaign, in the north of Kazakhstan. The nearest town was Atbasav, where there was no hotel. So we lived for several days on a special train. And to this train there came the chairman of the provincial soviet, a plump and jovial Kazakh, with an unmistakably Central Asian countenance. A banquet was swiftly conjured up. Our Kazakh host showed a remarkable capacity to pour a tumbler-full of cognac down his throat without any sign of swallowing it. After several such feats he turned to me and said, in Russian: 'Do you know the Kazakh language?' I replied that I did not. 'Would you like to hear Kazakh spoken?' Yes, I would. 'So', he said, 'I will now speak Kazakh.' And he addressed me in Yiddish. 'Hey', said I, 'that's not Kazakh.' He grinned and agreed it was not. 'Where did you learn it?', I asked. 'Before the war I was working in the Ukraine', he replied. And indeed, until the Germans destroyed them in 1941, there were compact Jewish communities there with their own schools and language. But it was odd all the same, coming from him, and on a train in the middle of the steppes of Central Asia.

A less agreeable surprise. In the winter of 1939–40 I was in the British army in northern France, very much in the ranks. We were stationed in a mining area, and most of the miners were Poles who had migrated there 20 years earlier. They lived in compact communities with their own schools. Some fellow-soldiers had caused damage to a village hall, and I was called on to interpret. I quickly discovered that the older Poles had not learnt French: they had previously worked in coal mines in Germany, and spoke some German. I did not know Polish, but admitted that I did know Russian. The news spread. And for the next few weeks Polish youths abused me as a 'Russian Yid'. Interesting. They had never been to their land, and they had probably never seen a Jew in all their short lives. But the bacillus was right there in their blood.

Luck was, however, with me throughout the war. Cut off from my unit, which was evacuated from Dunkirk, I and some other stragglers joined a scratch division, called after its commander's name the Beauman division. It was supposed to hold a segment of the front on the Somme, with the 51st Highland division to our left, the French on our right. We had practically no artillery, little signals equipment and hardly any medical staff. The Germans had no great difficulty in breaking through and getting around the rear of the Highlanders. My unit was based on Rouen, then back near Evreux. Four of us were in a van near the Seine, when we heard nearby machine-gun fire. A peasant said: 'Les allemands arrivent!' Luckily we got away. Rejoining our unit, we heard about the fall of Paris, and Petain's words came over the radio: 'Il faut cesser le combat.' Our last stop was in the telephone exchange in Caen, since we were using French civilian telephones. There were just three of us, on detachment. A French battalion made its way through the town. An officer said to us: 'There is nothing now between you and the Germans.' I telephoned our company commander, who said: 'Don't worry, stay put.' I also called French telephone exchanges in nearby towns (Lisieux, I recall) to ask if the Germans had got there yet. Soon the company commander came on the line: 'Get moving! Rendez-vous in Bayeux.' We arrived there and joined a motorised column which headed for Cherbourg. Occasionally we were machine-gunned by German planes and lay in ditches, but we did make it to Cherbourg. One ship was still there. I remembered sailing in her in prewar days: it was Belgian, the 'Princess Marie Joze', it used to do the Dover–Ostend run. The Germans did not bomb the port; they naturally wished to preserve it whole. I gather they arrived two hours after we left. I woke up in Southampton. Half of the Beauman division made it to Saint-Nazaire, and most were drowned when their ship was torpedoed. So I was doubly lucky. Trebly so, perhaps, when, in 1942, I was to sail to Murmansk as a sergeant-interpreter. War or no war, the Soviets required a visa for every British serviceman. My visa was refused, no doubt because of a suspect biography (born in Russia, anti-Bolshevik father). Later I heard that the ship I would have travelled on had been sunk, part of the ill-fated convoy of that summer. So I owe my life to the secret police!

Another surprise, of a different kind. On 14 July 1935 I was in Paris, and saw the huge Front Populaire demonstration pass the Place de la Bastille, the highpoint of Leon Blum's premiership (before the chickens came home to roost). Then, with a fellow-student, hitchhiking south to Toulouse. Then a train via Puigcerde to Barcelona. A cheap pension on the Ramblas. Next day I was to go to the post office, there to collect a few pounds sent to me by my mother to help pay for the intended holiday, but also the results of my final examination at the LSE. Instead – it was 19 July – we awoke to the sound of gunfire. The civil war had begun. The Ramblas was no-man's land, with a machine-gun nest at the top of the Columbus statue and some firing also from the Plaza Catalunya. We were stuck in the pension, eating whatever was in stock. When the republicans had won, it turned out that the bulk of the popular front were anarchist. Requisitioned vehicles were painted with the letters CNT/FAI. The communists, at that point of time, were not to be seen. A column of anarchist 'soldiers', in civilian clothes, brandishing rifles, with no supply column, crammed into buses, with mattresses on the roof as protection from air attack, set out 'to capture Saragossa', which, of course, they did not. They did, however, burn almost every church, in the name of bringing light into darkness and superstition. After a week, British subjects were evacuated on a destroyer. I think it was HMS Douglas to Marseille. Perhaps my money and exam results are still in the Barcelona post office . . .

Statistical probability? A few years ago I was sat next to a rather attractive lady at the Budapest opera. We talked about this and that and had absolutely no intention to meet again. A week later I was in Prague, in the old town square, looking at the procession of saints at the old clock, at 1 p.m. And there, standing right by me, was this same attractive lady. To repeat, there was no assignation, and we have never seen each other again. But what court of law would believe that this was just a coincidence? Or how about the following? I was due to give a lecture on the subject 'Marx and Russia'. It was clearly desirable to cite the 1881 correspondence on this very subject between Marx and Vera Zasulich. Somehow I had failed to look it up. It was 9 a.m. The lecture was at 11 a.m. Where, in which volume of which edition, would I find it? Before tackling this tiresome task, I opened the morning's mail. This included a paper (in English) by a Japanese scholar on the correspondence between Marx and Vera Zasulich, with photocopies of his rejected drafts. I was thus able to impress the class with my deep knowledge of the subject. Such luck seldom comes one's way. But there it is. Coincidence again, of a more homely kind. My grandson was married on 26 August. Shortly before, a relative wrote to me that *her* grandson was getting married – on 26 August! And if this was not enough, a few weeks later a granddaughter was travelling by train to Scotland, and got talking to a girl who was sitting next to her. This girl proved to be the same relative's other grandchild! Fate takes odd forms, does it not?

In November 1972 I was in Santiago, Chile, while Allende was holding precariously onto power. At that time the military was still to be more or less relied upon. A state of emergency was declared. My Spanish was up to this: 'estado de emergencia'. I noted the romantic name of the Santiago garrison commander: General Hector Bravo. What I did not note was that a curfew was declared. In French it is 'couvre-feu'. In German maybe 'Sperrstunde'. In Spanish? I was lucky not to be arrested, returning at a leisurely pace from visiting friends. Now I know the Spanish for curfew is 'toque di queda'. Tacsin for quiet. Shall not forget it again. When the coup happened, I was elsewhere. In Budapest actually.

Another wartime memory. As a Territorial, I was 'embodied' two days before the war actually began. We were in a camp on Salisbury plain. It was perhaps typical, but to me surprising, that when war was declared it occurred to none of the officers to tell us about it. I heard that war had been declared by listening to a radio behind the cookhouse. And the first song I heard as we marched was the highly militarist ditty which began, 'On Monday I touched her on the ankle/On Tuesday I touched her on the knee'. No wonder we won the war!

Thirty or so years ago I was flying from New York to Washington. My neighbour suddenly said: 'Do you know, you can still get real bread in New York, with a crust. Would you like to try it?' I agreed, and it did indeed have a crust. I said so. 'Say, you are not American, are you?' True, said I. 'Where are you from?' 'Scotland'. 'Scotland, and you are going to Washington. Are you going to the Scotch embassy?' Moral: there was hope for American bread. And sure enough, it is now possible to get good bread. Unlike 30 years ago, when it was all a sort of mush. A slightly different 'American' memory. The scene is Glasgow. The date – 1942. Sergeant Nove is asked by an American marine: 'Where can I get a drink?' Me: 'You see it's Sunday, and in Scotland the pubs are closed. In England they are open, but not here.' Puzzled marine, in reply: 'Gee. But doesn't Scotland belong to England?'

Back to Russia, and childhood. I must have been six years old, and it can be checked by the date of the event described. My mother was a busy doctor. But that evening she was very late home. Somebody asked why. She replied: 'At the hospital there was a very long line of people seeking medical certificates to show why they did not attend the spontaneous demonstration demanding the death penalty for the Social Revolutionaries.' Their trial was at the beginning of 1922. My scepticism about spontaneous demonstrations began in childhood, therefore. So I believe the story told, in 1956, at the time of Suez. The British embassy was besieged by an indignant mob. The ambassador called the police. A colonel of police arrived. Asked 'how long will this disgraceful business last?', the officer replied, looking at his watch: 'Another fifteen minutes.' 'Ah', replied a Russian to whom I told the story, 'but next day it *was* spontaneous.' Could be. It was Arthur Koestler who remarked that, under the old Soviet system, it was difficult for the truth to appear credible.

Finally, some of my favourite Russian experiences. Hélèn Carrère d'Encausse, French political scientist, wrote a book with the prophetic title *L'Empire éclaté*. Shortly afterwards in 1979, she (and I) attended an international political science congress in Moscow. She was met at the airport, and was asked: have you brought a copy of your book? Fearful of the possible consequences, she had not. 'Pity', said her Soviet colleague, 'I was particularly asked by the author of the *Pravda* review of the book to get him a copy. You see, he had not read it.' At the same congress, I was approached by two young men who said: 'You are professor Nove, and you have written an article "Is the USSR a class society?".' May we discuss it with you?' Me: 'Of course. Have you read it?' They replied: 'Our job is to follow Western interpretations of Soviet society. So in this capacity we are allowed to read whatever is put away behind two locks. Unfortunately, your article was behind *three* locks.' We had an amiable discussion about the *nomenklatura* system and graded privilege. The problem was not the exceptionally subversive author; I saw three of my books in the open catalogue of the university library. The problem was the subject. But how careful were the ideologues to keep even the selected specialists from ideological pollution. And did this not tell us something about their own lack of self-confidence, or of confidence in their own colleagues? Finally, when I was several times refused a visa (in the 1970s) my Russian friends reminded me of an old classic tale about the rabbit who was fleeing across the Soviet border. A second rabbit asked him why. 'Don't you know', said the first rabbit, 'they are arresting all camels?' 'But you are not a camel, you are a rabbit', said the second rabbit. 'That is true', replied the first rabbit, 'but, you see, I would have to prove it.'

Index